Managing Built Heritage
The Role of Cultural Significance

Derek Worthing
Faculty of the Built Environment
University of the West of England
Bristol

Stephen Bond
TFT Cultural Heritage
London

Blackwell
Publishing

© 2008 by Derek Worthing and Stephen Bond

Blackwell Publishing editorial offices:
Blackwell Publishing Ltd, 9600 Garsington Road, Oxford OX4 2DQ, UK
  Tel: +44 (0)1865 776868
Blackwell Publishing Inc., 350 Main Street, Malden, MA 02148-5020, USA
  Tel: +1 781 388 8250
Blackwell Publishing Asia Pty Ltd, 550 Swanston Street, Carlton, Victoria 3053, Australia
  Tel: +61 (0)3 8359 1011

First published 2008 by Blackwell Publishing Ltd

ISBN: 978-1-4051-1978-8

Library of Congress Cataloging-in-Publication Data

Worthing, Derek.
  Managing built heritage : the role of cultural significance / Derek Worthing and Stephen Bond.
     p. cm.
  Includes bibliographical references and index.
    ISBN-13: 978-1-4051-1978-8 (pbk. : alk. paper)
    ISBN-10: 1-4051-1978-0 (pbk. : alk. paper)
  1. Public buildings–Preservation.   2. Historic preservation.   3. Historic buildings.
4. Cultural property–Preservation.   5. Architecture–Conservation and restoration.
I. Bond, Stephen, MA   II. Title.
  TH3401.W675 2008
  363.6'9–dc22

                                                                    2007023180

A catalogue record for this title is available from the British Library

Set in 10/12.5pt Sabon
by Aptara Inc., New Delhi, India
Printed and bound in Singapore
by Fabulous Printers Pte Ltd

The publisher's policy is to use permanent paper from mills that operate a sustainable forestry policy,
and which has been manufactured from pulp processed using acid-free and elementary chlorine-free
practices. Furthermore, the publisher ensures that the text paper and cover board used have met
acceptable environmental accreditation standards.

For further information on Blackwell Publishing, visit our website:
www.blackwellpublishing.com

Contents

Chapter 1
Introduction to the Concept of Managing through Significance

In recent years, increasing focus has been placed upon the identification of social and cultural values that are enshrined in our built environment and in cultural landscapes. This approach is based around the notion that all buildings and spaces, whatever their age and however modest, make some form of contribution or have value to society.

This book is primarily concerned with how cultural heritage is managed in order to protect and enhance it. Although it focuses on built cultural heritage, we believe the principles and processes that we discuss are applicable to all aspects of cultural heritage.

This book brings together our experience of research, consultancy and practice over a number of years, and integrates this with current thinking on approaches to the management of built cultural heritage. It inevitably, and purposely, does this within the context of a discussion of the benefits and the value of conserving (built) cultural heritage.

We believe that this is a timely publication because there is now a strong agreement on the importance of effective management strategies and processes for the protection and enhancement of the built cultural heritage. Until recently there had been a tendency to focus concern, on the one hand, upon technical issues related to the care and repair of the historic fabric, and on the other to the integration of conservation activity into general land use planning. Although both of these continue to be important perspectives, their particular emphases left a gap. This meant that conservation activity was not being considered as holistically as it needed to be because the crucial role of management strategies and tactics was not being adequately considered, either as an activity in its own right, or, indeed, importantly as part of an integrated approach to the protection and enhancement of the built cultural heritage. In many cases and situations, management, at both a strategic and a 'day-to-day' level, tended to be left to take care of itself – partly one suspects because the idea of 'managing' was anathema to many conservation professionals.

This book is essentially about the important role that effective management plays in protecting and enhancing the historic environment. It concerns itself with what has now become known in some quarters as 'values-based management' but which we have referred to generally as 'significance-based management'. Essentially the book is concerned with the need to identify and assess what is important about a place, and with devising management strategies, processes and actions which focus on the need to protect and enhance those values.

The collection of values associated with a place of cultural value is generally referred to as 'cultural significance'. The idea of cultural significance has been around for some time, but it was perhaps clearly articulated for the first time, and more importantly linked specifically to the management of a place, by the Burra Charter (Australia ICOMOS, 1999).

Every place around us has a unique identity that is made up of the complete range of such social and cultural values that represents and embodies and which give it significance to our society. Thus, for example, the Tower of London, the Eiffel Tower, a war memorial in any town centre, a modern library or hospital, a bus station or the Royal Botanic Gardens at Kew all have particular value(s) to local communities and society at large. But the summations of that series of values, their cultural significance, are very different from each other. Modern conservation planning says that, by understanding the particular cultural significance of an asset, informed and better management decisions can be taken that will respect and potentially enhance that significance.

The basic premise behind this approach, then, is that in order to manage and protect a place of cultural heritage value you have to first of all be able to identify and articulate why a place is important and what the different elements of the place contribute to that importance – and how they do so. That is, we are concerned with determining why a place is valuable and what embodies and represents those values. This may seem like a simple and rather obvious concept – that you cannot protect something unless you:

- understand why it is important, and
- what it is about it that contributes to that importance;

but until recently this was not, at the least, an explicit approach.

However, if we accept, as most do, that as English Heritage (2007) observe:

> *Change in the historic environment is inevitable, whether caused by natural processes, through use, or by people responding to social, economic and technological advances*

then the key challenge in conservation is essentially about managing change to a place whilst protecting, and hopefully enhancing, its cultural significance. In order to meet this challenge it becomes vitally important that cultural values are clearly identified and assessed.

If cultural values and their interrelationships can be identified and fully comprehended, this knowledge can then be used to assist in taking management decisions now and in the future that will strengthen and enhance the benefits that accrue to society from that asset. The sense is that there needs to be an understanding of the cultural significance of a place to be able to articulate and justify designation, but it can also be, and in fact should be, both a focus and driver for managing the place.

The concern addressed in this book is the need to develop an approach that guides management planning so as to optimise the benefits that can be gained from a place without diminishing its value and potential for the future.

In this sense a management plan for the built cultural heritage is not dissimilar from approaches in other arenas which effectively ask a series of questions such as:

- Where do we want to be?
- What have we got?
- How do we get where we want to be?
- How are we doing?

In recontextualising this we can suggest that a coherent approach to the management of built cultural heritage, whether it be a single object or building, a site, an area (or indeed a town), will involve:

- An identification and measurement of cultural values.
- An identification of the attributes or elements of the cultural 'item' that embody and represent those values – so that it is clear what needs to be protected and hopefully enhanced.
- An identification of any factors that may adversely affect cultural values now and in the (measurable) future. That is, in what way are the values vulnerable and what are the processes and situations that may lead to an erosion and loss of those values? Therefore what are the actions that need to be put in place in order to avoid or nullify those threats – or at least mitigate them?
- An identification of opportunities to protect and enhance cultural significance – including by proactively seeking out opportunities for positive changes.
- An identification of 'where are we now' in relation to such matters as the condition and use of the place.
- The development of a management plan that links the assessment of cultural values to the operational needs and activities of the place and to the objectives of the organisation(s) that own and/or occupy it (and which integrates built cultural management planning into the general built asset planning on 'mixed' estates). Such a management plan must also focus actions, processes and priorities on the protection of built cultural heritage values, i.e. be primarily concerned with the implementation of management practices that maximise protection and enhancement of heritage values.
- The development of evaluation and review processes that address issues of 'how are we doing' whilst also considering the continuing validity of (heritage) objectives.

Acknowledgements

In addition to the instances where we have made direct reference, we would also like to acknowledge the following texts that informed some of our thinking on the development and content of this book:

The Conservation Plan (6th edition) by James Semple Kerr.
The Burra Charter.
Looking After Heritage Places – The Basics of Heritage Planning for Managers, Landowners and Administrators by Michael Pearson and Sharon Sullivan.

We also acknowledge with thanks the time generously given by staff at UNESCO's World Heritage Centre including Dr Mechtild Rössler, Giovanni Boccardi, Feng Jing, Guy Debonnet and Ron van Oers, to discuss their personal views on current issues in conservation planning and management. Lastly we would like to thank the members of Australia ICOMOS – too numerous to mention here – who were so generous in giving their thoughts and reflecting on their experience of conservation management.

References

Australia ICOMOS (1999) *The Burra Charter, The Australia ICOMOS Charter for Places of Cultural Significance.* Australia ICOMOS Inc.

English Heritage (2007) *Conservation Principles, Policies and Guidance for the Sustainable Management of the Historic Environment* (Second Stage Consultation). London, English Heritage.

Kerr, J.S. (2004) *The Conservation Plan* (6th edn). Sydney, National Trust of Australia (NSW).

Pearson, M. and Sullivan, S. (1995) *Looking After Heritage Places – The Basics of Heritage Planning for Managers, Landowners and Administrators.* Melbourne, Melbourne University Press.

Chapter 2
Asset Types, Their Managers and Management Implications

Introduction

The premise running through this book is that management decisions about the care and use of an asset will only prove to be sustainable in the long term if they have been shaped by a coherent understanding of its wider significance to society and the ways in which that significance has, is, or could yet be, compromised by change, misuse or neglect. Planning and decisions built from any other platform are likely to result in the cultural value of the asset being diminished in some way. A significance-based approach to management can be applied to any kind of cultural heritage or built asset. It is just as appropriate to use an evaluation of significance and vulnerability as a means of developing conservation management policies and consequent strategies for action for an historic area – for instance, the core of a town like Delft or a city such as Baalbek – as it is for a relatively simple historic monument such as Nelson's Column or the Taj Mahal. Indeed, a consideration of significance can be made at sub-regional or even regional levels, permitting this approach to heritage management to be fed beneficially into regional and national political processes.

Cultural heritage assets take many diverse forms. This chapter looks at the range of typical heritage asset types and examines in outline the management implications of each. For each asset type, we seek to define:

- Typical values that we might ascribe to such assets today.
- Who or what is likely to be responsible for managing use and change in and around the asset.
- The level at which management policy and action needs to be implemented to be effective in the sustainable care of the asset and its value to society.

Heritage assets and their management implications

Buried archaeology

Buried archaeology, by its very nature, is culturally precious. Physical intervention or investigation leads to its compromise or destruction. As an asset, it is unusual in that, under normal circumstances, its nature and extent cannot be fully comprehended and frequently can only be guessed at. This can make its management and care in the ground complex or problematic.

Buried archaeology consists of the surviving remains of earlier cultures and their environmental contexts. As a result, such deposits may be valued today for a wide range of reasons, including educational, artistic, social or religious significance. Extracting the complete range of cultural values from archaeological remains is a time-consuming and ultimately destructive process and, accordingly, is increasingly regarded with caution.

In the United Kingdom, the legal arrangements for the ownership of property (including land) mean that, in principle, buried archaeology may be the property and hence the management responsibility of individuals, any property-owning organisation, local or central government, or the Crown. This may be the case whether or not its existence is recognised and irrespective of any statutory protection that has been given to the asset through its designation as a scheduled ancient monument.

Archaeological remains are vulnerable to both inadvertent and purposeful damage. This may, at least in part, be associated with a failure to understand sufficiently the value of the asset. When the presence of buried archaeology is known or foreseeable, appropriate care to safeguard its value comprehensively necessitates active management to prevent any disturbance or intervention whatsoever. This sets an onerous level at which effective management needs to take place to safeguard the integrity and potentially unknown significance of the buried asset. When this is unavoidable, a watching brief should be kept of development works, and time and funding allowed for investigation and recording of data, as necessary.

Archaeological sites and monuments

In general terms, archaeological sites and monuments consist of a combination of buried archaeology and above-ground structures or, depending upon circumstance, of foundations and superstructure alone. Many such sites and monuments will be statutory protected, while others will be without protection despite their cultural value. Internationally, a growing number of archaeological sites are inscribed as being World Heritage Sites due to their 'outstanding universal value'. In the UK, this confers no additional statutory protection, although the presence of a World Heritage Site is a material consideration within the planning process and thus may have some influence on the eventual development of neighbouring sites. This will be discussed later in more detail.

Inevitably, 'archaeological sites and monuments' is a wide group of assets, running from the simple burial mound or barrow through multi-building and multi-phase sites such as Fountains Abbey to complex ruined cities such as Kandahar in Afghanistan or Byblos in Lebanon.

As with buried archaeological deposits, a wide range of cultural values may be ascribed to these assets, ranging from architectural, historical and archaeological values through social, cultural and religious to symbolic and economic values. Numerous archaeological sites and monuments are open to the public and contribute to the local economy through cultural tourism or spin-off enterprise.

In the UK, once again due to laws of land ownership, archaeological sites and monuments may be owned by individuals, by any organisation, institution or company which owns property, by local or central government, or by the Crown. In some situations, archaeological sites and monuments are managed actively and positively for their cultural value, but elsewhere their care is of marginal interest to the core activities of the owner/manager. Typical examples of the latter are where prehistoric burial places occupy valuable farm land in private ownership, or where a commemorative monument (such as a garden structure, obelisk or mausoleum) once formed an integral part of an estate which has now been split up or put to a very different use.

Active management of an archaeological site or monument in order to prevent compromise to its significance is likely to involve protection and preservation of its historic fabric (including its remaining buried archaeology) and, frequently, of its immediate setting or environmental context. A typical example of this focus is the management of cultural tourism to archaeological sites in ways that attempt to limit wear and tear and/or degradation resulting from large numbers of visitors, their requirements for facilities (toilets, orientation and signage, shops and restaurants), and the impact of their transport (pollution, vibration and car parking).

Individual historic structures and buildings

Undoubtedly, this category of historic property is the broadest and the most common. This makes generalised comment regarding management practice difficult. Conceivably, almost anywhere in the world, individual historic structures and buildings may variously be owned by individuals, a multitude of different types of organisations, institutions and companies, or by local or central government. Undoubtedly, the majority of individual historic structures are not fully appreciated for their heritage value, but are considered simply as a built envelope within which activities of one kind or another take place. They are generally managed accordingly.

In the UK, individual historic structures and buildings deemed worthy of protection are designated statutorily as 'listed buildings' and graded – according to perceived architectural or historic merit, close historical association with nationally important people or events, or group value within their wider setting – as being of 'exceptional' (grade I/A depending upon country), 'more than

(a)

(b)

Figure 2.1(a)–(c)   Ephesus is a well-known archaeological site in Turkey (a,b). The library of Celsus is shown in (c).

(c)

Figure 2.1   (*Continued*)

(a)

Figure 2.2   (a),(b) These examples of archaeological sites are to be found in Coventry.
(c) The *SS Great Britain*, which is moored in the Harbour at Bristol, is a Scheduled Monument.

(b)

(c)

special' (grade II*/B) or 'special' interest (grade II/C). A small number of historic structures and buildings are also designated for protective purposes as 'scheduled ancient monuments'. (Note: at the time of writing, in England, there are proposals to do away with separate categories for scheduled ancient monuments and listed buildings, the idea being to 'have a single national designation system with a single legislative base' (DCMS, 2007)).

Given the diversity of this group of assets, it is unsurprising that a very wide range of values may be variously ascribed to them by individuals, communities and society at large – including as being of historic, architectural, technological, associational, aesthetic, archaeological, educational, recreational, economic, social, commemorative, symbolic, spiritual, or ecological importance. However, as has already been mentioned, the great majority of historic structures are valued prosaically for housing day-to-day functions (in other words, their use).

Where statutory protection exists, depending upon circumstance, it is likely to seek to safeguard the structure's surviving historic fabric (including fossil archaeological evidence of previous use or change in the built fabric), plan form, external appearance, distinctive character, massing, materials, or long pertaining use. Thus, conservation management policies for individual buildings and structures tend to be focused (though not to exclusion) at this level of interest and attention. In the past, the starting point for conservation management generally – reflecting a strong cultural and philosophical bias towards the importance of the preservation of historic buildings and monuments – centred on a set of principles, including tenets such as minimum intervention, which lay at the heart of The Venice Charter (ICOMOS, 1964). At the time of writing, UK historic buildings legislation continues to retain this overarching focus, as examination of the Government's related policy guidance clearly reveals – see for instance, in England, sections within Planning Policy Guidance 15 '*Planning and the Historic Environment*' on 'Alterations and Extensions' (S3.12), 'The Upkeep and Repair of Historic Buildings' (S7) and 'Guidance on Alterations to Listed Buildings' (Annex C).

Management of protected buildings and structures involves some level of interaction between the owner or occupier of the property and the statutory authority responsible for administration of the relevant legislative procedures. Some of the problems with the current situation include:

- List descriptions that do not indicate what aspects of the building contribute to its significance, which means that the owners/occupiers do not know what it is that they are 'stewarding'.
- A widespread and mistaken concept that listing is intended to 'freeze' a place in time.
- An essentially adversarial relationship between the statutory authority and the owner/occupier.
- A lack of understanding of conservation ideas and principles by many owner/occupiers, which results in, amongst other things, a sense that the appearance of a building is of overarching importance (and therefore if elements

deteriorate or are damaged then as long as they are replaced with 'replicas' no loss has actually occurred).

Almost inevitably, many highly significant historic structures are left largely or entirely unprotected by national statute or are severely undervalued or misrepresented on descriptive lists of statutorily protected buildings. Management of unprotected buildings and structures is dictated more often than not by the short term goals and wants of the owner or occupier, irrespective of their long term impact or potential detriment to sustainable use.

Cultural landscapes

Under the heading of cultural landscape, we are including cultural routes, such as the ancient trade route, the Silk Road – which passed from the shores of the Mediterranean through Bukhara and Samarkand to Xian in Central China – and more modern aspects of heritage such as Brunel's Great Western Railway from Bristol to London. In devising the term 'cultural landscape' in 1925, Carl Sauer, an American cultural geographer, wrote:

> *The cultural landscape is fashioned from a natural landscape by a culture group. Culture is the agent, the natural area is the medium, the cultural landscape the result.*

More recently, the term has come to be highly inclusive. Another cultural geographer, Pierce Lewis, writing in 1979, observed:

> *It is proper and important to think that cultural landscapes are nearly everything we can see when we go outdoors... [Saying] that certain things in certain areas are somehow more historic than other things or places... is rather like saying that there is more geography in one place than another.*

This mirrors the more recent shift that has occurred in the conservation world – rather than in the discipline of cultural geography – where the term 'historic landscape' has been adopted to reinforce an appreciation that everything that surrounds us, whether in the town or country, is the result of ongoing cumulative change. As Peter Fowler has noted (2001, p. 77; 2002, p. 17):

> *By recognising cultural landscape, we have, almost for the first time, given ourselves the opportunity to recognise places that may well look ordinary but that can fill in our appreciation to become extraordinary; and an ability in some places to do that creates monuments to the faceless ones, the people who lived and died unrecorded except unconsciously and collectively by the landscape modified by their labours. The cultural landscape is a memorial to the unknown labourer.*

The cultural landscape represents a manifestation of a vital interaction between mankind and the natural environment (or perhaps more accurately the pre-existing cultural environments) over time. Values that may reside in a cultural landscape are diverse. Scazzosi (2002, p. 55) reflects that:

> *Places are. . . a document full of material and immaterial traces of man and nature's history. In this sense they are a vast archive, available to anyone willing and able to read it, that allows us to improve knowledge of culture, techniques, ways of life, as well as the nature, climate and vegetation of the past. . . When we use the term 'landscape', we stress the relationship between the world and ourselves: a window through which we can look at the world with the eyes of our cultural tradition.*

In UNESCO's 2005 operational guidelines for the implementation of the World Heritage Convention, cultural landscapes are sub-divided into three categories, the:

- **Clearly defined landscape** – designed and created intentionally by man (embracing gardens and parklands as landscapes constructed for aesthetic reasons);
- **Organically evolved landscape** – which results from an initial social, economic, administrative, and/or religious imperative and reflects a process of evolution in their form and component features; and
- **Associative cultural landscapes** – which have been called 'landscapes of ideas' and are distinguished by their associations with the natural environment rather than by their evidence of material culture, which may be minimal or entirely absent.

It has been noted that the range of natural features associated with cosmological, symbolic, sacred and culturally significant landscapes may be very broad, including mountains, caves, outcrops, coastal waters, rivers, lakes, pools, hillsides, uplands, plains, woods, groves and trees. Organically evolved landscapes fall into two categories, fossil or relic cultural landscapes. In the UK these are numerous – for example: the pre-historic landscape around Stonehenge; the industrial landscape of the Ironbridge Gorge; and the extensive surviving areas of historic landscaped elements, such as medieval ridge and furrow. Living cultural landscapes perhaps need less explanation, for they surround us everywhere – old and new gravel workings in the Thames Valley, fruit cultivation and its associated structures in the Vale of Evesham, the thatched villages of Devon and Cornwall, and so forth. It is being argued that our towns and cities are as much cultural landscapes as are designed rural landscapes, formal gardens or parkland, and that they should be interpreted and managed as such.

Places like the Indonesian island of Bali are being viewed as a single cultural landscape, since it reflects in a vital and deep-seated, often intangible, way the interaction between the natural landscape and Balinese Hindu culture and its unique cosmology over the last 1000 years.

Understanding the range of cultural landscapes that exist and their specific nature is fundamental to their proper management. If we want to safeguard and nurture such assets, we have to know where they exist, how they are characterised and why they are culturally valuable. Cultural landscapes are to be found in desert landscapes and oasis systems, in sacred mountains, in the vineyards of France and South Africa, as cultural routes such as the Silk Road, in the rice terraces of the Philippines, the canals and irrigation systems of the Fenlands and in the Netherlands, the Gardens of Versailles, the Darjeeling railway as much as Brunel's Great Western Railway, and the Cedars of Lebanon.

Until very recently, many cultural landscapes have not been recognised as such or as having overriding significance as a unified assemblage. As a consequence, some cultural landscapes are partially protected through the statutory designation of individual component parts, whilst the landscape as an entity is unrecognised in this way – an example of this situation is the important wider prehistoric landscape that includes both Stonehenge and numerous burial mounds in Wiltshire, England.

The universal presence of cultural landscapes means that their ownership and management patterns are often extremely complex. Some of the cultural landscapes referred to already cross modern national borders. Even the less dramatic are likely to be in multiple ownership and may extend across the boundaries of more than one planning authority. This makes the establishment or imposition of a unified beneficial management regime problematic and frequently impossible. As a consequence, caring for a valued cultural landscape often depends upon some form of designation or statutory protection. By and large, this will not achieve proactive day-to-day management, but provides a regulatory mechanism for managing large-scale physical change to such assets. Arguably, this is particularly inappropriate when dealing with continuing living cultural landscapes, since the inhibition of change may well destroy the essential characteristics of the landscape – in other words, its continuity of change.

As we have already noted, the values present in a cultural landscape may be diverse, including historic, archaeological, aesthetic, panoramic, scenic, educational, recreational, economic, social, commemorative, symbolic, spiritual, or ecological. Although the minutiae of the fabric of a cultural landscape may have, in some instances, relevance, management focus tends to need to occur at a higher level than for say individual historic structures and buildings, being involved with protection and care of rural and/or urban areas.

Landed rural estates

From the Norman Conquest onwards, large landed rural estates have been a significant feature of the landscape, society and economic well-being of the United Kingdom and, indeed, much of Europe. The aggregation of massive land holdings has been equated with power throughout much of our history. As just one example, within twenty years of the Norman Conquest, the Baron William de Mohun held 56 Manors in Somerset, 11 in Dorset and one each in Devon and Wiltshire. The family name is thus repeated in, for instance, National Trust information

(a)

(b)

Figure 2.3(a)–(c)   Silbury Hill in Wiltshire (a) lies in close proximity to the standing stones at Avebury. They are both part of the wider cultural landscape in this area that includes Stonehenge. Silbury Hill is the largest man-made mound from prehistoric Europe (at 40 metres). Its purpose is unknown. Silbury Hill was built approximately 4600 years ago at about the time that Avebury was being completed.

(c)

Figure 2.3   *(Continued)*

today in properties in Cornwall, Devon and Somerset. Equally, the Acland family of the nineteenth and twentieth centuries is often referred to in the National Trust's literature for the same area of the country. At the end of the nineteenth century, roughly 90% of rural England and Wales was tenanted: land ownership was dominated by families who generally depended upon the income from their estates for their livelihood. However, this long-standing pattern was about to change with the effects of the Industrial Revolution, taxation, agricultural depression, World War I and subsequent sweeping social change. The 1874 return of *Owner's of Land* recorded that 17% of England was occupied by large estates in excess of 3000 acres and 24% by great estates in excess of 10 000 acres. Over the twentieth century, the pattern of land holding changed dramatically. The number of land holdings over 700 acres in size increased fourfold between 1950 and 1970, yet behind this lay a fundamental change in the pattern of ownership and management responsibility. By 2001, Kevin Cahill (2002) found that the top ten landowners in the UK were: The Forestry Commission, 972 000 hectares; The Ministry of Defence 303 750 hectares; The National Trust 222 750 hectares; Pension Funds 202 500 hectares; Utility Companies 202 500 hectares; Crown Estate 155 520 hectares; The Duke of Buccleuch and Queensberry 112 470 hectares; The National Trust of Scotland 71 280 hectares; Duke of Atholl's Trust 59 940 hectares; The Duchy of Cornwall 57 105 hectares.

Landed rural estates have been defined (Bettey, 1993) as: 'any landholding of at least 3,000 acres, subject to a single owner, whether an institution or an individual, not necessarily made up of a single compact territory, but which has been

Figure 2.4   Subak in Bali – a cultural landscape shaped by centuries of use and Hindu custom.

administered as a unit and where the effects of a single ownership can be recognised'. For our purposes, we may take a wider view of the landed rural estate to include smaller holdings in the ownership of individuals as well as larger estates (in foreign ownership), non-governmental organisations (NGOs) and government departments. In short, day-to-day management control and decision making will normally be in the hands of the tenant or a professional manager, unless the holding is essentially owner occupied. It seems readily apparent from the foregoing that the great majority of the UK's surviving historic landed estates are managed not for their heritage but for their economic value. This undoubtedly influences the day-to-day decisions that are made and implemented.

Arguably, historic landed rural estates can and perhaps should be regarded as being cultural landscapes. In their entirety, they are each an organically evolved landscape of a continuing nature. Many will also contain other distinct cultural landscapes – for instance, relict medieval ridge and furrow landscapes or significant areas of mineral or stone extraction – or they may be bisected by a significant cultural route such as a canal or railway. The whole estate may have coalesced around a mansion and its pleasure grounds and parkland, in itself a clearly defined cultural landscape. Such hierarchies of heritage assets must be recognised and understood in order that appropriate management strategies and planning can be put in place for the individual and distinct areas.

Historic urban estates

Urban estates can be contrasted distinctly with landed rural estates. Inevitably, because of their context they tend to be significantly smaller (in terms of land area), whilst usually containing buildings whose total floor area far exceeds their rural counterparts. These buildings may well be subjected to considerably greater use pressures, and demand a style of management that is very different from the rural estate.

Although small in area in comparison to expansive rural estates, some historic estates can dominate and dictate the character and culture of whole towns and cities. The University of Oxford and the University of Cambridge are good examples of where a major part of the cultural and economic values of modern cities continues to be focused on historic estates that lie at their core. Other urban estates may be woven deeply into the historic grain of an urban area, whilst being less obvious to the uninformed visitor – the widespread ownership of property around Bloomsbury in London by the Bedford Estates in London is a typical example. Here, a substantial part of the valuable urban area separating the West End from the City of London has been owned and managed by the Duke of Bedford's estate since 1669. Undoubtedly, this has had a dramatic impact upon its development, form and significance.

The types of estates already cited are interwoven into the fabric of towns and cities, but are essentially dispersed and, to a greater or lesser degree, outward looking. Others are more self-contained and introspective, more like walled or defended complexes: Royal Palaces, residential estates – such as the *Spaarndammerplantsoen* in Amsterdam which has three public housing blocks designed by Michel de Klerk, or Albany off Piccadilly in London – and governmental estates fall into this category.

Where historic structures predominate in these various urban estates, it may seem reasonably obvious that management should take account of their historic interest (although this is often not the case). More problematic for the general estate manager is the situation where a largely twentieth century portfolio of structures of little architectural significance (but, of course, potentially rich in other cultural values) contains one or a small number of protected historic structures – typical examples might be Post Office estates, underground railways, hospital complexes and the like. In such cases, standard prescribed management processes devised for the estates as a whole may well not act in the best interests of the individual historic building or element. Conversely, adaptation of the estate-wide management arrangements and procedures to suit the needs of historic components may render the management organisation as a whole inefficient, cumbersome or costly.

By circumstance, historic urban estates will rarely – in the UK at least – be owned by individuals. Most will be in the ownership of institutions, trusts, central and local government, management companies, pension funds or the Crown. Management tends to be in the hands of professional managers or their agents.

The implications of the foregoing are critically important. Many historic urban estates contribute substantially to the primary urban grain and/or character of modern towns and cities. They may also play an important part in maintaining or contributing to the economic health and sustainability of the wider area or sub-region. Despite this, many will be managed on a day-to-day basis, with little regard to their historic interest, let alone their overall cultural significance.

(a)

(b)

Figure 2.5(a)–(c)   The Colleges of Oxford University are a Historic Urban Estate.

(c)

Figure 2.5   (*Continued*). Photograph (c) courtesy of Lee Stickells.

This implies that they may well not be managed (to echo Brundtland (United Nations, 1987)) to optimise their benefit to society whilst safeguarding the needs and interests of future generations. Unsustainable management is surely bad management.

Historic areas and urban landscapes: towns and cities

As at 2007, there are somewhere in the region of 10 600 historic areas in cities, towns and villages around the UK that are recognised for their special character, having been designated as Conservation Areas [England – around 9400; Scotland – 628; Wales – 500; Northern Ireland – 59]. There are substantially more areas of historic interest throughout the UK that are not recognised or protected in any way. Indeed, as we have already noted, we regard the historic environment as involving everything around us.

Currently, there is considerable debate as to whether historic areas of settlements and conurbations, and urban landscapes more generally, should be regarded as being 'extreme' or ultimate forms of cultural landscape. On the one hand, just as with other cultural landscapes, historic areas and urban landscapes have undeniably been 'fashioned from a natural landscape by a culture group' (Sauer, 1925). However, others would argue that the natural landscape contributes almost nothing to such places. In our view, this would deny that

(b)

(a)

Figure 2.6(a),(b)   The *Spaarndammerplantsoen* in Amsterdam is another example of a Historic Urban Estate.

(a)

(b)

Figure 2.7(a),(b)   The Barbican development in the City of London is yet another example of a Historic Urban Estate.

topography and 'natural' features (for instance, rivers and undulating land) frequently play a major part in urban morphology. We believe that, as an asset type, historic areas and urban landscapes should be accepted as being a separate grouping of cultural landscapes. However, in terms of management, they are characterised by some quite distinct features that are not shared by other cultural landscapes.

By their very nature, whether protected or unprotected, historic areas usually contain numerous individual properties, frequently in separate ownership. Management responsibility is thus often split amongst numerous individuals and/or property-owning companies or institutions. In the UK, the public areas and spaces will be vested in and managed by a local authority. If protected as a conservation area, that same authority may hope to encourage good management practice of the individual premises within the area. This can be encouraged either positively by providing design and care guidance, or administratively (and restrictively) by removing certain permitted development rights and by regarding the special character of the area as a material consideration during the planning process. Where historic areas are unprotected statutorily, their significance is exposed to diminution by the management decisions of individual property owners, except in so far as the normal planning process might apply some protective control.

Management of a historic area can and should take place at several levels. Gradual erosion of the quality of an area's character frequently occurs through ill-judged intervention with historic fabric, especially those interventions involving changes in traditional material usage or to external elements such as the profile of roofs or design of windows. Equal damage can be occasioned within a short time by the accretion of modern communications equipment, such as satellite dishes or television aerials to external elevations and chimney-stacks. However, historic areas also need to be managed in terms of building heights, building lines, massing, street patterns, vistas and so forth. The remarkable historic grid of Barcelona is an excellent example of a situation where, if this aspect is to be retained, management needs to take place at a strategic level far removed from cares about retention or intervention with historic fabric.

The multi-layered value of historic areas and the need for multi-layered management have been described beautifully by Feilden and Jokilehto (1993):

> *For the pedestrian, there are many subtle qualities in streets, lanes, even canals and bridges, and these urban spaces combine to give visual drama by the sensations of compression, expansion, surprise and the careful location of fine architectural set pieces. Views of the principal buildings from various places provide reassuring reference points. Citizens who know the history of the place will enjoy the rich feeling of participating in its history, and a sense of continuity and identity. Some of the key buildings are symbolic; without them, the place would never be the same.*
>
> *In an historic town, the substance and archaeological potential that embody historic values and material authenticity lie in the structures of all*

buildings and in the infrastructures. Often a large part of urban fabric may consist of simple buildings without special artistic qualities, anonymous architecture connected by open squares, lanes, streets and parks. It is these structures and urban spaces in which the life of the town has evolved that distinguish the concept of historic town from a group of monuments. Since their demolition or neglect would deprive the town of its essence, a policy for their treatment should be established.

What Feilden and Jokilehto observe in the historic town is mirrored within the historic quarters of cities and, indeed, by entire cities themselves. As Brand (1994) has written, 'While the regions provide myth, cities express history'. It is this expression of history that gives comfort to people and gives value to urban life, as David Lowenthal (1985) has demonstrated in *The Past is a Foreign Country*. Our towns and cities are mostly intensely complex historical documents. Yet, though these are interpreted and understood by exceedingly few, their historicity is appreciated by the many.

Spiro Kostoff (1991) has noted that 'Cities are amalgams of buildings and people. They are inhabited settings from which daily rituals – the mundane and the extraordinary, the random and the staged – derive their validity... The city is the ultimate memorial of our struggles and glories'. As inhabited settings, the intimate characteristics of nearly every urban district are a reflection of a vital contest that has taken place over time between socioeconomic forces of change and the remarkable persistence of the city's most enduring feature, its physical build. This is the case block by block, street by street, site by site. This is not just another theoretical way of viewing urban space, it is basic raw reality. It is the 'how' and the 'why' that explains every aspect of physical form in the streetscape – from the 'puzzles of premeditated and spontaneous segments [of urban form], variously interlocked or juxtaposed' to the 'small incident, the twisted street, the rounded corner, the little planted oasis unexpectedly come upon'.

Everyone – it seems – has some innate and instinctive recognition of the value of this developmental complexity in our towns and cities. Peter Larkham (1996), explaining the theoretical approach to townscape management of M.R.G. Conzen, has put it thus:

Landscapes embody not only the efforts and aspirations of the people occupying them at present, but also those of their predecessors. In this way, the townscape may be seen as embodying the spirit of society in the context of its own historical development in a particular place... It becomes the spirit of the place, the genus loci. In Conzen's view, it is an important environmental experience for the individual, even when it is received unconsciously. It enables individuals and groups to take root in an area. They acquire a sense of the historical dimension of human experience... Viewed in this way, townscapes represent accumulated experience... and are thus a precious asset.

(a)

(b)

Figure 2.8(a)–(c)   In Conservation Areas, the buildings and the spaces between buildings are important.

(c)

Figure 2.8   *(Continued)*

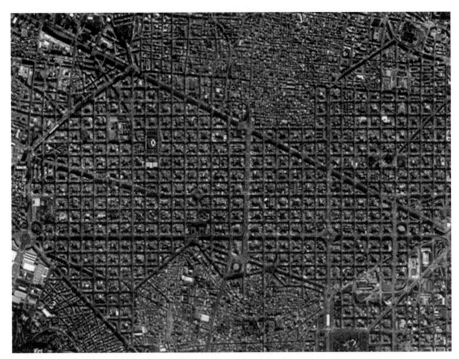

Figure 2.9   The remarkable survival of Barcelona's historic city plan. Copyright QuickBird ©
Digital Globe, 2001, distributed and by courtesy of Eurimage.

ICOMOS's Washington Charter (ICOMOS, 1987) which was concerned with
'the conservation of historic towns and urban areas', noted that such areas 'embody the values of traditional urban cultures'. The Charter advised that the
management of historic urban areas 'should be an integral part of coherent policies of economic and social development and of urban and regional planning at
every level'. Specifically, it recommended that:

> *Qualities to be preserved include the historic character of the town or
> urban area and all those material and spiritual elements that express this
> character, especially:*
>
> - *Urban patterns as defined by lots and streets;*
> - *Relationships between buildings and green and open spaces;*
> - *The formal appearance, interior and exterior of buildings as defined by
>   scale, size, style, construction, materials, colour and decoration;*
> - *The relationship between the town or urban area and its surrounding
>   setting, both natural and man-made; and*
> - *The various functions that the town or urban area has acquired over
>   time.*

Active management of historic areas and urban landscapes needs to consider and
respect all these many and varied attributes to be successful and sustainable in
its effects.

Figure 2.10   The Sydney Opera House is a World Cultural Heritage Site.

World heritage sites/cities

The *Convention Concerning the Protection of the World Cultural and Natural Heritage*, more commonly referred to as 'The World Heritage Convention', was adopted by UNESCO in November 1972. It was ratified by the UK in 1984. At the time of writing, 56 national states have ratified the Convention.

The Convention requires that a World Heritage List be maintained by an inter-governmental World Heritage Committee. The World Heritage List identifies cultural and natural properties which are to be protected under the Convention. The Convention (Article 1) defines 'cultural heritage' under three headings:

- *monuments: architectural works, works of monumental sculpture and painting, elements or structures of an archaeological nature, inscriptions, cave dwellings and combinations of features, which are of outstanding universal value from the point of view of history, art or science;*
- *groups of buildings: groups of separate or connected buildings which, because of their architecture, their homogeneity or their place in the landscape, are of outstanding universal value from the point of view of history, art or science;*
- *sites: works of man or the combined works of nature and of man, and areas including archaeological sites which are of outstanding universal value from the historical, aesthetic, ethnological or anthropological points of view.*

Article 2 of the Convention defines 'natural heritage' as:

- *natural features consisting of physical and biological formations or groups of such formations, which are of outstanding universal value from the aesthetic or scientific point of view; geological and physiographical formations and precisely delineated areas which constitute the habitat of threatened species of animals and plants of outstanding universal value from the point of view of science or conservation;*
- *natural sites or precisely delineated natural areas of outstanding universal value from the point of view of science, conservation or natural beauty.*

UNESCO's 2005 *Operational Guidelines for the Implementation of the World Heritage Convention* allow for the inscription of mixed cultural and natural heritage sites (Paragraph 46) and, as we have already seen, for cultural landscapes as cultural properties, representing the 'combined works of nature and of man' (Paragraph 47).

As the description of each category of cultural and natural heritage makes clear, the defining characteristic is that, in every case, the asset or property must be of 'outstanding universal value'. This is defined as:

cultural and/or natural significance which is so exceptional as to transcend national boundaries and to be of common importance for present and future generations of all humanity. As such, the permanent protection of this heritage is of the highest importance to the international community as a whole.

Currently, 10 criteria are used to establish outstanding universal value. Properties being nominated for inscription on the World Heritage List must meet one or more of the following:

(i) *represent a masterpiece of human creative genius;*

(ii) *exhibit an important interchange of human values, over a span of time or within a cultural area of the world, on developments in architecture or technology, monumental arts, town-planning or landscape design;*

(iii) *bear a unique or at least exceptional testimony to a cultural tradition or to a civilization which is living or which has disappeared;*

(iv) *be an outstanding example of a type of building, architectural or technological ensemble or landscape which illustrates a significant stage(s) in human history;*

(v) *be an outstanding example of a traditional human settlement, land-use, or sea-use which is representative of a culture (or cultures), or human interaction with the environment especially when it has become vulnerable under the impact of irreversible change;*

(a)

(b)

Figure 2.11(a),(b)   Pamukkale in Turkey is an example of a natural site on the World Cultural Heritage list.

Figure 2.12   Ha-Long Bay in Vietnam is another example of a natural site on the World Cultural Heritage list.

    (vi) *be directly or tangibly associated with events or living traditions, with ideas, or with beliefs, with artistic and literary works of outstanding universal significance;*

   (vii) *contain superlative natural phenomena or areas of exceptional natural beauty and aesthetic importance;*

 (viii) *be outstanding examples representing major stages of earth's history, including the record of life, significant ongoing geological processes in the development of landforms, or significant geomorphic or physiographic features;*

   (ix) *be outstanding examples representing significant ongoing ecological and biological processes in the evolution and development of terrestrial, fresh water, coastal and marine ecosystems and communities of plants and animals;*

   (x) *contain the most important and significant natural habitats for in-situ conservation of biological diversity, including those containing threatened species of outstanding universal value from the point of view of science or conservation.*

Clearly, not all are relevant to cultural heritage assets.

Inscribed cultural World Heritage Sites range from individual monuments and sites through to historic areas and cities such as Bath, Brasilia, Toledo and Venice and the Lagoon.

In some countries, World Heritage Sites are provided with additional statutory protection under national planning/development legislation. That is not the case in the UK, although the outstanding international importance of the site does constitute a key material consideration to be taken into account by local planning authorities in determining planning and listed building applications. Local authorities are also required to formulate specific planning policies for protecting World Heritage Sites.

The Operational Guidelines require that nominated properties 'should have an appropriate management plan or other documented management system which should specify how the outstanding universal value of a property should be preserved, preferably through participatory means' (Paragraphs 108 and 109) – the purpose being to ensure effective protection for present and future generations. The Guidelines also recognise that 'Management systems may vary according to different cultural perspectives, the resources available and other factors. They may incorporate traditional practices, existing urban or regional planning instruments, and other planning control mechanisms, both formal and informal' (Paragraph 110). However, it is suggested that to be effective, management arrangements could include (Paragraph 111):

a) *a thorough shared understanding of the property by all stakeholders;*
b) *a cycle of planning, implementation, monitoring, evaluation and feedback;*
c) *the involvement of partners and stakeholders;*
d) *the allocation of necessary resources;*
e) *capacity-building; and*
f) *an accountable, transparent description of how the management system functions.*

This is potentially onerous where the World Heritage Site includes numerous properties in private ownership. (For instance, the City of Bath, see Figures 2.14a–d.) In the end, as the Guidelines make clear, the State Party is 'responsible for implementing effective management activities for a World Heritage property', doing so 'in close collaboration with property managers, the agency with management authority and other partners, and stakeholders in property management' (Paragraph 117). As ICOMOS's tourism handbook for World Heritage Site Managers sombrely comments, 'The management of urban historic sites is perhaps the most complex of all sites. They are living organisms, often densely populated, with deteriorating infrastructures and enormous development pressures. The management of these sites is often fragmented among various local and national government agencies' (ICOMOS, 1993). In the worst case, this might necessitate direct intervention by a national Government to correct ineffective management of a World Heritage Site, if the World Heritage

(a)

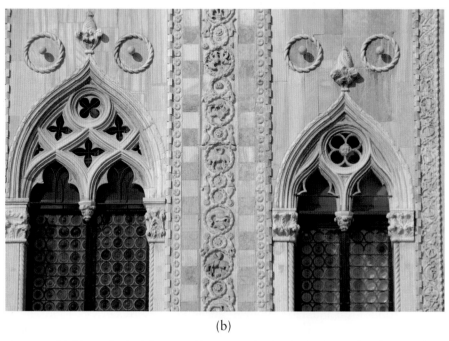

(b)

Figure 2.13(a)–(c)   Venice (and the Lagoon) is an example of a city that is a World Cultural Heritage Site.

(c)

Figure 2.13   (*Continued*)

Committee had concluded that the situation was placing the outstanding universal value of the asset in jeopardy.

Buffer zones and urban settings to major heritage assets

Increasing attention is being paid to the urban settings of World Heritage Sites, historic monuments and other cultural heritage assets and to their potential to act as part of a planning buffer zone to protect the major heritage asset at their core. Whilst in every respect, these settings are simply historic areas and sometimes urban landscapes in their own right, in our view, this focus seems likely to intensify still further in the next few years. For this reason, we have separated them out for individual consideration in this brief overview of heritage asset types.

This section deals specifically with urban situations. In this context, there is no agreed definition of what constitutes the setting to a historic site or area. In England, the Government's Planning Policy Guidance 15 states that 'In some cases, setting can only be defined by a historical assessment of a building's surroundings' – in other words, identification of setting may well vary with circumstance and, specifically, according to historical development. A buffer zone is rather easier to define. Paragraph 104 of UNESCO's 2005 *Operational Guidelines for the Implementation of the World Heritage Convention* states that 'a buffer zone is an area surrounding the nominated property which has complementary legal and/or customary restrictions placed on its use and development to give an added layer of protection to the property'. Whilst this is intended to relate only to World Heritage Sites, replacing the words 'nominated property' with 'heritage asset' provides a satisfactory definition for all situations. UNESCO's Operational Guidelines go on to expand upon the definition by stating that a buffer zone: 'should include the immediate setting of the nominated property, important views and other areas or attributes that are functionally important as a support to the property and its protection'. Again, this seems apposite to all other buffer zones as well.

Settings to urban historic sites (or areas), like all other historic areas, will usually contain numerous individual properties that will be in separate ownership. Management responsibility is thus often split amongst many individuals and/or property-owning organisations. Just as with other historic areas, settings encapsulate a multitude of cultural values for the local community.

It is worth repeating the words of Feilden and Jokilehto (1993) quoted above whilst considering 'historic areas or urban landscapes':

> *Often a large part of urban fabric may consist of simple buildings without special artistic qualities, anonymous architecture connected by open squares, lanes, streets, and parks. It is these structures and urban spaces in which the life of the town has evolved that distinguish the concept of historic town from a group of monuments.*

(a)

(b)

Figure 2.14(a)–(d)   The City of Bath is a World Cultural Heritage site; much of it is also defined as Conservation Areas. In addition, it contains many individually protected scheduled monuments and listed buildings.

(c)

(d)

Figure 2.14   (*Countinued*). Photographs (c and d) courtesy of John Bailey.

Obviously, this describes the urban setting of a heritage asset just as well as any other 'typical' historic area. We have suggested in looking at historic areas and urban landscapes generally that 'as inhabited settings, the intimate characteristics of nearly every urban district are a reflection of a vital contest that has taken place over time between socio-economic forces of change and the remarkable persistence of the city's most enduring feature, its physical build' (Kostoff, 1991). Again, that is as true of architecturally mundane settings for major urban heritage assets as it is for large parts of other urban grain.

However, unlike other historic urban areas, for reasons that are arguably both good and bad, the conservation world has come to regard the character of urban settings to more major – often, monumental – heritage assets as being, to a degree, selectively expendable in the interests of 'proper' management of the latter. In simplistic terms, we seek to impose a conceptual relationship of master and subordinate on major historic assets and their urban settings. As we have seen, in England, PPG15 states that 'In some cases, setting can only be defined by a historical assessment of a building's surroundings'. In theory, this approach risks subordinating the history and values of the setting into being but a subset of the history and values of the more major historic place itself. It defines the setting as being principally an attribute of the heritage asset with little value as an organic area in its own right. Literature and guidance relating to the setting of monuments and other historic places are in short supply – what little there is, expressly or implicitly, reflects this same attitude. The Venice Charter states that 'conservation of a monument implies preserving a setting which is not out of scale (ICOMOS, 1964). Wherever the traditional setting exists, it must be kept'. Whatever one's sympathy with the intent behind this, once again it does impose a master and subordinate relationship between the historic place and the setting. It demands that the ongoing 'vital contest' within the setting (which after all until then has not affected the survival of its 'traditional' nature) be curtailed and subordinated to the perceived needs of the major asset for protection from change and the inappropriate world outside. Of course, the very notion that the setting may be 'traditional' is a solecism. Every urban space and hence every setting without exception is the result of historical decisions and activity that according to Larkham (1996) 'embody . . . the efforts and aspirations . . . of predecessors' and thus, in Kostoff's eyes (1991) represent 'the ultimate memorial of our struggles and glories'.

The present-day urban setting of the Tower of London provides a vivid illustration of the serious misrepresentation inherent in this attitude and the dangers that it can bring.

As a composition of fortifications, imposing buildings and spaces, the Tower is an internationally recognised icon of England's heritage. It receives more than 2 million paying visitors each year and there are at least as many again who tarry to admire and photograph without entry. In terms of designation and statutory protection, the Tower's intrinsic worth is well-recognised: it is a World Heritage Site, a scheduled ancient monument and virtually every structure within its walls is a listed building in its own right. More potently, perhaps, it is a living symbol of the power of the Crown through almost a thousand years of cultural development. The Tower of London has been at the heart of so much that defines the nation. Its involvement in the history of the state is familiar to all, but it has also been the birthplace and home of many major political and cultural institutions – for instance, the Board of Ordnance, the Ordnance Survey, the Royal Observatory, the Public Records Office, the Royal Mint and, through the Royal Menagerie, even London Zoo. In simple terms, it is one of the most vital and important heritage assets in the land. As such it should be treasured.

With this as background, it would seem axiomatic that the modern setting of the Tower should be rich in 'sense of place'. Bewilderingly, nothing could be further from reality, for the area is epitomised by diminished social and cultural values and wasted opportunity. Despite a number of determined attempts in the last fifty years by those seeking to improve and regenerate, little value has been ascribed or added to the environs of the Tower in the post-war reshaping of this quarter of London until recent alterations have made some improvements to the open space immediately beside the monument. Superficially, it is difficult to comprehend how this situation could have developed. Despite the recent improvements, the architectural amphitheatre and open space surrounding the Tower are blighted by the visual and environmental impact of a dual carriage highway which cuts across the open land immediately to the north of the Tower. The road forms an impenetrable barrier and the pavements alongside it are, for the most part, so narrow that pedestrians are encouraged to use subways for 'safe' passage around the environs. Above ground, the public open spaces are so seriously ravaged by traffic noise and pollution as to feel like roadside verge.

However impoverished the current setting of the Tower might be in environmental and aesthetic terms, it is an important historic space in its own right. It just cannot be read as such very easily today. Across many centuries, the primary defensive function (both real and overtly symbolic) of the Tower of London was not to protect the capital from river-borne invasion but to impose the will of the Crown upon the often reluctant City of London, and its administrators and inhabitants. The history of the development of the surrounding urban area (as distinct to the history of the Tower of London) is a fascinating one. Innumerable examples might be quoted of the continuing open and deep-seated conflict between these two powers from the Tower's construction in the late eleventh century through to the mid-to-late 1800s. During this time, the wider urban area (which also happens to be the setting of the fortress) can be viewed as a political, social and cultural 'battlefield', with the ongoing history of physical development, ownership and rights reflecting the ebb and flow of power and influence between these two forces, as well as the 'efforts and aspirations' of the many generations of local people.

Crucially, the current urban setting of the Tower is the direct inheritance of several generations of part-implemented planned comprehensive solutions to the area's problems. Master plans, developed with the best of intents to address urban blight and squalor in the 1930s, 1950s, 1960s and 1970s, all concentrated on the importance of the Tower and its history to the exclusion of anything else. On each occasion, the Tower was conceived as being a self-contained historic

Figure 2.15   The Tower of London and its modern urban setting in 2006.

monument that was solely responsible for any significance and cultural value in the wider locality. Its environs were only regarded as the means of approach to the monument, not as being a cohesive and meaningful historic area in its own right. This attitude has repeatedly pervaded re-planning of its future. The result has been sequential piecemeal yet radical restructuring of the environs as a setting for the Tower of London and no more. In the long term, this approach has been of no benefit. Critically, it has not re-engendered any sense of place. Instead, with each cycle of change, the principal outcome has been merely to leave further residues of discordant and inharmonious elements as a legacy to the future.

   This situation is far from unique. On many occasions, there are very real risks in treating the urban setting of a monument as being to some extent subordinate, without a development history of its own, and therefore open to shaping or stultification of change to suit the perceived needs of its influential neighbour. This approach reinforces the belief that our towns and cities consist, in essence, of isolated historic jewels or cores of elegance (each of which should ideally be protected by an umbra of appropriateness) surrounded by the historically or culturally valueless and dispensable. The lasting effect of this attitude is the total concealment of the importance of the 'vital contest' (between socioeconomic forces of change and persistence of the built historic grain) to urban existence. The importance of buffer zones is already enshrined within the Operational Guidelines for World Heritage – as will be discussed below. At that level, undoubtedly, there is a strong justification for ensuring wider protection of assets of 'outstanding universal value' (although the shortcomings with the setting of the Tower of London – itself a World Heritage Site – must remain an object lesson to the unwary). The problem is exacerbated, however, when dealing with the need to protect more modest heritage assets from the deleterious influence of unsatisfactory development in their setting. It is conceivable that, in the coming years, pressure will grow to protect some historic urban areas of note by the designation of a setting or buffer zone in which additional planning controls can be applied. At that level, the 'sacrifice' of one area's ongoing organic development to benefit another could well prove hard to justify. The key will be in the nature and derivation of the additional planning controls applied to the setting/buffer zone. If these are built from an understanding of the value and significance of the setting, the arrangement may provide sustainable solutions; if they are based solely upon the significance and needs of the dominant historic area, unsustainable and ultimately damaging change will occur.

The foregoing suggests that the management of change in settings to heritage assets and, by implication in protective buffer zones, can be a challenging issue – perhaps more so and for different reasons than is generally recognised. There is one further matter – specifically relating to the buffer zones of World Heritage Sites – that needs to be aired whilst considering responsibilities for the management of change within settings. As we have already seen, in the UK, it is generally held that inscription of an asset as a World Heritage Site confers no additional statutory protection, although the presence of a World Heritage Site is a material consideration within the planning process and thus may have some influence on the eventual development of neighbouring sites. Indeed, for England, PPG15 (S2.22) (Department of the Environment and the Department of National Heritage, 1994) states this to be the case unequivocally, as does Historic Scotland's 1998 Memorandum of Guidance on Listed Buildings and Conservation Areas (S2.24). In 2006, Christina Cameron, Canada Research Chair on Built Heritage at the University of Montreal, pointed out a substantive flaw in this argument. Paragraph 107 of UNESCO's 2005 Operational Guidelines declares that 'any modifications to the buffer zone subsequent to inscription of a property on the World Heritage List should be approved by the World Heritage Committee'. As Cameron (2006) notes, 'Now, countries are under a fairly onerous obligation to obtain international approval for activities in the buffer zones of their World Heritage Sites. Furthermore, recent decisions by the [World Heritage] Committee suggest that this obligation extends beyond the formal boundaries of buffer zones to include views and vistas'. In this discussion, 'activities' within buffer zones and wider vistas would seem specifically to include development proposals. The implication is that inscription as a World Heritage Site does, through the wording of Paragraph 107 of the Operational Guidelines, confer certain additional international statutory protection, irrespective of the original intent of the relevant national Government through application of its legislative planning and development controls. Overlooked until now, this could have far-reaching ramifications for the management of change in the wider settings to urban World Heritage Sites.

Intangible heritage

This book deals with the sustainable management of the built cultural heritage. Whilst intangible values are often a vital and significant component of such assets – and are discussed in Chapter 3 – an assessment of management issues affecting intangible heritage (for example, language, folklore and assets such as sacred mountains) lies beyond our current scope. For this reason, intangible heritage will not be covered in this brief review of cultural heritage assets.

Owners, managers and management approaches

The analysis of historic asset types set out above has sought to demonstrate that assets, individually or as an estate, are subjected to different management regimes and approaches according to ownership patterns. This is a fundamental point to comprehend.

Individual property owners or tenants view the act of management and the nature of their management responsibilities in a very different manner to corporate, institutional or governmental asset managers. Not the least, organisations as property managers must often have regard to the influence and expectations of external stakeholders. By and large, individuals manage the buildings they own or lease solely for their own needs and interests. It would be incorrect, as well as being potentially invidious, to suggest that one or other group takes better management decisions or cares more for the special interest of a historic asset. They are exposed to very different pressures and influences, and manage in contrasting ways.

For as long as their freehold or leasehold interest exists, individual owners or tenants provide continuity in property management. Conversely, the individual is very unlikely to perceive their use, care and alteration of the historic building as equating to 'management'. Therein lies the inherent threat that such 'managers' pose to the special interest, value or cultural significance of their property. Without a framework of management policies and strategies, it is unlikely that they will readily associate individual actions with the potential to inflict lasting damage on vulnerable aspects of significance.

The professional manager frequently comes with very different baggage. To some, property management is merely a 9am to 5pm job undertaken using someone else's money. Whilst this does not necessarily prevent the care that they give to a historic asset being entirely professional, for better or worse, it will hardly equate to the devotion applied by a proud home owner. Of course, neither is guaranteed to achieve appropriate sound care of the historic building; both can have highly undesirable results. They are, however, fundamentally different management approaches, which are likely to influence the nature of ongoing change in the asset.

Generalist (as in non-heritage) property managers are no more likely to manage in a way that respects the cultural significance of a historic site than the average individual freeholder or lessee. Often, the application of standard 'one size fits all' management approaches and procedures across a mixed portfolio of building types (in other words, a combination of modern and historic assets) is likely to result in undesirable or ill-judged repairs or changes to the historic structure.

It might be assumed that heritage management organisations are *per se* better equipped to manage historic buildings in a sustainable way than generalist property or portfolio managers. It is arguable that this is not always borne out in practice. Heritage management organisations tend to be somewhat idiosyncratic and self-absorbed. They are certainly frequently fraught with unique tensions between those with responsibility for aesthetics, maintenance and works managers, and commercial and operational managers whose fundamental objective is to get things done to improve the standard of facilities and income generation.

There are two fundamental problems that pervade both non-heritage and heritage property management organisations. First, with frequent personnel changes, all are prone to iterative loss of 'understanding' about the assets under their control and loss of ownership of planned initiatives. This can lead to weakening of focus, much wasted expenditure and the tendency to reinvent the wheel with astonishing regularity. Second, the quality of property management is very often seriously compromised by the inability to cascade understanding and ownership down to those whose job is to action day-to-day maintenance and repair tasks. This puts the vulnerable heritage asset at continuous risk of compromise or lasting damage, since works will tend to be undertaken without comprehension of their sensitivity, in a manner which suits the maintenance operative rather than the specific needs of the historic property and its significance.

Whatever the nature of the manager of a historic asset, therein lies the challenge to conservation planning as a management approach. Unless the decision maker(s) and the day-to-day operatives possess shared ownership of the management process and of the assessment of the significance of the place, they are unlikely to reach sound strategic decisions and also implement appropriate physical actions that respect and seek to enhance its wider special interest and value.

References

Bettey, J.H. (1993) *The Estates and the English Countryside*. London, Batsford.
Brand, S. (1994) *How Buildings Learn: What Happens After They're Built?* New York, Viking Penguin.
Cahill, K. (2002) *Who Owns Britain*. Edinburgh, Canongate Books.
Cameron, C. (2006) Protecting important views? Recent case studies from the World Heritage Committee. Paper presented to the *ICOMOS Canada 2006 Conference*, November, Carleton University, Ottawa, Ontario.

DCMS (Department of Culture, Media and Sport) (2007) *Heritage Protection for the 21st Century (White Paper)*. London, DCMS, p. 11.

Department of the Environment and the Department of National Heritage (1994). *PPG 15: Planning and the Historic Environment*. London, HMSO.

Feilden, B.M. and Jokilehto, J. (1993) *Management Guidelines for World Cultural Heritage Sites*. Rome, ICCROM.

Fowler, P. (2001) Cultural landscape: great concept, pity about the phrase. In: *The Cultural Landscape – Planning for a Sustainable Partnership between People and Place* (eds R. Kelly, L. Macinnes, D. Thackray and P. Whitbourne). London, ICOMOS UK, pp. 64–82.

Fowler, P. (2002) World Heritage Cultural Landscapes, 1992–2002: a review and prospect. In: *UNESCO World Heritage Papers 7 – Cultural Landscapes: the Challenges of Conservation*. Paris, UNESCO.

Historic Scotland (1998) *Memorandum of Guidance on Listed Buildings and Conservation Areas*. Edinburgh, Historic Scotland.

ICOMOS (1964) International charter for the conservation and restoration of monuments and sites. *IInd International Congress of Architects and Technicians of Historic Monuments*, Venice, Article 6. [Known as 'The Venice Charter'] [Available online at www.international.icomos.org/charters.htm]

ICOMOS (1987) *Charter for the Conservation of Historic Towns and Urban Areas* (adopted by ICOMOS General Assembly, Washington DC). ICOMOS, Paris. [Known as 'The Washington Charter.]

ICOMOS (1993) *Tourism at World Heritage Cultural Sites: the Site Manager's Hand Book*. Paris, ICOMOS.

Kostoff, S. (1991) *The City Shaped*. London, Thames and Hudson.

Larkham, P. (1996) *Conservation and the City*. London, Routledge.

Lewis, P. (1979) Axioms for reading the landscape: some guides to the American scene. In: *The Interpretation of Ordinary Landscapes: Geographical Essays* (ed. D.W. Meinig). New York, Oxford University Press, pp. 11–32.

Lowenthal, D. (1985) *The Past is a Foreign Country*. Cambridge, Cambridge University Press.

Sauer, C. (1925) Morphology of landscape. In: *University of California Publications in Geography*.

Scazzosi, L. (2002) Landscape and cultural landscape: European Landscape Convention and UNESCO Policy. In: *UNESCO World Heritage Papers 7 – Cultural Landscapes: the Challenges of Conservation*. Paris, UNESCO.

UNESCO (1972) *Convention Concerning the Protection of the World Cultural and Natural Heritage*. Paris, UNESCO.

UNESCO (2005) *Operational Guidelines for the Implementation of the World Heritage Convention*. Paris, UNESCO.

United Nations (1987) *Report of the World Commission on Environment and Development*. New York, UN. [Also published as *Our Common Future* by Oxford University Press, 1987.]

Chapter 3
Cultural Significance

Conservation is about negotiating the transition from past to future in such a way as to secure the transfer of maximum significance
(Holland and Rawles, 1993, p. 19)

The Getty Conservation Institute (CGI) report *Values and Heritage Conservation* observes that 'The creation of cultural heritage is largely derived from the way people remember, organise, think about and wish to use the past and how material culture provides a medium through which to do this' (Avrami et al., 2000, p. 8). But as Zancheti and Jokilehto (1997) observe, 'Conservation is a process that can only exist if society attributes values to the urban structure'.

Much of the literature in conservation refers to the values which are embodied in, or represented by, the built cultural heritage, and it uses the idea of protecting these values in order to explain and justify the purpose of conservation and its importance for individuals, groups and nations. The idea of protecting values is fundamental to the notion of conservation activity. The CGI report, for example, suggests that 'The ultimate aim of conservation is not to conserve material for its own sake but rather to maintain (and shape) the values embodied by the heritage – with physical interventions or treatment being one of many means towards that end' (Avrami et al., 2000, p. 7).

The term 'cultural significance' is now commonly used to refer to the collection of the various values associated with a place which together identify why it is important. The Burra Charter (Australia ICOMOS, 1999, p. 2) suggests that 'Cultural significance is embodied in the place itself, its fabric, setting, use, associations, meanings, records, related places and related objects'. The identification, measurement, protection and enhancement of cultural significance form the basis of what has come to be referred to as 'values-based management'.

It is suggested that societies protect certain aspects of the built environment because conservation brings benefits. This assertion raises the question not only of what these qualities are, but how they are identified, by whom, and for what reasons (and who benefits).

It is then the sense that the built cultural heritage embodies and represents a range of, often complex, sometimes conflicting values that bring benefits which is behind the idea of conserving the built cultural heritage. As Mason observes (2002, p. 8), 'Heritage is valued not as an intellectual enterprise but because (as one aspect of material culture) it plays instrumental, symbolic and other functions in society'. This point is reflected in the document *Power of Place* (English Heritage, 2000, p. 4) which observes, 'The historic environment is what generations of people have made of the places in which they lived. It is all about us. We are the trustees of that inheritance. It is in every sense a common wealth'.

Benefits of conservation

In his seminal book *The Past is a Foreign Country*, David Lowenthal (1997) discusses the 'benefits and burdens of the past'. He observes that although there is a general consensus about past related benefits (and he is concerned not just with the built environment here), they are seldom articulated, and so he sets out these categories (pp. 38–52):

- *Familiarity:* *The surviving past's most essential and pervasive benefit is to render the present familiar. Its traces on the ground and in our minds let us make sense of the present. Without habit and the memory of past experience, no sight or sound would mean anything; we can perceive only what we are accustomed to.*
- ***Reaffirmation and validation:*** *The past validates present attributes and actions by their resemblance to former ones.*
- ***Identity:*** *The past is integral to our sense of identity... Ability to recall and identify with our own past gives existence meaning, purpose and value... Even traumatically painful memories remain essential, emotional history.*
- ***Guidance:*** *The past is most characteristically evoked for the lessons it teaches.*
- ***Enrichment:*** *A well loved past enriches the world around us.*
- ***Escape:*** *... besides enhancing an acceptable present, the past offers alternatives to an unacceptable present. In yesterday we find what we miss today. And yesterday is a time for which we have no responsibility and when no one can answer back.*

Lowenthal says that 'No sharp boundaries delimit these benefits' and he observes, for example, that a sense of identity is also a mode of enrichment and that familiarity provides guidance. He also observes that some of these benefits are in conflict and gives as an example 'using the past to enrich present day life is at odds with wanting to escape from the present'. Indeed, escape from the present is seen as a negative aspect of an 'obsession with the past' associated with what

Robert Hewison identified as 'The Heritage Industry' in his well known and rather polemical book of the same name (Hewison, 1987).

It can be suggested that the value of conservation in a general sense might include the five points discussed below.

1. That there are significant benefits to the social, psychological and political well-being of individuals, groups and nations – or indeed collections of nations

In essence, the benefits that Lowenthal (1997) refers to are congruent with these social, psychological and political concerns. The notion is that the physical evidence of the past holds meaning for individuals and/or groups. Mason (2002, p. 11) suggests that 'The capacity of a site to convey, embody or stimulate a relation or a reaction to the past is part of the fundamental nature and meaning of heritage objects.' In part, this is related to relatively intangible concepts such as the idea of a collective memory and the sense that the physical remains of the past can embody and represent and stimulate this. The argument is that the ability to connect to the past is important because it, amongst other things, 'gives existence, meaning, purpose and value' (Lowenthal, 1997). This might work at a national level with often symbolic values being at play – the role of the restoration, or in many cases re-creation, of iconic buildings or structures following war or other disasters is an obvious example. But it can of course happen at a smaller group level, where a building can symbolically represent the development and or values of particular factions and therefore play a positive role in reinforcing and acknowledging shared values and reinforcing notions of community identity. However, it can have the opposite effect, and polarise and exclude by reinforcing and validating a particular view of the past.

Hubbard in a paper entitled 'The value of conservation' (1993, p. 266) asserts that 'it is apparent that the townscape must be considered extremely important for stabilising individual and group identities, particularly in times of stress'. In addition, he quotes Rowntree's 1981 comments that 'loss of cultural identity can be alleviated through the creation of shared symbolic structures that validate, if not actually define, social claims to space and time'. Hubbard suggests that this notion of shared but constructed value is important for community cohesion in a fragmented world. Thus the designation of places as having cultural value means the built environment can have a special function in creating and stabilising group identity. Stokols and Jacobi (1983) suggested that the bond between place and identity can give cultures a sense of historic perspective and belonging, but that the process for doing this may not be necessarily conscious and that the values may be difficult to discern or disentangle. Hubbard concludes that conserved environments generally create a sense of place and that this is imbued by people with cultural meaning.

The European Charter of the Architectural Heritage (Council of Europe, 1975, p. 1) picks up on some of these themes when it states that:

> *The past as embodied in the architectural heritage provides the sort of environment indispensable to a balanced and composite life. In the face of a rapidly changing civilisation in which brilliant successes are accompanied*

by grave perils, people today have an instinctive feeling for the value of this heritage. This heritage should be passed onto future generations in its authentic state and in all its variety as an essential part of the memory of the human race. Otherwise, part of man's awareness of his own continuity will be destroyed.

In a 1983 essay, entitled *Do we need a past?*, the Swedish philosopher, Sören Halldén, wrote:

The intensity of the awareness of life's continuity depends on the extent to which a society is enlivened with history. Monuments and settlement patterns contribute a great deal to the process of enlivening International conservation.

Why do we need such an enlivened environment in much the same way that animals need biological territory? With a few exceptions, most living creatures find it rewarding to live in an environment enriched with memories. Knowing what it is all about makes one feel more secure. This very basic biological fact is still valid within environments that we have made relatively safe by other means (by social welfare, for example). In our context, cultural identity is the sense of belonging created by many aspects of the physical environment that remind us of links between the present generation and the historical past.

The notion that there may also be benefits to groups of nations is also well established (if not necessarily agreed upon). For example, the Council of Europe (2005) refers to the common heritage of Europe, which, it states, consists of:

a *all forms of cultural heritage in Europe which together constitute a shared source of remembrance, understanding, identity, cohesion and creativity, and*
b *the ideals, principles and values, derived from the experience gained through progress and past conflicts, which foster the development of a peaceful and stable society, founded on respect for human rights, democracy and the rule of law*

and the United Nations Educational, Scientific and Cultural Organisation (UNESCO) has suggested that 'the cultural heritage of each is the cultural heritage of all' and that 'damage to cultural property belonging to any people whatsoever means damage to the cultural heritage of all mankind, since each people makes its contribution to the culture of the world' (ICOMOS, 1954).

At the 1984 ICOMOS General Assembly held in Germany, the Rapporteur, Dr Roland Palsson, spoke of the crucial importance of peace and international co-operation as a basic prerequisite for the conservation of cultural heritage (ICOMOS, 1987a). He recognised that the concept of cultural heritage was widening as the differences in the traditions and context of cultures and societies were taken into account. This increasing awareness of cultural diversity and pluralism gives hope for increased tolerance and respect for ethnic and religious minorities and for local opinions. Most particularly, cultural identity, having dimensions in both time and space, provides an essential framework for people's lives and activities.

The hope for peace and international co-operation is picked up by UNESCO, which operates its World Heritage programmes as a core part of its mission to 'create the conditions for dialogue among civilizations, cultures and peoples. . . encompassing observance of human rights, mutual respect and the alleviation of poverty'. Elsewhere, the World Bank invests in cultural heritage programmes in tandem with making major infrastructure loans to developing and transition national economies (frequently as part of post-conflict rehabilitation), because it sees this as being a powerful way to engender economic stability and growth. Cultural heritage can be a beneficial and benign tool in the search for peace, international stability, communication amongst and the forging of linkages between peoples, the sharing of common values, and respect for cultural diversity.

2. That there are significant educational benefits – that we can understand aspects of past societies not only through analysis of the physical remains of the past but also the historic environment is a focus and an opportunity for a less 'expert' engagement with the lives and experiences of previous generations

In the same way that we suggest that the buildings we construct today reflect the values of modern society, those from the past can help us to understand the political, social, economic and cultural values of previous societies. As *Power of Place* (English Heritage, 2000) observes, 'The historic environment is an incomparable source of information. For people in the distant past and for more recent generations whose history was never recorded it offers the only route towards an understanding of who they were and how they lived'.

3. That as existing buildings, they are a resource that should be reused for (environmental and financial) sustainability reasons

The Architectural heritage is a capital of irreplaceable spiritual, cultural, social and economic value. Each generation places a different interpretation on the past and derives inspiration from it. This capital has been built up over the centuries: the destruction of any part of it leaves us poorer since nothing new that we create, however fine, will make good the loss. Our society now has to husband its resources. Far from being a luxury this heritage is an economic asset which can be used to save community resources   (Council of Europe, 1975)

4. That the historic environment contributes to a sense of place through its character and its visual aesthetic

In many cases the built cultural heritage is a strong defining force or anchor for a sense of place (genus loci) that can be identified and appreciated by inhabitants and visitors. For some, the extent and intensity of such identification may be determined by the knowledge and understanding of the place that the person or group has, particularly in relation to factors such as present and previous uses and/or the nature and meaning of events which may have taken place there. The place may be important as the repository of a cultural memory that reinforces group identity.

5. That historic buildings and areas attract significant tourist revenue and make significant contributions to local, regional and sometimes national economies and employment

This point needs little further expansion here, for we have already observed that the World Bank recognises the considerable potential of cultural heritage programmes to assist in the stabilisation and re-invigoration of regional and national economies damaged by conflict. In most such situations, this will be reliant upon the development of a significant cultural tourism industry.

The benefit of both the built cultural and natural heritage to stable developed economies is demonstrated by numerous case studies – two from the United Kingdom will suffice to illustrate the point. Using data from Maeer and Millar (2004), eftec (2005, p. 62) report that:

> *the restoration of the Kennet and Avon Canal has also generated economic benefits for the leisure and tourism industry. Work carried out for British Waterways suggests that spending within local economies [following major investment in the canal's restoration] had risen to £26 million per year by 2002, a 20% increase on 1995. Of this, £21 million is attributed to towpath visits and £5 million to boating. In employment terms, the canal is estimated to support around 1,000 tourism and leisure jobs, 180 of which have been created since 1995.*

In a similar vein, a report published by ONE North East in 2004 (ONE North East, 2004, pp. 4–5) found that five protected landscape areas in the North East of England (Durham Heritage Coast, Northumberland National Park, Northumberland Coast Area of Outstanding Natural Beauty, the North Pennines Area of Outstanding Natural Beauty, and the North Yorkshire and Cleveland Heritage Coast) were directly generating an estimated £165 million of annual tourism expenditure in the region and supporting 5163 jobs. Taking into account indirect and induced effects, the total contribution of these protected landscapes to the region was estimated to include business turnover of more than £700 million and support for 14,000 jobs.

English Heritage (1997) articulates most of these benefits when they suggest that:

> *Historic buildings are a precious and finite asset, and powerful reminders to us of the work and way of life of earlier generations. The richness of this country's architectural heritage plays a powerful part in our sense of national identity and our enjoyment of our surroundings*

and The Charter for the Conservation of Places of Cultural Heritage Value (ICOMOS New Zealand, 1992) states that:

in general such places:
- *have lasting values and can be appreciated in their own right;*
- *teach us about the past and the culture of those who came before us;*
- *provide the context for community identity whereby people relate to the land and to those who have gone before;*
- *provide variety and contrast in the modern world and a measure against which we can compare the achievements of today*
- *provide visible evidence of the continuity between past, present and future.*

In a similar vein, The Burra Charter (Australia ICOMOS, 1999) suggests:

there are places worth keeping because they enrich our lives – by helping us understand the past; by contributing to the richness of the present environment; and because we expect them to be of value to future generations.

To a large extent these are potential rather than actual benefits. For example, realising educational benefit not only requires the active engagement of people but also a commitment of the owners and managers of historic places to inclusive access strategies and the development of objective interpretation strategies. *Power of Place* (English Heritage, 2000, p. 23) recognised this need to deliver actual benefits in observing that:

many feel powerless and excluded [when] the historical contribution of their group to society is not celebrated. Their personal heritage does not appear to be taken into account by those who make decisions...if the barriers to involvement are overcome the historic environment has the potential to strengthen a sense of community and provide a solid basis for neighbourhood renewal.

The various benefits can also be in tension. The obvious one being that of maximising the financial aspects at the expense of the social ones, particularly perhaps at tourist sites where the physical fabric and the 'spirit of the place' may be damaged by a mass influx of people and the service provision that is thought necessary to support them (and maximise income). Concerns about the impact of tourists at such well known tourist sites as Florence, Venice, Machu Picchu and Angkor Wat are echoed in various other cultural hotspots and also mirror concerns expressed about, say, national parks and other aspects of the natural environment.

Understanding value

Understanding the cultural value of a particular place – and being able to articulate what those values are and what aspects of the place embody and represent them – has become to be seen as an important, or rather a crucial task in 'value led management' of the built cultural heritage. As Mason (2002, p. 5) points out, 'assessment of the values attributed to heritage is a very important activity in any conservation effort, since values strongly shape the decisions that are made'. It follows that to achieve effectiveness it is important that there is an integration of value-led decision making at all levels (in an organisation) which addresses the issues of what to protect, how to protect it, how to prioritise and how to address conflicting interests.

We would suggest that the idea of values-based management is centred upon:

- The principle that in order to protect and manage a place you need to know why it is important, and what elements contribute to that importance.
- The point that the importance of the site (and what it is that contributes to that importance) cannot be inferred or assumed, but needs to be demonstrated through understanding the place and assessing its significance through a rigorous, transparent and objective process.

Development in the idea of values

We can see that the basis of today's conservation values, at least in a western, or, perhaps more specifically a northern European context, were articulated in the Victorian period through the writings of William Morris and John Ruskin. These two men, in inspiring the development of the early conservation movement, articulated the idea of the stewardship of existing resources, the spiritual and educational value of the built cultural heritage and a concern for the fabric of these buildings as a physical manifestation that embodied and represented these values. At the same time, they honoured the skill, artistry and spirit of those who had created them. Such ideas emphasised the sense of the uniqueness of the authentic fabric of historic buildings, which was a physical expression of cultural values and concerns – and a resource for education and social development.

In the UK, despite the concerns of the early conservation movement about the importance of the work of the craftsmen and the value of 'everyday buildings', protection was originally focused on protecting monuments – either empty buildings, ruins or iconic buildings. The idea of protecting a wider range of buildings evolved over the first half of the twentieth century, culminating in the setting up of the listing system in the period following World War II – a position that was at least partly influenced by the destruction of (historic) buildings during the air raids. However, the dominant ethos was still one of architectural aesthetics and a focus on individual prestigious buildings of historic value or artistic achievement (based on class and power), combined with notions of protecting pleasing amenity views. It was damage of a different kind, or rather from a different source, that encouraged the setting up of conservation areas in the 1960s. Their creation was originally, at least in part, a response to the perceived damage to the context, and therefore the integrity, of listed buildings, caused by new roads, slum clearances and urban development projects which often left them physically and 'spiritually' isolated.

In recent years the focus has moved away from what to protect (although the listing of post-war structures has re-ignited that debate) to a development in the ideas about what qualities are to be valued. Perhaps the most important shift in attitude is towards the acceptance of a wider-ranging and more inclusive idea of what is of value. The idea that 'the everyday' (particularly where it traces the development of a wider range of social movements or where it embodies associations and memories for different social groups) might be as valuable as the iconic high points of artistic and historical development has come to be accepted – if not entirely acted upon.

International Charters

It is possible to track some of these changes, in ideas of the value and the benefits of conserving the built cultural heritage, through developments in the concerns raised and focused on by various international Charters.

After WWII the United Nations and its agencies, such as UNESCO, were formed. The founding of the Institute for International Conservation (IIC) in 1950 by scientists concerned with the conservation of museum artefacts formally initiated a phase that has been described by some commentators as 'scientific conservation'. UNESCO founded ICCROM in 1959 to promote scientific conservation of cultural property. Key individuals from UNESCO, ICCROM and other internationally focused organisations drafted the Venice Charter, which was approved by the *Second Conference of the International Union of Architects* (IUA) in 1964 and adopted by ICOMOS on its foundation in 1966.

The Venice Charter of 1964 laid down a framework which considered the courses of action that were acceptable in deciding on how to protect 'monuments'. It was very much a product of its time: an attempt to deal with individual, usually iconic, monuments, where redevelopment was seen as a severe threat to the historic environment. Although it made reference to 'a common heritage' and referred to more 'modest works of the past which have acquired cultural significance with the passing of time', it nevertheless did seem to emphasise works of art rather than the more 'everyday'. Article 3, which stated that the 'intention in conserving and restoring monuments is to safeguard them no less as works of art than as historical evidence' (ICOMOS, 1964, p. 1), illustrates this point.

The Venice Charter has been criticised for its 'euro centric' perspective and for concentrating on monuments (although the term has a more inclusive sense in the rest of Europe than it has in the UK). However, the Charter was of vital importance and a marker for its time, as it stressed the need to preserve the authenticity and integrity of the 'monument', and the need for proper documentation before, during and after essential interventions.

In the latter part of the 1960s and through the 1970s there was an increasing emphasis on the importance of 'the everyday', and a sense that those places that were not considered important under the criteria of art history and age were nevertheless of value. Bell (1997) draws attention to UNESCO's concerns in the latter's 1976 document *Recommendation Concerning the Safeguarding and Contemporary Role of Historic Areas* and its emphasis on the importance of recognising the 'significance and message' of the composition of minor buildings in long-established settlements. There was also in this period a growing awareness of the need to place conservation in its wider context, and we start to see it being related to what we now see as issues of sustainability – in relation not only to physical resources, but also in economic and social terms. The *European Charter of the Architectural Heritage* (Council of Europe, 1975), for instance, picks up the various strands of 'sustainable development' (the social, the economic and the environmental) and links this clearly to the protection of the built cultural heritage – and it also implies that cultural values are not inherent but are reinterpreted by each generation:

> *The architectural heritage is a capital of irreplaceable spiritual, cultural, social and economic value. Each generation places a different interpretation on the past and derives new inspiration from it. This capital has been built up over the centuries; the destruction of any part of it leaves us poorer since nothing new we can create, however fine, will make good the loss. Our society now has to husband its resources. Far from being a luxury this heritage is an economic asset which can be used to save community resources.*

Charters such as The Washington Charter of 1987 (ICOMOS, 1987b), which looked at historic towns and urban areas, continued the examination of broader concerns and the need for holistic and integrative policies for conservation which related to wider economic and social development issues and the general spatial planning context. The Nara document on Authenticity (ICOMOS, 1994) reflected the sense of a growing acknowledgement of a range of values associated with the built cultural heritage. This is reflected in that document's statement that:

> *all judgements about values attributed to cultural properties as well as the credibility of related information sources may differ from culture to culture and even within the same culture. It is thus not possible to base judgements of value and authenticity within fixed criteria.*

The Charter on the Built Vernacular Heritage (ICOMOS, 1999) captured the idea of the social value of heritage when it stated that:

> *The built vernacular heritage occupies a central place in the affection and pride of all peoples. It has been accepted as a characteristic and attractive product of society. It appears informal, but nevertheless orderly. It is utilitarian and at the same time possesses interest and beauty. It is a focus of contemporary life and at the same time a record of the history of society. Although it is the work of man it is also the creation of time. It would be*

unworthy of the heritage of man if care were not taken to conserve these traditional harmonies which constitute the core of man's own existence.

The built vernacular heritage is important; it is the fundamental expression of the culture of a community, of its relationship with its territory and, at the same time, the expression of the world's cultural diversity.

Vernacular building is the traditional and natural way by which communities house themselves. It is a continuing process including necessary changes and continuous adaptation as a response to social and environmental constraints. The survival of this tradition is threatened world-wide by the forces of economic, cultural and architectural homogenisation. How these forces can be met is a fundamental problem that must be addressed by communities and also by governments, planners, architects, conservationists and by a multidisciplinary group of specialists.

Other key developments in the recent evolution of conservation thinking have spread from, on the one hand Eastern Europe and, on the other, from East and South East Asia. Political turmoil in many Eastern European countries after 1989 led to the birth (or reappearance) of a number of nations and new cultural alliances. People began to dream of the revitalisation of their cultural roots, as a potent symbol of newly won or regained identity. Basic components of international heritage, which in many cases had been suppressed or prohibited for decades or more, came to be considered as being vital elements in supporting and sustaining people in the process of nation building (or rebuilding).

At the same time, it became evident elsewhere in the world that economic development strategies designed around Western models could not be applied rigidly or simplistically to communities with very different cultural traditions. At international gatherings, representatives from Pacific Rim countries raised awareness of intangible aspects of heritage, since traditionally these cultures and societies had been permeated with spiritual and other intangible values and associations that were poorly served by the 'monumental' focus of Western-dominated thinking on heritage protection. In the early 1990s, recognition grew that urgent action was needed to protect the Region's extensive intangible cultural heritage, which was under threat from rapid social change sparked by strong economic growth.

These two contemporaneous catalysts initiated a period of extensive international debate on intangible heritage issues, much of which occurred within forums provided by international organisations such as UNESCO and ICOMOS. Opinion and accepted wisdom on the nature of cultural heritage and the value of its intangible aspects have evolved radically in the past fifteen years. UNESCO's 2003 *Convention for the Safeguarding of the Intangible Cultural Heritage* acknowledged that intangible cultural heritage (or 'living heritage') is the mainspring of our cultural diversity and its maintenance proffers a guarantee for continuing creativity (UNESCO, 2003). Over the past 60 years, the Western world has become increasingly secular and material in its focus – at times, seemingly besotted by transience and ephemera. As a result, many find it hard to recognise or appreciate the importance of intangible values. The 2003 Convention provides a marker, reflecting a growing understanding that our intangible cultural heritage is traditional and living at the same time. It sees intangible cultural heritage as being manifested in oral traditions and language, the performing arts, social practices, rituals and festive events, knowledge, and craftsmanship. As such, intangible cultural heritage is:

- *transmitted from generation to generation;*
- *constantly recreated by communities and groups, in response to their environment, their interaction with nature, and their history;*
- *provides communities and groups with a sense of identity and continuity;*
- *promotes respect for cultural diversity and human creativity;*
- *compatible with international human rights instruments;*
- *complies with the requirements of mutual respect among communities, and of sustainable development.*

The reawakening of awareness of the intangible dimension to heritage has had a profound effect upon the practice of conservation around the world in the last decade, including in the United Kingdom. The notion of living heritage and our growing concentration on the concept that the historic environment involves everything around us are compatible and convergent views.

As conservation practice has expanded into this new territory, it has become clear that different considerations prevail and other management tools are required. Some thirty years ago, in a conservation world dominated by tangible elements of heritage and physical acts of preservation, conservation was often regarded as being an artistic activity aided by scientific and historical knowledge. This notion sits less comfortably when dealing with, say, the management of change in a cultural landscape, the protection of vulnerable intangible cultural heritage or even safeguarding the character of a historic urban area threatened by modern developments such as tall buildings.

Initially developed as an appraisal tool for use on natural landscapes and national parks, the potential of the conservation plan for application to heritage assets was explored first in Australia in the mid- to late-1980s. With care, the conservation plan and its variants can provide a means of evaluating the contribution of both tangible and intangible heritage and as such now lie at the heart of 'conservation planning': a value (or significance)-based approach to the management of the historic environment that has come to dominate international conservation in the past five years or so. In parallel with the conservation plan – and providing the philosophical bedrock for today's conservation planning – Australia ICOMOS produced the Burra Charter in 1988. Based on the Venice Charter, this has proven to be an immensely useful document for conservation practice everywhere, providing guidance on the conservation and management of places of cultural significance. Perhaps more than any other post-WWII Charter, it has helped conservation to evolve. As this has happened, the Charter itself has been adapted, with the critical recognition of the less tangible aspects of cultural significance, including those embodied in sense of place, and the meanings and association that places have for people.

In the early years of the twenty-first century, conservation is no longer mainly or solely about the repair and protection of monuments and a philosophy based on the notion of authenticity. That aspect of conservation has not been banished to the waste heap of history as a fashion of the nineteenth and twentieth centuries, but, internationally, it is no longer pre-eminent. For many in the western world, this has involved a dramatically changing conceptual landscape as increasing emphasis is placed upon economic, social and cultural processes. As Feilden and Jokilehto observe, 'the tendency today is to understand cultural heritage in its broadest sense as containing all the signs that document the activities and achievements of human beings over time' (Feilden and Jokilehto, 1993, p. 11).

Value characterisation – typologies

As we have observed there has, over the last few years, been increasing debate and a re-examination of a range of cultural social and economic values embodied in and represented by the built cultural heritage and the means by which these can be identified and evaluated. However, until relatively recently there has been little attempt at clearly articulating a common understanding of what those values are and how they might be expressed and utilised.

The values represented by the built cultural heritage are diverse and complex. Older sites have multiple layers of history but newer sites can also be complicated because of the range of values that are or may be represented. Values are also sometimes difficult to 'measure' and it is partly because of this that attempts to do so have been avoided, but there have also been concerns expressed about the usefulness and the possible negative effect of categorising heritage values from both a conceptual and a pragmatic viewpoint. Avrami et al. (2000, p. 8) observe that 'Though the typologies of different scholars and disciplines vary they each represent a reductionist approach to examining very complex issues of cultural significance'.

Despite the difficulties and concerns, we would suggest that it is important to have a range of values stated, rather than a situation where value judgements are clearly being made but where they are not being adequately articulated or made available for discussion and debate. That is, it is necessary to have a more definite reference point for measuring, articulating and justifying the case for suggesting that a particular place is important and should be protected. It is also, we would suggest, necessary to have a clear articulation of the cultural value of a place in order to inform decision making in the context of 'value driven management'.

The other important aspect of this is that clearly setting out a values framework could be the basis for increasing accountability at both the level of identifying places worthy of protection and in respect of managing them, because it would allow for more openness and transparency about decision making by producing better opportunities for debate as well as scrutiny. It would also encourage and allow a greater understanding of the place for a wider constituency.

A value typology or categorisation needs to acknowledge the range of possible values in a place, to the extent that all stakeholders recognise that their interests are represented – and it follows from this that no one category should be assumed to be more worthy than another. The articulation of significance in this way is never going to be an 'absolute' definition of the value of a place. However, its usefulness is as a flexible framework which broadly acknowledges a range of values that ought to be considered in most situations, and allows, as Mason suggests (Mason, 2002, p. 9), for a starting point of common references and comparisons that will be modified to take account of the particular qualities of a place.

There have been various attempts to characterise and categorise heritage values over the years. Some of the differences accentuate the problems of reaching an agreement on the range of values and what constitutes those values (and indeed the meanings of specific terms), but the differences also reflect the particular context and the time at which these were developed.

Table 3.1 shows some of the better known value categories that have been developed and proposed by individuals and organisations.

Table 3.1   Examples of cultural value typologies.

Riegl (1902)	Feilden and Jokilehto (1993)	English Heritage (1997)
• Age • Commemorative • Use • Newness	Cultural values: • Relative artistic or technical • Rarity Contemporary socioeconomic values: • Economic • Functional • Educational • Social • Political	• Cultural value • Aesthetic value • Recreational value • Resource value • Economic importance
Mason (2002, p. 10)	**Feilden (2003, p. 6)**	**Throsby (2006, p. 43)**
Sociocultural values: • Historical • Cultural/symbolic • Social • Spiritual/religious • Aesthetic Economic values: • Use (market) value • Non-use (non-market) values: – existence – option – bequest	• Emotional • Cultural • Use	• Aesthetic • Spiritual • Social • Historical • Symbolic • Authenticity

The rationale for which aspects of the built environment we should conserve has been traditionally dominated explicitly by (value) judgements that emphasise age and/or rarity and the idea of celebrating high art and culture as well as the icons of power and influence. Although Morris and Ruskin referred to age value (Ruskin wrote that 'the greatest glory of a building is its age') and artistic value (Morris referred to 'ancient monuments of art'), they also implicitly set out a wider range of values including educational and social values (Ruskin, 1989; Morris, 1877).

Riegl's (1902) is perhaps the most oft quoted next attempt to articulate heritage values, and is particularly interesting because of the way in which he links the categories to conservation actions. For example, of age value he wrote:

in principle it condemns every effort at conservation, every restoration, as nothing less than an unauthorised interference with the reign of natural law

which he saw as being in tension with historical value by suggesting that:

Prior disintegration by the forces of nature cannot be undone and should, therefore, not be removed even from the point of view of historical value. However, further disintegration from the present day into the future, as age value not only tolerates but even postulates, is from the standpoint of historical value, not only pointless but simply to be avoided, since any further disintegration hinders the scientific restoration of the original state of a work of man. Thus the cult of historical value must aim for the best possible preservation of a monument in its present state.

The Burra Charter (Australia ICOMOS, 1999) categorises values under the following headings:

Aesthetic: *Aesthetic value includes aspects of sensory perception for which criteria can and should be stated. Such criteria may include consideration of the form, scale, colour, texture and materials of the fabric; the smells and sounds associated with the place and its use.*

Historic: *Historic value encompasses the history of aesthetics, science and society (and therefore to a large extent underlies all of the values). . . . A place may have historic value because it has influenced, or has been influenced by, an historic figure, event, phase or activity. It may also have historic value as the site of an important event. For any given place the significance will be greater where evidence of the association or event survives in situ or where the settings are substantially intact, than where it has been changed or evidence does not survive. However some events or associations may be so important that the place retains significance regardless of subsequent treatment.*

Scientific: *The scientific or research value of the place will depend on the importance of the data involved, on its rarity, quality or*

> *representativeness and on the degree to which the place may contribute further substantial information.*
>
> **Social value:** *Social value embraces the qualities for which a place has become a focus of spiritual, political, national or other cultural sentiment to a majority or minority group.*

In 2007 English Heritage proposed a 'family' of values under headings which it explains as follows:

> **Evidential:** *Evidential value relates to the potential of a place to yield primary evidence about a past human activity. [The document subdivides this family heading into 'Natural' and 'Cultural'.]*
>
> **Historical:** *Historical value relates to the ways in which the present can be connected through a place to past people, events and aspects of life. [The document subdivides this into 'Illustrative' and 'Associational'.]*
>
> **Aesthetic:** *Aesthetic value relates to the way in which people derive sensory and intellectual stimulation from a place. [The document subdivides this into 'Design', 'Artistic', 'Artless Beauty' and 'Sublime'.]*
>
> **Communal:** *Communal value relates to the meanings of a place for the people who relate to it, and whose collective experience or memory it holds. Communal values are closely bound up with historical (particularly associational) and aesthetic values, but tend to have additional and specific aspects. [The document subdivides this into 'Commemorative/Symbolic', 'Social' and 'Spiritual'.]*

The English Heritage document reinforces the point that we made earlier when it states that these are 'not intended as the definitive checklist of heritage values but to prompt comprehensive thought about the values of a place'.

In our experience of writing conservation plans we have found that the following categories of values have been useful and have worked well.

Aesthetic

In the UK the term 'aesthetic' is sometimes used in this context, mainly in relation to visual perception rather than all the senses. As we have noted, The Burra Charter (Australia ICOMOS, 1999) uses 'aesthetic' in this wider connotation, as does the aforementioned English Heritage document. The Burra Charter states:

> *Aesthetic value includes aspects of sensory perception for which criteria can and should be stated. Such criteria may include consideration of the form, scale, colour, texture and materials of the fabric; the smells and sounds associated with the place and its use.*

The English Heritage document (2007) interestingly includes 'intellectual' as well as 'sensory' stimulation.

In a sense we are essentially talking about character and what makes a 'sense of place'. Appearance will of course be part of the character of a place but there is a real danger that this dominates an assessment of this wider value category, in part because it is easier to measure and articulate. There are many examples where the appearance of a place has been 'enhanced' but the aesthetic of the place has been damaged. Sometimes this has occurred because of a misplaced desire to 'tidy up' and 'improve' the place, but often because the use and feel of the place – and its noises and smells and activities – have neither been understood nor their importance appreciated.

In relation to the visual aesthetic, English Heritage use the term 'artless beauty' to refer to an aesthetic value that is not the result of 'conscious design'. They illustrate the idea by reference to 'the seemingly organic form of an urban or rural landscape and the relationship of its buildings, structures and their materials to their setting' and 'the harmonious (but not consciously designed) relationship of one building to another'. They make the point that 'artless beauty' often derives from a combination of natural and artificial elements, or the action of nature on human works. We agree that this is a notion that needs to be represented in any 'palette' of values, although the word 'beauty' is perhaps marginally misleading. Amongst many other values, a partially overgrown old cemetery with higgledy-piggledy, moss-covered headstones may well exhibit and be important to many for this value. It is not 'beauty' in the sense that many would define the word, perhaps more an emotive unstaged cameo or an intangible sense of place. Nonetheless, we retain the term 'artless beauty' since it is more fitting to some other instances.

Scenic and panoramic

These are closely associated visually aesthetic values. Panoramic value belongs to sweeping **outward** vistas, whereas scenic value may be related more to beauty in a reasonably confined setting and may include the subject place or be experienced looking from it.

Architectural/technological

Architectural value is concerned with innovation, development and perhaps pinnacles of achievement (as in 'the finest example of. . .') in relation to architectural ideas and movements, and also in the work of individuals. This value would also embrace the work of craftsmen and the development of materials. Some of the architectural values might be related to developments and high points in technical achievement, but a place may have technological value represented by structures, etc. which would fall outside the concept of architecture – an obvious example would perhaps be a bridge.

Because architecture and technology (or indeed art) are not created in a vacuum, the social, cultural, political and economic context, which informed their development, will also be represented by the architectural and technical achievement.

Historical

Clearly the concept of historical value is of primary importance in the notion of built cultural heritage, and to a large extent it underpins and validates many of the other values. Here we are concerned with, as Mason puts it, 'The capacity of a site to convey, embody or stimulate a relation or reaction to the past is part of the fundamental nature and meaning of heritage objects' (Mason, 2002, p. 11).

English Heritage refers to 'the perception of a window that provides links between past and present people' (English Heritage, 2007, p. 25), and clearly historical value is closely linked to social value and associational values.

Associational

Clearly a site may be important because of its associational links with a person or event. But how symbiotic that link is needs to be considered: that is, the link should be substantial – and generally it should not be transitory. The intactness of the place in relation to the period, and activity related to the association, and/or its 'spiritual quality' in relation to the association are also key factors. Another facet might be some evidence that the place had an impact on the activity or work of the person or on the event(s) in question. The Burra Charter observes, however, that (guidelines to significance) that 'some events or associations may be so important that the place retains significance regardless of subsequent treatment' (Australia ICOMOS, 1999, p. 12).

Archaeological

As the English Heritage document *Conservation Principles* (English Heritage, 2007) observes, this is linked to educational value and relates to the ability of the place to be a source of information about the past through scientific investigation. In part, its archaeological potential may be related to its representativeness and its completeness. As the English Heritage document states (p. 25), 'Material remains of past human activity are the primary source of evidence about the substance and evolution of places and of the people and cultures that made them. Their evidential value is proportionate to their potential to contribute to our understanding of the past'. The document also observes that, in the absence of written records, archaeological evidence may be the only source of evidence about the distant past, as well as of poorly documented aspects of the more recent past.

This is not just a one-off process, as even the most well known and apparently well investigated and documented place can sometimes continue to reveal new information. A good example of this is the moat at the Tower of London, which has continued to reveal important evidence about the development of the medieval fortress and its entrance in recent years, despite the amount of attention that has been paid generally to the archaeology of the site over many decades. However, the converse of this must be appreciated just as well. As has often been stated, archaeological excavation is a destructive process – once something has been 'dug out', the capability of future generations to learn more from the same archaeological strata and material is either greatly reduced or erased altogether.

There is another, in some ways more esoteric value, in the archaeology which is buried and remains essentially unseen but which has a mystery and therefore an almost spiritual value.

Economic

This can be seen at a very simple level as pertaining to the quantification of how much money is generated by heritage places, either directly through admissions and sales of services and goods at the site, or indirectly in the sense of visitors to a place purchasing goods and services in the wider area. The effect of heritage value on attracting visitors to the wider region, or indeed a particular country, is also an economic value that can be measured in terms of direct and indirect investment and employment opportunities and realities. This important value is of course, as we have mentioned previously, not necessarily without negative effects for the place itself.

Another way of measuring economic value is by asking people what they are prepared to pay for it – whether it be how much they are prepared to pay to enter a particular place or how much public money they think they would be prepared to see spent on it (in the context of perhaps higher taxes or in relation to other things of public value such as healthcare or street cleaning). Throsby (2006, p. 41) refers to this latter point of gauging a person's willingness to pay to preserve (*sic*) the heritage when that same person is not gaining a direct benefit from it (in the same way as a visitor), and identifies them as 'non use values'. He suggests that these may relate to: the asset's existence value (people value the existence of the heritage item even though they may not consume its service directly themselves); its option value (people wish to preserve the option that they or others might consume the asset's services at some future time; and its bequest value (people may wish to bequeath the asset to future generations).

But there is also a more prosaic value, and that is the value of the place as 'real estate', including its development value. The issues that a 'valuer' might take into account will vary depending on whom they are valuing it for, but often the fact that a place is protected may reduce its monetary value because of perceived restrictions on how it can be managed and developed. Clearly also, the potential development value may lead owners and users to propose changes that damage its cultural value. However, the potential to develop the place through a new use may be what actually effectively protects the place – as long as the new use is compatible with its cultural significance.

Educational

In part, educational value is derived from the historical value of the place. This can work at an informal level, in that a place may invite and stimulate a person's interest through curiosity. That person may then go away and, through other media, investigate the place, its context and the society that created it. To a certain extent this may be triggered by how powerful or astonishing the atmosphere of the place is – Machu Picchu is a good example of this. Or it may be a combination of wonderment of the atmosphere combined with interest in the artistic or even technical achievements – such as engendered by, say, a cathedral or perhaps the Alhambra Palace or Sydney Opera House. But that curiosity is also likely to be stimulated by wanting to understand more about less grand places that the person is unfamiliar with but with which they feel some connection or association. However, and as we have already observed, in many instances educational values will only truly be realised through effective interpretation strategies, although the sense of place can sometimes be reduced by poor, and in some cases any, interpretation.

Recreational

Clearly many built cultural heritage places are enjoyed as sources of recreation, in which an engagement with the past may be a primary or a secondary reason for the visit. Their value is essentially that of an amenity.

English Heritage (1997, p. 4) have suggested that 'the historic environment plays a very significant role in providing for people's recreation and enjoyment. Increasingly the past and its remains in the present are a vital part of people's everyday life and experiences'.

Artistic

This again may be closely related to historical value. Artistic value may be related to the work of a particular person or an artistic or architectural movement, and may be important because it is a unique example or it may be pivotal or representative.

Social value

This is largely about the meaning that a place might have for individuals or groups because of some kind of association they have with it, or with events that occurred there. It refers to the benefits of social cohesion and group identity. Social value may be related to events that occurred in the relatively distant past and which are connected to the present through oral history traditions anchored by the place in question, but the event(s) may also be relatively recent. English Heritage (2007, p. 29) suggests that the place 'may have fulfilled a community function that over time has developed into deeper attachment, or shaped some aspect of community behaviour or attitudes'. This value category is often closely linked to perhaps one of symbolism.

It is an important value to identify and measure, but is it also often produces difficulties and controversy (this is explored in more detail in Chapter 4). However, it is interesting, and perhaps pertinent, to observe that in the case of recent buildings (such as post-war social housing estates) there is often a shying away from attributing social values. Possibly this is because it is more difficult, and also perhaps because it is more contentious – e.g. in regard to social housing. In these instances the case for protection is often met on largely less contentious, though still contested, grounds. The problem here is that if the 'true' or one of the key criteria is not openly acknowledged and debated then that value can be lost in decisions on management and change.

Another way of looking at social value is in the facility a place provides for the community related to its perhaps original function, such as, say, a place of worship or swimming pool, or its changed use, such as a youth club or just as a more general community amenity value such as the grounds of a manor house.

Commemorative values

These are different from associational values in that the commemorative place may or may not be located where the event actually took place. War memorials are an obvious example of this.

Symbolic/iconic

The symbolism of places is a widely referred to value. Very often the symbolic values that a place holds are interpreted differently by different groups. In some cases different interpretations are relatively harmonious and positive and reinforce the importance of a place, but sometimes they are negative, particularly where they are seen by, for instance, minority groups, as celebrating past events which oppressed or damaged them. There can be benefits in conserving places precisely because they are reminders of past wrongdoings, attitudes and events that are to be condemned. Whether that benefit is realised will depend on perceptions and interpretations.

In a slightly different way, the very human sense of belonging can attach symbolic or iconic value to a place, both for individuals and also arguably for whole sections of a community. The sense of home is important to many people. Irrespective of the amount of time they have lived at the place that they feel to be 'home', people may experience the warmth of homecoming every time they approach or see a particular landmark, scene, vista or place that they associate with their journey home. Sometimes that symbol of home may be many miles away from the place itself. Whilst this is a very personal value, in towns and cities, by the very nature of things, many people may associate precisely the same symbolic trigger with the same value (albeit that a different 'home' is the object of that symbolism). In some ways, this implies there is also a separate value to do with 'belonging' – not the symbolic attachment to a place other than home as part of the ritual of homecoming, but the strong value received when standing in the 'bosom' of one's community, or perhaps the cameo view of the world gained from your own window, or the value many people place in their birthplace or first home.

Related to this form of symbolic value is the importance that many people, when travelling, place on landmarks and the like as symbols of arrival at a gateway. An example of this is given later in this section for the Wellington Monument, the UK's tallest obelisk standing at the end of a dominant range of hills overlooking a busy motorway in the south-west of England. There, many thousands, perhaps millions of travellers associate the Monument with arrival to and departure from their holidays. This is an extremely powerful symbolic value placed on this asset.

Spiritual and religious

As Mason (2002, p. 12) observes, '[these] spiritual values can emanate from the beliefs and teachings of organised religion, but they can also encompass secular experiences of wonder, awe, and so on, which can be provoked by visiting heritage places'.

At the most obvious level, places of worship are likely to have spiritual value to both worshippers and other members of society, including (sometimes) adherents of other religions. Equally, a place such as Highgate Cemetery may well have spiritual value to many visitors, including atheists, as well as being important for its artless beauty and its historical, associational, commemorative, social and educational values. All of these combine together to create its essential 'sense of place'.

The point has just been made that, undoubtedly, atheists can experience spiritual value, whether in a setting like a cemetery or in certain inspirational places. The cultural values 'religious', 'spiritual' and 'inspirational' (the latter being discussed in more detail below) are closely related to each other, but may be experienced concurrently or individually. They are appreciably different, but belong to one family of intangible values. Not all inspirational places have spiritual value. Arguably, atheists do not personally experience religious value, but they will find spiritual value in certain spaces and places.

This leads to another crucial consideration regarding significance – there is a difference between perceiving or appreciating value and receiving or experiencing it personally. An open-minded atheist can appreciate that a believer finds religious value in a place of worship, irrespective of whether he/she personally identifies that same place as having spiritual value. Providing you are open to the experiences of others, you can develop a sound assessment of significance for a place without necessarily experiencing the complete range of cultural values that it holds for the whole of society. Indeed, for some value-rich places, it is extremely unlikely that one person can ever personally experience the complete palette of values that are present, because, most often, the same place holds very different values for different communities and individuals.

In some ways, spiritual value is one of the harder intangible values to pin down – it is so very personal. What is a spiritual mountain to millions in a Pacific Rim country is but a mountain to even more people elsewhere around the world – albeit, quite possibly an awe-inspiring, panoramically or scenically valued piece of natural heritage.

Inspirational

Inspirational values have been referred to briefly already. Like the spiritual and religious, this is a cultural value that can be hard to define unambiguously and with precision, because of its very personal nature. Nonetheless, millions of people may derive enormous inspirational drive or emotions from the same place. The contrast between inspiration as a driver and as an emotion is an interesting one and is key to appreciating that, perhaps more than most other values, inspiration can be gained from an astoundingly diverse group of places and assets.

Sometimes inspiration is to be connected with the 'awe-inspiring'; at other times, it is not a sense of positive or wondrous awe, but a very different drive to do good or better that is derived through inspiration. Thus, an unscientific poll of friends and colleagues whilst writing this text produced the following disparate list of places or assets exhibiting powerful inspirational value: Angkor Wat, Machu Picchu, the Taj Mahal, the Great Wall of China, Stonehenge, the terracotta warriors at Emperor Qin Shihuang's Mausoleum in Shaanxi, Mayan ruins, the Pyramids of Giza, Eisenman's 2005 Holocaust Memorial in Berlin, Auschwitz and Dachau, the Parthenon, Chartres Cathedral, Coventry Cathedral, the complex of Hue monuments in Vietnam and the Washington Monument.

This list illustrates the different forms of inspiration that can be felt by different people on different occasions. Assessments of significance need to be able to explore such diversity, but reaching conclusions on relative values when inspiration is involved can be extremely problematic.

Ecological

Ecological values are perhaps easier to understand and assess in terms of relative importance than something as intangible as inspiration. Conversely, assessments of significance produced for built cultural heritage assets in the UK, including those to be found within conservation plans, have often dealt with ecological significance very poorly, since such assessments tend to focus over-much on traditional building conservation themes like archaeology and history and not tackle value holistically. Particular focus is needed to overcome this aspect.

Environmental

Environmental value is often confused with ecological interest, but they are and should remain quite distinct. Landscapes can have environmental value without being ecologically significant; equally, a park in a city can also provide important environmental value to the local community, not least by acting as a 'green lung' to reduce pollution.

As with ecological value, this has often been undervalued and under-represented in assessments of significance.

Some examples of places and their values

As we have suggested, any given place will have a number of cultural values. As an example we can imagine what the range of values might be for the following places.

Sydney Harbour Bridge (Figure 3.1) is significant amongst other things for its iconic status, as an entry to and symbol of Sydney and Australia, its place within panoramic views, as an architectural composition, socially for communication and linkage value, as an economic driver related to tourism and so forth.

The Eiffel Tower (Figure 3.2) similarly has strong iconic, panoramic/scenic and economic values, arguably technologically it is more significant than Sydney Harbour Bridge and it has particular associational value.

Figure 3.1   Sydney Harbour Bridge.

Figure 3.2   The Eiffel Tower.

Coventry Cathedral (Figure 3.3) is a post-war building that stands alongside the ruins of the old Cathedral which was bombed in 1940. There are obvious spiritual, commemorative and historical values represented here, as well as architectural and artistic ones.

The Royal Botanic Gardens at Kew (Figure 3.4), a World Heritage Site, is particularly strong in educational, ecological and recreational values, as well as being important for its historical, architectural and associational significance.

The Byker estate in Newcastle upon Tyne (Figure 3.5) has strong architectural and townscape value and social value related to its concept and execution, including the way that the community was involved in the design and planning process.

St Paul's Cathedral (Figure 3.6) is a particularly iconic building with extremely powerful associational, symbolic, inspirational, historical, architectural and townscape values.

The Bauhaus, Dessau (Figure 3.7), is one of the most iconic buildings of the twentieth century. It has powerful architectural, historical symbolic and commemorative values, in relation not only to the 'art, craft and architecture' of the Modern Movement but also its associated social and political ideas and ideals.

The Radiator Building and the Empire State Building (Figure 3.8), New York are both iconic buildings which represent architectural, technological, historical and symbolic buildings, particularly in relation to the confidence and energy of American capitalism in the period between the two world wars.

The Lutyens War Memorial (Figure 3.9) on Tower Hill in London also has powerful associational, historical and architectural values, but beyond this it has a very strong commemorative significance.

The list could go on. We do not pretend that the foregoing assessment is scientific, objective or comprehensive – our purpose in providing these rough-and-ready 'pen portraits' of nine well-known heritage assets is merely to make one vital point. In the end, through careful analysis, significance can be identified and, in a comparative way, quantified. This helps to build up a picture of the holistic value of an asset which, at least to a degree, can be likened to a unique 'fingerprint' that defines its special interest to society today. If you understand and can define that 'fingerprint', you can begin to make rational management decisions that build upon the asset's real value to society.

Issues in value assessment

> *Objects, collections, buildings and places become recognised as 'heritage' through conscious decisions and unspoken values of particular people and institutions and for reasons that are strongly shaped by social contexts and processes*   (Avrami et al., 2000, p. 6)

The sense that value is a subjective judgement clearly raises issues not only about the benefit of conserving the built cultural heritage but also about the process(es)

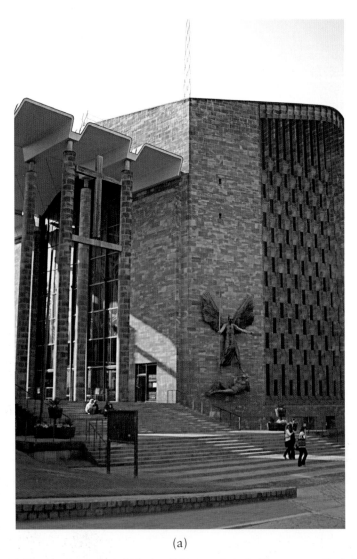

(a)

Figure 3.3(a)–(c)   Coventry Cathedral. The 'new' Coventry Cathedral is a post-war Grade I listed building (a). It contains many specially commissioned works of art, including Graham Sutherland's tapestry of Christ (b). The ruins of the medieval Cathedral were incorporated into the new design (c).

(b)

(c)

Figure 3.4   The Palm House at Kew Gardens.

by which certain elements of the built environment are chosen as being worthy of protection (and by implication some are said to have little or no value), and how those elements are protected and managed.

Any particular place may or may not contain all of the values indicated in a particular typology, but it is likely to have a range of values. As Impey (2006, p. 80) observes, 'historic places do not have just one immutable value, but many overlapping values that reflect differing viewpoints'.

Typologies need to be understood in terms of both meaning and intent by a range of groups. They should also reflect a variety of perceptions of what is valuable and why, and not just reflect how 'experts' and professionals view heritage. A value typology therefore needs to acknowledge the range of possible values in a place to the extent that all stakeholders recognise that their interests are represented. That is, there needs to be a development of value categories which is more wide ranging, holistic, pluralistic and inclusive (particularly in acknowledging the views of those who have associations with the site) than the sort of typology that even in recent times favoured the art-historical view of what constituted cultural heritage. This is a situation that, in part at least, can be seen to have been due to the fact that decisions about what should be protected, and why, were decided by a relatively small, and some would suggest, elite group of experts, drawn from a relatively narrow constituency.

Value categories should be conceived of as being fluid and not mutually exclusive. The value of categories is in having a reference point, but they should be designed and intended to stimulate divergent thinking. The intention should be

(a)

(b)

Figure 3.5(a),(b) The Byker Estate in Newcastle upon Tyne.

Figure 3.6   St Paul's Cathedral, London.

to help order thinking about the place, but not to restrict it. It is also important not to oversimplify – complexity needs to be acknowledged and worked with.

The fact that, in most cases, a site will have multiple values will usually reinforce its importance and therefore the case for its protection. However, multiple values will also probably mean that different individuals or groups will see the place, and particular aspects of the place, as being important for different reasons. Also where the values of a place are embodied in a particular object a situation can arise where different groups see the same thing as important but for different reasons, and this can cause problems in its management and protection. Sometimes these different values (and perspectives) complement and reinforce each other but sometimes they are in tension or conflict. Also the credibility and/or the value attached to different types and different sources of evidence may vary between different cultural groups in the community, between the community and the experts and possibly between experts with different backgrounds and perspectives. Different disciplines will give different priorities and see things in different ways. This emphasises that the attitude of and make-up of the team which is undertaking a value assessment is important, and it reinforces the point that the process of value measurements, as well as the results, needs to be open and democratic. There may also be problems with interpretations of terms and even meanings. So it may seem that different groups perceive the same value as being embodied in the same aspect or element of the place (say aesthetic value), but in reality they conceive and interpret that value in different ways.

(b)

(a)

Figure 3.7(a), (b)   The Bauhaus, Dessau.

Figure 3.8   The Radiator Building (foreground) and The Empire State Building, New York.

It is important that no one particular value category should be assumed to be more worthy or important than another, and should not be allowed to dominate the assessment of significance nor decisions flowing from it. Also, following on from an assessment, this balance needs to be maintained to ensure that one set of values does not obscure other values in terms of either celebrating the place or managing it (and it is in the management of the place that values are likely to be 'lost'). It is, for example, not uncommon for age value to dominate to such an extent that more recent aspects of the site are seen as relatively insignificant.

The articulation of values into a typology is never going to be an 'absolute' definition of the cultural significance of a particular place, but its usefulness

Figure 3.9   Lutyen's Great War memorial on Tower Hill in London.

is as a framework which can be an organisational tool and a reference point whilst being fluid and flexible. A typology should broadly acknowledge a range of values that ought to be considered in most situations and which allows for common reference points and comparisons as a starting point, which will be modified to take account of the particular qualities of a place. That is, the typology should not be used in a way that assumes that all the values do or should exist at a particular site, nor, more importantly, that any typology encapsulates all aspects of value. Most commentators suggest that the values statements are useful frameworks, but which probably need to be broken down into more precise categories as knowledge and understanding of the site increases.

We can suggest that the categories are further defined in response to the characteristics of the particular place, and that for any given place the typology should be used to engage with the site and tease out its particular characteristics and attributes. On this latter point it is worth noting the observation in The Burra Charter Guidelines (Australia ICOMOS, 1999, p. 12) that its categories are only 'one approach to understanding the concept of cultural significance. However more precise categories may be developed as understanding of a particular place increases'.

Although they may have to be 'deconstructed' and developed for the particular situation in order to make a better fit with the place, there is clearly a value in setting out such a typology which effectively categorises a range of values that may contribute to the significance of a place. Mason suggests that the purpose is to 'move conservation stakeholders closer to having a *lingua franca* in which all parties values can be expressed and discussed', and he suggests that devising and debating the typology are a means of stimulating participation (Mason, 2002, p. 9).

It is important to understand the following points about values and value typologies.

What is regarded as valuable about a particular place will not only vary between individuals and groups but will change over time – as will value categories themselves. That is, significance is dynamic and subjective and evolves within the context of changing social, cultural and political contexts. In other words, changing social perceptions considerably influence the value that we put upon our historic environment. For example, most generations struggle to appreciate the architecture of their own period along with that of their immediate predecessors. Georgian architecture was reviled by the Victorians, yet arguably it is appreciated more than any other age/style today. Most of the high Gothic Victorian architectural masterpieces that we acknowledge today were decried forty years ago as monstrosities. Current debates about the value of twentieth century buildings reinforce this point. It may be extremely difficult to predict how and when such a reappraisal of value may occur, but consideration of this is an important part of the equation in seeking to optimise benefits accruing today without compromising the value that might be placed on that asset by future generations.

In looking at how conservation was discussed in the relatively recent past, an attitude can be perceived amongst some that the buildings and sites in question were self-evidentially valuable (and that the values are now self-evident because the sites are designated); that is, they were treated as though there were some intrinsic value involved. However, cultural values are not intrinsic in the sense of being fixed or absolute. Essentially, places, sites and objects become culturally significant because people – often from a rather small and narrow constituency – have ascribed values to them. Value in this sense is essentially a social construct that can vary between people and over time. As Avrami et al. (2000, p.11) observe:

> *Objects and places are not in and of themselves what is important about cultural heritage; they are important because of the meanings and uses that people attach to these material goods and the values that they represent. These meanings, uses, and values must be understood as part of the larger sphere of socio cultural processes... As a social activity conservation is an enduring process, a means to an end rather than an end in itself. The process is creative and is motivated and underpinned by the values of individuals, institutions and communities.*

It is important then to remember that cultural values are in fact dynamic, relative and subjective (as are the value typologies). It is worth noting, however, Mason's observation (2002, p. 13) that '[This] intrinsic value argument in heritage conservation would be analogous to the "intrinsic" argument in environmental conservation, through which it is assumed that "natural" characteristics (wildness) are intrinsically valuable'. There are, in one sense, widely accepted values – age and rarity, for example (at least in western cultures, although even in Europe the notion is not uncontested) – and of course some characteristics that are considered to be of value may be intrinsic to particular sites or buildings. However, the idea that conserving something, for example, just because it is old is a social construct. Significance, then, is seen to represent what people feel about the historic environment, rather than reflecting any inherent qualities of the place. We should 'understand significance as growing out of the needs of contemporary societies rather than existing independently, within the relics of past cultures' (Carman, 1996, p. 11). Consideration of the idea that we are not dealing with absolute values also emphasises that what we choose to protect is not a means of preserving the past *per se* (particularly by choosing some elements and not others), so much as it is the holding up of a mirror to our present-day values. As Lowenthal (1997) states, ' However faithfully we preserve, however authentically we restore, however deeply we immerse ourselves in bygone time, life back then was based on ways of being and believing incommensurable with our own... we cannot help but view and celebrate it through present day lenses'.

However, it is worth acknowledging that, as Impey observes (2006, p. 80), values 'are liable to evolve along with changes in people's own perceptions and interests although longstanding attachment of value to places itself confers a species of value and adds substance to the idea of "established" value'.

Assessing significance – comparisons and relativity

We have already observed that it should be assumed that all value categories should be considered to be of equal standing. This should be the working premise when carrying out the assessment of a place, as should the assumption, initially at least, that the full range of values is represented (and indeed as we have also observed the investigation of the site may reveal other values). The process of assessment should then normally follow these procedures:

- The identification and assessment of the overall and particular values embodied in and represented by the site.
- An assessment of how valuable the site is related to comparable sites.
- An evaluation of what aspects and what elements of the site contribute to the overall significance of the place – and in what way they do so.
- Following from the above, an evaluation of the relative significance of the various aspects and elements of the place.

It can be seen that at the heart of this process is an assessment of value which is looking outwards at comparisons and looking inwards at relativity.

Comparative significance is best expressed by using a hierarchy of ascending or descending levels of value. A number of different hierarchical systems are in use today, but the three most common would appear to be a traditional structure built around international/national/regional/local levels, high/medium/low grading or several variants of a hierarchy proposed by Kerr (2004) which typically might consist of:

- **Exceptional:**   features of exceptional/international significance or which contain elements with a significance beyond national boundaries
- **Considerable:**   features of considerable/national significance, possibly reflected in statutory designations such as Scheduled Ancient Monument, Listed Building or equivalent nationally graded sites (including those of ecological and nature conservation value)
- **Some:**   features of some significance, important at regional level either individually or for group value
- **Limited:**   features of limited/local significance
- **Unknown:**   features of unknown significance resulting from a lack of sufficient information on which to base sound analysis of its value
- **No:**   features of no significance to the study area

In many cases a further category – 'negative significance' – is also identified in this kind of hierarchy in order to identify features that are thought to have such a deleterious effect that they detract from the overall significance of the place, or from elements of it. Such an approach may have value if it is properly considered, but it can cause difficulties since, conceptually, negative values are difficult to contend with and there is a real risk that users of the hierarchy will begin to confuse significance with character. There is also the practical problem that the element is likely to have a function, but at least the negative value can be taken into consideration in future decision making.

Whatever hierarchical system is chosen, it is vital that the levels are fully explained within the introduction to the assessment of significance so that readers can comprehend the adopted gradings unambiguously. There is a real danger in trying to read out and compare assessments from one conservation plan to another, although in our experience this is occasionally attempted.

The (heavily edited) examples below are from recent conservation plans that we have been involved in and are intended to provide an indication of how attributions of significance might be made. The first example – The Bodleian Library, Oxford – is a complex place and it is inappropriate and impractical to go into more detail here. Likewise, the second example, an assessment of significance of the Wellington Monument in Somerset for the National Trust, is not a complete analysis as that would be far too detailed to cite here, but the closing summary of significance of this less complex site is shown.

Example 1 – The Bodleian Library

The Bodleian Library is located in the heart of the city of Oxford, principally on a block of land delimited by Broad Street (to the north), the High (to the south), Catte Street (east) and Exeter College (west). The New Library building lies to the north of this land on the corner of Broad Street with Parks Road.

Physically, the Bodleian Library complex today is made up of a number of historically distinct elements:

- The Divinity School (fifteenth century)
- Duke Humfrey's Library (fifteenth century)
- Selden End (seventeenth century)
- The Convocation House and the Chancellor's Court (both seventeenth century)
- The Old Schools Quadrangle (seventeenth century)
- The Sheldonian Theatre (seventeenth century)
- The Clarendon Quadrangle (seventeenth century)
- The Clarendon Building (eighteenth century)
- The Radcliffe Camera (eighteenth century)
- The New Library (twentieth century)

All buildings within the complex are Grade I listed structures. The city defences, which pass through the centre of the site under the main buildings, are collectively a Scheduled Ancient Monument. The whole site falls within a Conservation Area.

Today, the Bodleian can justly claim to be the very heart of the University of Oxford. Architecturally, its importance cannot be overstated – the Old Schools Quadrangle alone was described by Pevsner (Sherwood and Pevsner, 1974) as being 'a formidable building... without parallel in the secular architecture of [its age]'.

The Bodleian is generally considered to be the first major public library in Britain. It was founded both to serve the University of Oxford and also, as is recorded in words attributed to Sir Thomas Bodley in an inscription over the entrance to the Proscholium through the west side of the Library's Old Schools Quadrangle, 'the republic of the learned'. The statutes, by which it is governed, require it to be maintained 'not only as a university library, but also as an institution of national and international importance'. Since 1610, the Bodleian has been a library of legal deposit. As a result of this – and also through gifts, bequests and purchases – it has over almost four centuries accumulated great collections of books, manuscripts and other sources of information which place it in the first rank of international libraries. By 2000, the library housed 6 500 000 printed books and manuscripts. Today, the Bodleian is housed on eleven separate sites, including eight specialist or 'dependent' libraries – the Bodleian Law Library, the Radcliffe Science Library, the Indian Institute Library, the Bodleian Japanese Library, the Oriental Institute Library, the Institute for Chinese Studies Library, the Philosophy Library, and the Rhodes House Library (for North American and sub-Saharan African materials).

Every year, the Old Bodleian receives in excess of 300 000 visits from readers wishing to use Duke Humfrey's Library, Selden End, or the Upper and Lower Reading Rooms. It is also a significant tourist attraction within the city of Oxford, drawing approximately 530 000 non-paying visitors per annum into the Old Schools Quadrangle, of whom around 200 000 enter the Divinity School.

A detailed conservation plan for the central Oxford complex was prepared in 2000/01. In summary, this defined the significance of the various principal elements as being:

Saxon and medieval defences across the site

Architecture: some significance
Archaeology: exceptional significance
Townscape: considerable significance
Artefacts: some significance
Social value: some significance
Associated personalities: little significance

Pre-University elements

Architecture: little significance
Archaeology: considerable significance
Townscape: considerable significance
Collections: considerable significance
Social value: considerable significance
Associated personalities: little significance

The Divinity School and Duke Humfrey's Library

Architecture: exceptional significance
Archaeology: considerable significance
Townscape: exceptional significance
Collections: some significance
Social value: exceptional significance
Associated personalities: exceptional significance

Bodley and his library

Architecture: exceptional significance
Archaeology: considerable significance
Townscape: exceptional significance
Collections: exceptional significance
Social value: exceptional significance
Associated personalities: exceptional significance

The Old Schools Quadrangle and Seldon End

Architecture: exceptional significance
Archaeology: some significance
Townscape: exceptional significance
Collections: exceptional significance
Social value: exceptional significance
Associated personalities: exceptional significance

The Sheldonian Theatre

Architecture: exceptional significance
Archaeology: some significance
Townscape: exceptional significance
Collections: little significance
Social value: exceptional significance
Associated personalities: exceptional significance

Example 2 – The Wellington Monument, Wellington, Somerset (see Figure 5.4)

History

Although initially conceived as a tribute to the Duke of Wellington's internationally significant victory at Waterloo and his earlier military campaigns, the Monument's commemorative association with the Duke has been greatly complicated by the prolonged time taken over its construction. The changing public perception of the Duke during that period fundamentally altered the nature of the Monument. Had the Duke not entered into politics with such controversial and anti-progressive vehemence in the early 1820s, it is probable that public opinion might still have regarded him with sufficient favour for the necessary subscriptions to be raised and the Monument completed, as first intended. If this had been the case, it would have been Lee's 1817 design, not the current configuration that now stands upon Wellington Hill. The fact that, essentially, it is Giles' 1853 structure that we see today is fundamentally related to the innate complexities of Wellington's character, to the course of his political career and to the contemporary international sociopolitical atmosphere of upheaval, unrest and change. In this sense, there is an intimate connection between the Monument's evolution and the course of early-to-mid nineteenth century political and domestic history that shapes its significance. Irrespective of its form and size, the Monument also has considerable prominence amongst the plenitude of contemporary dedications and monumental tributes to the Duke of Wellington. This is because it was the principal act of public homage to the man and his military achievements by the community whose name he had adopted and elevated to international renown. Its siting on his own estate also gave eminence to its comparative importance as a memorial and tribute.

Assessment of significance: exceptional

Architecture

Although quite unheralded as such in any medium, the Wellington Monument occupies a prominent position amongst the world's great obelisks. It is the tallest in the UK and the second tallest in Europe, after the Wellington Testimonial in Phoenix Park, Dublin. It is the fifth tallest stone obelisk in the world and, again, outside of the United States, it is second only to the Wellington Testimonial in the world. It is far and away the tallest three-sided obelisk of any material in the world.

Assessment of significance: exceptional

Social

Somewhat ironically for a memorial originally intended to commemorate the early nineteenth century epitome of heroic individualism, the Monument has, since the twentieth century, become a focus for familial and organisational outings (within the National Trust archives, there are numerous accounts of barbecues and events held on the site by local associations). Undoubtedly, it was the obelisk itself that drew families and groups to the site, and this continues to be the case. To this extent, the Monument provides a catalyst for recreation that is essentially unrelated to its historical and commemorative values. Instead, it depends on the sheer magnetism of its form and size, on its ready accessibility and panoramic rural environs and, to a lesser degree than might normally be the case, on the pulling power of the National Trust's 'badge' of ownership.

Assessment of significance: limited

Panoramic

The Monument and its immediate environs afford extensive panoramic views across the surrounding region and beyond. Conversely, its exposed location on the highest point in the vicinity ensures that the inward vistas to the Monument are just as dramatic, especially at dusk when the obelisk is floodlit.

Assessment of significance: some

Symbolic/iconic

Quite distinct from the Monument's direct symbolism as a homage to the military might of early nineteenth century Britain and the nation's predominance as a world power, it has also come to hold an iconic status for many millions of motorists every year, who see the obelisk silhouetted against the skyline from the M5 motorway. The Monument affords a strong and unforgettable geographical symbol for travellers to and from the south-west, forming a landmark by which many undoubtedly measure their progress. To an extent, therefore, the Monument and its profile on the leading edge of the Blackdown Hills are symbolic of the Taunton Deane area and the sub-region as a whole. Irrespective of its commemorative value, the Monument marks the passage from Somerset to Devon (and vice versa) for the nation's motorists and, accordingly, it has both regional and national iconic significance.

Assessment of significance: considerable

Ecological

Whilst the immediate environs of the Wellington Monument are not necessarily unique within the Area of Outstanding Natural Beauty in which they are located, the site forms a characteristic and representative part of the Blackdown Hills range. It supports a relatively diverse spectrum of flora and fauna. The Monument itself acts as shelter to butterflies, moths and nesting birds, and provides habitat for various lichens and moss. Otherwise, ecologically, the structure is of limited value, given its severely inhospitable and inclement micro-climate.

Assessment of significance: limited

Economic

Although, arguably, the Wellington Monument may be regarded as a historic asset of some potential prestige, given its architectural significance and its place in popular consciousness, it has always proven a serious economic burden to its managers. Ironically, the instigators of both principal nineteenth century phases created a structure that was so inherently flawed by their own economising measures that it would prove a substantial ongoing drain on the resources of their successors. Whilst there may be some potential to exploit the Monument to a greater extent for its economic value, there is no prospect that this will balance out or even approach the investment that will be required to support its long-term care.

Assessment of significance: none (arguably, negative) significance

Overall, the assessment concluded that the Wellington Monument is of very considerable, perhaps exceptional, cultural significance.

As we have said, as well as this overall picture of the cultural significance of the place, it will also be necessary to determine what elements embody and represent the values – and therefore how they contribute to its significance and the degree to which they do so. This should be done holistically of course by looking at the whole site first. But it will also probably be necessary to assess the significance of all the elements individually (whilst understanding that a group or sub-group of elements, say buildings, taken together may be more important than looking at them individually might suggest).

This is not a simple process particularly on complex sites. The issue of how a range of values, sometimes co-existing and reinforcing each other, but sometimes competing with each other, can be clearly identified and accommodated, and then protected and enhanced, without producing something which lacks coherence and cohesion can be difficult to resolve. If such a situation occurs then not only will it be a source of confusion and probably controversy it will be impossible to produce an effective management plan.

Some would argue against the idea of relative significance, in the sense at least of actually classifying and grading elements, particularly when, as in most cases, the relative significance of aspects, elements or components is assessed not only to help in articulating the overall significance of the site but also in order to make decisions about managing change on most sites of any complexity. That is to say, fabric may be lost as a result of these decisions to state what elements absolutely must be protected and which are less important.

It should be borne in mind that an element that is considered less significant than another may still be vital to an understanding of the value of the more significant element because it might be contextually important.

There is also a general concern about deciding that something has no signif-icance. On a complex site, documentary evidence may not be available about every aspect of the place (it may have been lost, overlooked, or there is no evidence because it was not thought important in the past – even though it may be now). This raises the question of whether on an evidence-based assessment a lack of evidence supporting the significance of something means that it is not significant. It could be argued that 'the precautionary principle' should apply and that elements should only be placed in this category if it can be actively demonstrated that they are not important, rather than assuming they are not just because there is no evidence to support their value. Schaafsma (1989, p. 49) suggested that 'our problems in cultural resource management persist because we have failed to develop means to identify insignificant sites satisfactorily'. For him, the historic resource was significant until proven otherwise. Whilst such an approach may not be entirely or always practical, it is perhaps a valuable 'mindset' to adopt in that it adds to and reinforces the notion of rigorous assessment.

Example 2 above, the assessment of significance of the Wellington Monument, does not include a relative assessment of the contribution of significance made by individual parts of the site and structure. Indeed, for a simple architectural form such as a monumental obelisk, it is doubtful if this type of evaluation can be meaningfully achieved. Some also suggest that the more cohesive the site, the less necessary is an assessment of relative significance. However, for more complex structures and sites, as we have suggested this is an important step if priorities are to be established for action.

The assigning of a relative value is not a quantitative exercise and is not meant to be a scoring system – it is rather a means of making comparisons. It is important to assign 'soft' criteria which, whilst differentiating, do not give the impression of absolutes or the sense that such things can be easily measured, particularly as we are dealing with comparative judgements. Kerr suggests (2004, p. 19) 'that the hierarchy developed to present the level of significance should (therefore) be chosen to suit the place and that it should be explained with clarity'.

It is this area, the extent to which ideas of relative significance can be agreed upon, that can cause the most difficulties, both conceptually and in practice, but upon which the success of any plan arising out of an assessment of significance will, to a large extent, rest. This is because, in effect, its purpose and role is derived from the idea that a 'values-based' approach to managing the built cultural heritage acknowledges that there may be different values embodied in the place, and that these might be embodied both alone and in various combinations in the different elements and aspects. The value of a plan is that it is an attempt to identify values as separate, whilst understanding and celebrating their connections and intricacies and the way that they contribute to the whole – but nevertheless at the same time judging and balancing their worth in order to provide the substance of a single cohesive and coherent plan. Also as The Burra Charter observes, 'Relative degrees of cultural significance may lead to different conservation actions at a place' (Australia ICOMOS, 1999).

However, Pearson and Marshall (2005) make an interesting and valid point about using the idea of relative significance in a Conservation (Management) Plan they wrote for the National Library of Australia.

It is not very prudent to indicate an absolute ranking of significance, as the ranking can change as the perspective of the assessor changes. An attribute of the place either is or is not significant in relation to the criteria used. Attributing degrees of significance depends very much on the context in which the judgement is made—for example, is the architectural value of one element of the building more or less important than the historical value of another? Nor does attributing levels of significance necessarily have direct implications for setting management and conservation priorities—for example, a component of 'high' significance might need less effort to conserve, and hence have a lower funding priority, than a component of 'moderate' significance. Both need conserving, but the priorities are not driven solely by levels of significance. A more useful approach is to consider the sorts of actions and change that might have an impact on significance, and identify how sensitive to change a range of significant attributes might be. Actions and change might include such things as introducing new built elements, removing or altering original fabric, changing use, changing frequency of maintenance, or undertaking conservation works. Different actions will have different potential impacts on significance, depending on the nature of the heritage values of the particular element (of the Library). It is therefore useful to indicate the degree of sensitivity that components of the place might have to changes in their conservation, use or management... The level of sensitivity to change is based on the vulnerability of the component to loss of heritage values through change.

High sensitivity   *High sensitivity to change occurs where a change would pose a major threat to a specific heritage value of the component affected, or the Library as a whole. A major threat is one that would lead to substantial or total loss of the heritage value.*

Moderate sensitivity   *Moderate sensitivity to change occurs where a change would pose a moderate threat to a specific heritage value of the component affected, or would pose a threat to a component of heritage significance in another part of the building. A moderate threat is one that would diminish the heritage value, or diminish the ability of an observer to appreciate the value.*

Low sensitivity   *Low sensitivity to change occurs where a change would pose no appreciable threat to a specific heritage value of the component affected, and would pose no appreciable threat to heritage significance in another part of the building. Components of the Library with no individual identified heritage values are likely to have a low sensitivity to change (rising to moderate if the proposals affect adjacent areas having values).*

The level of sensitivity will depend on the specific values of the space involved, and any one space might have a range of heritage values that have high, moderate or low levels of sensitivity to the same proposal. Assessment of proposals should therefore consider all values. An example would be a proposal to refurbish a significant reading room. The heritage values of the reading room might include its long-term historical use as a reading room, the design values of its wall cladding and fitout, and its being part of a rare suit[e] of rooms reflecting the original design of the Library. If a proposal to reclad the reading room in new materials were made, the room would have high sensitivity to change in relation to the design of its wall cladding, high to moderate sensitivity in relation to its impact on a suit[e] of rooms, and low sensitivity in relation to use (which would remain unchanged).

Understanding the relationship between values and impacts of change will help in modifying proposals and avoiding loss of significance.

To a large extent, assessing the overall significance of a place is based on comparisons. Therefore, it is all about relative significance, particularly in terms of what we might call traditional conservation criteria (e.g. the best example of an architectural period, the first time such and such a technique was used, etc.). But it is arguably less so with other perhaps newer criteria in that, for example, you cannot really measure the value of a site to one community compared to the value of another site for another community – although you can of course measure how many people value it, etc. Therefore part of the process of assessment may well involve a knowledge of comparative information about say building types – for example how does this nineteenth century workhouse compare in terms of, say, its design and layout and use in relation to other workhouses regionally and nationally, for example:

Is it the most complete?

or

Does it perhaps have a design and layout which represents or illustrates some change in social policy regarding how the poor were regarded by society and how they were treated?

or

Is it a representative example of its type (which might be the most valuable quality)?

Other useful examples might be:

If it is the work of a particular architect does it represent, say, an early example of their work, or a particularly fine example of it?

If it is good example of a particular style of architecture – say, Arts and Crafts or Modernism – is it the only known example in that area or a pioneering example?

Such comparisons provide a context that will help to assess and then to justify, explain and illustrate significance. However, it is important that such comparisons do not produce too much of a straightjacket for the assessment, which could overshadow the unique qualities and values of the particular place.

Kerr (2004, p. 16) suggests that the quality of the assessment of significance will depend on the assessor's contextual and comparative knowledge of the subject and period. He refers to the need to establish how:

- Early
- Seminal
- Intact
- Representative
- Rare, or
- Climactic

an example is.

We would suggest that these categories are extremely useful for comparative purposes in helping to assess importance (and some are of course explicit or implicit values), and we would make the following observations on Kerr's list (to which we have added age and vulnerability):

Age: The fact that something is old is often considered as in itself demonstrating value. Indeed, in some countries such as the UK age is an overriding factor in determining whether a building should be listed. Whether something should be automatically considered valuable simply on the basis of its age is clearly a debatable point – and has been since the time of William Morris. The point that the emphasis on age is one of the factors which increases the vulnerability of more recent buildings of cultural value, particularly perhaps from the post-WWII period, is an obvious one but nonetheless important.

Early: Obviously the quality of being an early example is a different concept to age, as it can just as easily mean an early example of a telecommunications site as it can an early example of a medieval timber-framed farmhouse.

Rarity: The characteristic of something being rare is another reference point for demonstrating its importance. The sense that just because something is unique it is valuable is generally accepted, although it is interesting to reflect on why this should be necessarily so. There is perhaps a distinction to be made between something which is now the only remaining example of an important building or place and something which is rare because it was the only one of its kind – in which case, we might value its uniqueness because this might tell us something about a society or the forces that created a 'one off'. If it is a less important object it might be considered a 'curiosity' and therefore of interest value rather than of significance.

Vulnerability: The question of whether we perhaps see things as being more significant if they are in danger is an interesting one. It is not that we see them as more significant perhaps, but that we value them more because they are vulnerable and likely to be lost.

Completeness: The extent to which something is complete and/or in good condition will make it valuable because of what we can learn and understand from the whole (physical) picture. But many sites are valuable because they are incomplete. Pompeii and Machu Picchu are examples where the atmosphere created by the ruins is arguably as important as the story to which the ruins testify.

Representativeness: This is an important characteristic and some have argued that it is more important than significance. It can be viewed at two levels. One is the sense of being representative of its type – in which case (as Kerr suggests) the extent to which it is complete may be important. The other is more related to a perhaps more fundamental issue about identifying what should be protected and why. In turn, this is related to the point that, if one of the purposes of conservation is for present and future generations to understand more about past societies then, for example, when the iconic or rare is favoured over that which represents the ordinary and the everyday, the picture is distorted.

Seminal: Places or buildings that influenced and shaped ideas, on not only the built form but also the function or purpose represented by that built form, will clearly be significant (for example, in representing and illustrating changes in public policy in, say, the treatment of offenders, care of the mentally ill, etc.).

High point: That which is considered perhaps the developmental peak of, say, architectural or technical achievement, or perhaps a social idea which is reflected in the built form.

Conservation principles

Development of conservation principles

Within western cultures we can trace a concern for preserving certain physical artefacts back many centuries, although perhaps the first stirrings of what we might discern as a conservation consciousness only really began to develop in the eighteenth century. However, in the UK it was not really until the formation of the Society for The Protection of Ancient Buildings (SPAB) in 1877 that a coherent philosophy was articulated and developed. The driving force behind this early conservation movement was William Morris, who was much inspired by the thoughts and writing of John Ruskin. It is interesting to note the extent to which the ideas formulated during this period still inform much of current thinking about approaches to the care of the built cultural heritage. However, some of the rather dogmatic assertions about the 'evil' of restoration have been contextualised by the idea of the overriding importance of establishing and protecting cultural significance.

As we have observed previously, we can see in the development of this early movement the identification of the value of stewardship of existing resources (Morris (1877) said that 'we are only trustees for those who come after us'), as well as an emphasis on the spiritual and educational value of the built cultural heritage and a concern for the dignity and pleasure to be gained from skilled creative work. Ruskin (1989) felt that old buildings were to be revered because they were the results of a living popular art.

Morris developed a manifesto for SPAB that implicitly and explicitly set down a number of principles, which still have relevance and resonance and can be seen as informing the basis of ideas in a number of charters and guidelines. Amongst the key ideas were:

- The uniqueness and therefore the importance of the fabric of buildings as a physical expression of the cultural values of the place as well as a source of education and understanding
- The importance and significance of all the developments contained within these buildings and respect for all historic materials found
- The importance of maintenance:

> *put Protection in the place of Restoration, [to] stave off decay by daily care*
> (Morris 1877)

> *take proper care of your monuments, and you will not need to restore them*
> (Ruskin, 1989, p. 196)

In the early days of the conservation movement there was a very strong emphasis, often to the exclusion of any other considerations, on the need to protect the original and/or authentic fabric of the structure, based on the idea that it represented the skill and art of the originator and, as mentioned previously, that age in itself conveyed cultural worth. This 'archaeological' perspective is still a strong theme today, and appropriately so – at least for certain buildings and certain situations. The 'archaeological' perspective, with its reverence for the work of the 'original hand' and the emphasis on respecting that art by not falsifying/copying or damaging it, was reinforced by the concerns of the art historian which would unequivocally be antagonistic to attempts to 'repair' say a work of art painted by a great artist. The same concept would be applied to the buildings that were protected, based on the idea that they were also examples of great artistic achievement (and indeed those that were chosen were to a large extent singled out for that reason). This situation reinforced the anti-restoration rhetoric of SPAB and others, and underlined the basic tenets or principles of conservation philosophy – especially those of minimum intervention and honesty.

It is important to acknowledge that the ideas developed by Morris and Ruskin and the early pioneers of the conservation movement – particularly minimum intervention and honesty – still form the core of what we might call 'conservation principles' as witnessed by the various international conservation charters and guidance. For example:

> *Conservation should show the greatest respect for, and involve the least possible loss of, material of cultural heritage value*
> (ICOMOS New Zealand, 1992)

> *Conservation is based on a respect for the existing fabric, use, associations and meanings. It requires a cautious approach of changing as much as necessary but as little as possible*   (Australia ICOMOS, 1999)

> *The unnecessary replacement of historic fabric, no matter how carefully the work is carried out, will have an adverse effect on the appearance of a building or monument, will seriously diminish its authenticity, and will significantly reduce its value as a source of historical information*
>   (Brereton, 1991, p. 8)

These principles of honesty and minimum intervention, although developed in reference to the fabric, apply equally to all interventions in relation to the built cultural heritage – from decisions about maintenance of the fabric to alterations, changes of use and indeed the development of new buildings in historic areas.

Conservation principles have been developed from these early ideas, with the most commonly adopted ones being perhaps:

Authenticity

The idea of authenticity is fundamental to conservation principles. Bell (1997, p. 28) suggests that 'Authenticity is not an easy concept. Each part of a site's development is authentic in its own right, as a reflection of its time', and Feilden and Jokilehto (1993, p. 16) observe that 'Authenticity is ascribed to a heritage resource that is materially original or genuine and as it has aged and changed in time' and that 'The contributions of all periods to the place must be respected'. In practice, determining authenticity is closely linked to assessments of value – and can cause problems when, for instance, the idea of age value influences decisions about the relative value of more recent developments to the place.

The importance of the fabric

As The Burra Charter observes (p. 3), 'Conservation is based on respect for existing fabric, use, associations and meanings'. The Charter also emphasises the importance of the fabric in understanding the place when it suggests that 'the traces of additions, alterations and earlier treatments to the fabric of a place are evidence of its history and uses which may be part of its significance' (p. 3).

The importance of maintenance

This is emphasised in many charters and other guidance as a key activity in protecting the cultural significance which is represented by fabric, and in reducing the need for inappropriate interventions. The Venice Charter, for instance, states that 'Protection must involve a continuing programme of maintenance'. Maintenance management is discussed in further detail in Chapter 5.

Minimum intervention

This can be interpreted at two levels. The notion emphasises the importance of the fabric as evidence in understanding the development of the place, as reference

Figure 3.10 The story that the fabric of a building can tell is illustrated by the town walls of Spoleto. It is important that all the significant developments of a place are respected. (Photograph courtesy of Tony Bryan).

is often made to being able to read the building and to allowing the building to tell its own story.

> *Conservation is based on respect for fabric and it should involve the least possible physical intervention. . . Intervention should not distort the evidence provided by the fabric.*   (Australia ICOMOS, 1999)

But minimum intervention does not just refer to the fabric, it refers to all actions in the place, including additions, new buildings and changes in use. The idea is not to stifle change but to ensure that any changes protect and enhance cultural significance. The Burra Charter emphasises a cautious approach to change and says 'do as much as necessary to care for the place and to make it useable, but otherwise change it as little as possible so that its cultural significance is retained'.

Truth and honesty

The idea of truthfulness or honesty has been an important aspect of conservation principles for certain architectural movements for some time. The neo-Gothic architect A.W.N. Pugin refers to the idea as did John Ruskin in his discourses on architecture, for example in the *Seven Lamps of Architecture* (Ruskin, 1989). It is also one of the central themes, for instance, in the Arts and Crafts Movement and the Modern Movement. The concern in such architectural movements is that, with such concepts, you do not disguise but rather you should celebrate the materials that have been used in its construction. Furthermore, you should be able to understand by observing the building how it was put together and how its structure works, and also that its function should be decipherable by its design – and indeed that its form should be derived from its function. The idea of truthfulness and honesty has also long been a key conservation principle. One of the catalysts for the formation of The Society for the Protection of Ancient Buildings (SPAB) was the concern of Morris and others about the implications of the restoration of churches back to some previous state of Gothic purity, mostly a state that was imagined or based on conjecture. Ruskin, for example, suggested that 'Restoration. . . means the most total destruction which a building can suffer. . . The thing is a lie from beginning to end' (Ruskin, 1989, p. 194). This anti-restoration stance has implicitly and explicitly driven much of the thinking on conservation actions, particularly in the UK, for some time. For example, the current document from SPAB states:

> although no building can withstand decay, neglect and depredation en-
> tirely, neither can aesthetic judgment nor archaeological proof justify the
> reproduction of worn or missing parts. Only as a practical expedient on
> a small scale can a case for restoration be argued   (SPAB)

However, other guidance, particularly where it uses cultural significance as a reference point, has put this anti-restoration idea into perspective – whilst still showing a cautionary stance about it. So, for example, in the English Heritage document *The Repair of Historic Buildings* (Brereton, 1991), Brereton acknowledges that the restoration of lost features may be justified as long as there is no loss of historic fabric and that sufficient evidence exists for accurate replacement. But restoration can involve both adding something and/or taking it away, and on this latter point Brereton states that 'Additions or alterations including earlier repairs are of importance for the part they play in the cumulative history of a building or monument. There should always be a strong presumption in favour of their retention'. He goes on to state that any potential and architectural gains must be balanced against any likely loss of historic integrity. The Burra Charter (Australia ICOMOS, 1999) defines conservation as being 'all the processes of looking after a place so as to retain its cultural significance'. It goes on to expand on this by observing that 'Conservation may, according to circumstance, include the processes of: retention or reintroduction of a use; retention of associations and meanings; maintenance, preservation, restoration, reconstruction adaptation and interpretation; and will commonly include a combination of more than one of these'. The Charter qualifies this by stressing that restoration (and reconstruction) should only happen where it will reveal culturally significant aspects of the place, and only if there is sufficient evidence of an earlier state of the fabric. The Charter reinforces this by stating that 'Changes to a place should not distort the physical or other evidence it provides nor be based on conjecture'.

The issue with restoration, particularly of, say, major parts of the place, is not just an issue of truthfulness, it is also a process that, unless it is handled sensitively, negates the development of the place by suggesting that one era is more important than another. Also that it may go against the principle of minimum intervention. Nevertheless, it is generally accepted that – with the provisos stated above – restoration may be an appropriate action but this should only be done after the cultural significance of the place has been established.

The English Heritage document, *Conservation Principles, Policies and Guidance for the Sustainable Management of the Historic Environment* (English Heritage, 2007), states in regard to restoration (p. 43):

> *Restoration is an intervention made with the deliberate intention of revealing or recovering some elements of heritage value that has been eroded, obscured or previously removed, rather than simply maintaining the status quo. It may also achieve other conservation benefits, for example restoring a roof on a roofless building may make it both physically and economically sustainable in the long term.*

The document goes on to say that:

> *Restoration of a significant place should be acceptable if all the following criteria are met:*

> - *the heritage value of what would be revealed or recovered decisively outweighs the value of what would be lost;*
> - *the work proposed is justified by compelling evidence of the previous form of the place, and is executed in accordance with that evidence;*
> - *the current state of the place, the form in which it survives, is not the result of an historically significant event;*
> - *there would be no obvious incongruity, through creating something that has never previously existed as an entity;*
> - *resources are available to maintain what is restored.*

But the idea of truth and honesty is not just related to the issue of restoration. A basic principle of conservation is that all interventions in the fabric should be handled 'truthfully' to make clear what is 'original' and what has changed, in order to avoid producing a parody or facsimile of the past or pretending that something is what it is not. The Venice Charter (ICOMOS, 1964) states that

'Replacements of missing parts must. . . be distinguishable from the original so that restoration does not falsify the artistic or historic evidence'. In part, this is harking back to a Ruskin/Morris concept of respecting the work of previous generations, but it is also concerned with not obscuring the 'reading' of the building and the understanding that all developments of the place have value. Brereton (1991) makes the point that 'The authenticity of an historic building depends most crucially on the integrity of its fabric and on its design, which may be original or may incorporate different periods of addition and alteration'.

As with the concept of minimum intervention, the idea of honesty is most often perhaps used in reference to repairs to the fabric. However, as a principle, it should be applied to all intervention in the historic environment, including alterations, additions and indeed new buildings – which generally should respect the historic context and certainly not detract from its significance, but should also be clearly distinguishable from new work. The issue is one of truthfulness, but it also acknowledges that changes made now are part of the continuing history and development of the place.

Reversibility

To some extent reversibility is a relatively pragmatic principle, in that it allows current actions to be substituted for future, possibly more appropriate, options – perhaps where a repair, for instance, is not functioning properly or where it is causing unforeseen damage to adjacent material. But something that is reversible also has an implied subservient quality in reference to the 'original' material, and could be taken to imply a hierarchy mainly based on age and the perceived (un)worthiness of modern intervention – that what we do now has less value than that done in the past. However, new interventions are, an often important, part of the 'story' of the place. As with other principles, reversibility could equally apply to actions other than repairs – for example, with the physical aspects of the introduction of a new use where the design might allow for the removal of the new structure without adverse impact on the 'original' fabric.

Fit the new to the old

This again works at a number of levels and covers 'moulding' the new to the old because this will usually reduce the amount of original material lost in repair work – and may, for instance, reinforce the value of 'plastic' repairs in stonework. Equally, as with reversibility, it should concern how new uses, additions and new buildings are 'fitted in' with the existing.

The importance of the relationship of a site with its surroundings

The sense that the context of a building was important and that its loss would detract from its cultural significance led to the creation of Conservation Areas in the UK. The Venice Charter (ICOMOS, 1964) was emphatic in saying that 'A monument is inseparable from the history to which it bears witness and from the setting in which it occurs'. The Burra Charter (Australia ICOMOS, 1999) states that 'Conservation requires the retention of an appropriate visual setting and other relationships that contribute to the cultural significance of the place' and that 'other relationships such as historical connections may contribute to interpretation, appreciation, enjoyment or experience of the place' and 'the contribution which related places and related objects make to the cultural significance of the place should be retained'.

This principle also extends to the idea that buildings should not be moved. Again as The Burra Charter states, 'The physical location of a place is part of its cultural significance. A building, work or other component of a place should remain in its historical location'. The SPAB document, *SPAB's Purpose*, says that 'As good buildings age, the bond with their site strengthens. A beautiful interesting or simply ancient building still belongs where it stands however corrupted that place may have become'.

The importance of records

Creating a record of the built cultural heritage is part of the process of establishing its significance and also of managing the care and protection of the place. The need to record all actions in order to help others to understand 'the story' of the place is also an important conservation principle. The Burra Charter states that 'existing fabric, use, associations and meanings should be adequately recorded before any changes are made to the place'.

The maintenance and development of an accurate record is a key process in managing the care and protection of heritage sites. As the ICOMOS Charter (1990) on recording states, '[historic buildings] must be treated responsibly, and the understanding that is essential to their proper treatment can only be reached by making the best possible use of information about them and by ensuring too that future generations understand what the present generation has done for their care'.

Recording and interpretation of the built cultural heritage are pre-requisites for processes related to the effective management of the built cultural heritage, for example: defect analysis; maintenance; visitor management.

Reasons for recording historic buildings include:

- To collect information in order to aid in the understanding of cultural significance. As Cooper (1991) observes, 'We record buildings because we want to discover certain things about them'. This may be primarily related to identifying the changes that have occurred over a period of time.
- To provide information for interpretation and public understanding of the building.
- To enable the reconstruction of part or the whole of the building (or 'object') in the event of its damage or destruction. An accurate record of a historic building is required for any reconstruction, necessitated by, for example, fire, flood or perhaps even theft (of course, whether or not such a reconstruction has value in cultural heritage terms is a matter of debate – and context).
- As part of the process of proper management of the place in relation to maintenance, repair or conversion projects where:

- the information is used to inform decision making about the effect that proposed changes will have on the historic fabric;
- an archival record of that which is inevitably lost or changed (even routine maintenance work can involve loss or change) is established. As Rosier (1996, p. 20–22) points out, 'prior recording can ensure that the removal or obstruction of historical evidence can be "preserved by record" while the agreed alterations allow the buildings a new lease of life';
- hidden features revealed during the works can be recorded before they are re-concealed.

Given the above requirements and uses, we can see that the recording of a historic building is not a 'one-off' event but a continuous process that is a prerequisite of many conservation management activities. The ICOMOS (1990) guidelines say that 'The record of a building should be seen as cumulative with each stage adding both to the comprehensiveness of the record and the comprehension of the building that the record makes possible'.

It is important to recognise that recording is not value free. It is, as stated, part of the process of understanding and interpreting the building – of establishing cultural significance – and therefore attributing value to the structure. 'The essence of the record lies in coming to an understanding of the building and of its development and structure, and that all recording should have as its objective the elucidation and illustration of this understanding' (ICOMOS, 1990). Similarly, Molyneux (1991) observes that 'The purpose of analytical recording is not merely to ascertain the initial form of the building but rather how the use of the structure has responded to and reflects social cultural and economic change through time'. Recording should therefore, so far as possible, not only illustrate and describe a building but also demonstrate significance.

Clearly, as mentioned before, decisions on how and what to record will involve varying measures of subjective judgement of the relative values embodied in, or represented by, the building. However, it is also clear that the process used to communicate or disseminate the analytical record may in itself influence the interpretation of the building and therefore the understanding of its significance.

Records are discussed further in Chapter 4.

New uses

A general principle is that the original use of a place is the most appropriate use, and certainly where the use of a place is of cultural significance it should be retained. But from a financial perspective, finding a new use may be the only effective way of retaining the building or place. However, because of operating requirements, some uses that are the same as the original may be more intrusive now than if the place was put to a different use – for example, hospitals with changing perspectives on service delivery, and requirements for security, based on sight lines, in many buildings.

New uses that reduce the building to a façade are rarely justifiable in conservation terms. (The visual amenity that is kept is almost always a poor reason/

substitute for the loss of the building and encourages the sense that appearance is the main value.)

If a place is to have a new use it should be a compatible use (The Burra Charter: Australia ICOMOS, 1999). The basis of judging compatibility could be related to reducing interference with the fabric, and therefore any use that can fulfil its function without damaging the fabric may be compatible. However, the idea of compatibility may also relate to considering the use from an 'ethical' point of view (reuse of churches as some social good rather than, for instance, something with a purely commercial purpose), or one that retains the same sort of 'spirit of place' associated with noise, atmosphere, etc.

Whilst finding a new use may be absolutely necessary to the continuing use of the place from a financial perspective, if the main, or a major aspect, of cultural significance is related to the type of use then clearly this will be problematic.

Some reuses have been achieved by inserting a whole new structure within an original space in such a way that it does not damage fabric (minimum intervention), is constructed of modern material with a modern design (honesty) and can be dismantled and removed (reversibility – even though if successful it will became part of the story of the place).

References

Australia ICOMOS (1999) *The Burra Charter, The Australia ICOMOS Charter for Places of Cultural Significance*. Australia ICOMOS Inc.

Avrami, E., Mason, R. and de la Torre, M. (2000) The spheres and challenges of conservation. In: *Values and Heritage Conservation, Research Report*. Los Angeles, The Getty Conservation Institute.

Bell, D. (1997) *The Historic Scotland Guide to International Conservation Charters*. Edinburgh, Historic Scotland.

Brereton, C. (1991) *The Repair of Historic Buildings*. London, English Heritage.

Carman, R.J. (1996) *Valuing Ancient Things*. London, Leicester University Press.

Cooper, N. (1991) Architectural records: recording evidence and recording facts. In: *Recording Historic Buildings*. London, RCHME.

Council of Europe (1975) *European Charter of the Architectural Heritage*. Available online at www.international.icomos.org/charters.htm

Council of Europe (2005) *Framework Convention on the Value of Cultural Heritage for Society*. CETS Number 199. Available online at www.coe.int

eftec (2005) Valuation of the historic environment – the scope for using results of valuation studies in the appraisal and assessment of heritage-related projects and programmes. Final Report. *Report to English Heritage, the Heritage Lottery Fund, the Department for Culture, Media and Sport and the Department for Transport*. London, eftec.

English Heritage (1997) *Sustaining the Historic Environment*. London, English Heritage.

English Heritage (2000) *Power of Place, the Future of the Historic Environment*. London, English Heritage.

English Heritage (2007) *Conservation Principles, Policies and Guidance for the Sustainable Management of the Historic Environment (Second Stage Consultation)*. London, English Heritage.

Feilden, B. (2003) *Conservation of Historic Buildings*. London, Architectural Press. [Imprint of Elsevier, Oxford]

Feilden, B. and Jokilehto, J. (1993) *Management Guidelines for World Cultural Heritage Sites*. Rome, ICCROM.

Halldén, S. (1983) *Behövs der Förflutna?: en bok om det Gåtfulla Vardagslivet*. Stockholm, LiberFörlag. [Trans. Do we need a past?][In Swedish]

Hewison, R. (1987) *The Heritage Industry; Britain in a Climate of Decline*. London, Methuen.

Holland, A. and Rawles, K. (1993) Values in conservation. *Ecos* **14**(1), 14–19.

Hubbard, P. (1993) The value of conservation. *Town Planning Review* **64**(4), 359–373.

ICOMOS (1954) *Convention for the Protection of Cultural Property in the Event of Armed Conflict*. Available online at www.international.icomos.org/hague/

ICOMOS (1964) *International Charter for the Conservation and Restoration of Monuments and Sites (The Venice Charter)*. Available online at www.international.icomos.org/charters.htm

ICOMOS (1987a) *ICOMOS Monograph: 7th General Assembly and Symposium Rostock–Dresden, 1984*. Berlin, VEB.

ICOMOS (1987b) *Charter for the Conservation of Historic Towns and Urban Areas (The Washington Charter)*. Available online at www.international.icomos.org/charters.htm

ICOMOS (1990) *Guide to Recording Historic Buildings*. London, Butterworth.

ICOMOS (1994) *The Nara Document on Authenticity*. Available online at www.international.icomos.org/charters.htm

ICOMOS (1999) *Charter on the Built Vernacular Heritage*. Available online at www.international.icomos.org/charters.htm

ICOMOS New Zealand (1992) *Charter for the Conservation of Places of Cultural Heritage Value*. ICOMOS New Zealand.

Impey, E. (2006) Why do places matter? Paper in: *Capturing the Public Value of Heritage*. London, English Heritage.

Kerr, J.S. (2004) *The Conservation Plan* (6th edn). On behalf of The National Trust of Australia. Sydney, NT.

Lowenthal, D. (1997) *The Past is a Foreign Country*. Cambridge University Press.

Maeer, G. and Millar, G. (2004) Evaluation of UK waterway regeneration and restoration projects. *Municipal Engineer* **157**(2): 1 June, 103–109.

Mason, R. (2002) Assessing values in conservation planning: methodological issues and choices. In: *Assessing the Values of Cultural Heritage, Research Report* (eds E. Avrami, R. Mason and M. de la Torre). Los Angeles, The Getty Conservation Institute, pp. 5–30.

Molyneux, N. (1991) English Heritage and recording: policy and practice. Paper presented at the *Recording Historic Buildings* symposium. London, RCHME, pp. 24–30.

Morris, W. (1877) The Principles of the Society (for the Protection of Ancient Buildings) As set Forth upon its Foundation. Available on SPAB website http://www.spab.org.uk/html/what-is-spab/the-manifesto/

ONE North East (2004) *The Economic Value of Protected Landscapes in the North East of England: Report to ONE North East – Executive Summary*. Leeds, SQW Ltd.

Pearson, M. and Marshall, D. (2005) *National Library of Australia, Conservation Management Plan*. Canberra.

Riegl, A. (1902) The modern cult of monuments: its essence and its development (trans. Karin Bruckner with Karen Williams of *Der moderne Denkmalkultus*) In: *Historical and Philosophical Issues in the Conservation of Cultural Heritage* (eds N.R. Price,

K. Talley Jr and A.M. Vaccaro). Los Angeles, The Getty Conservation Institute, pp. 74–76.

Rosier, C. (1996) PPG and recording: the Oxfordshire experience. *Context*, No. 52, 20–22.

Rowntree, L.B. (1981) Creating a sense of place: the evolution of historic preservation of Salzburg, Austria. *Journal of Urban History* 8(1), 61–76.

Ruskin, J. (1989) The lamp of memory. In: *The Seven Lamps of Architecture* (reprint of 1880 edition). New York, Dover Publications, Chapter 6.

Schaafsma, C.F. (1989) Significant until proven otherwise: problems versus representative samples. *Archaeological Management in the Modern World* (ed. H. Cleere). London, Unwin Hyman, pp. 38–51.

Sherwood, J. and Pevsner, N. (1974) (reprinted 1999) *The Buildings of England: Oxfordshire*. London, Penguin Books, p. 260.

SPAB. *SPAB's Purpose*. Available on SPAB website: http://www.spab.org.uk/html/what-is-spab/spabs-purpose/

Stokols, D. and Jacobi, M. (1983) The role of tradition in group environmental relations. In: *Environmental Psychology: Directions and Perspectives* (eds N. Fiemar and E.S. Geller). New York, Plenum Press.

Throsby, D. (2006) The value of cultural heritage: what can economics tell us? Paper in: *Capturing the Public Value of Heritage*. London, English Heritage.

UNESCO (1976) *Recommendation Concerning the Safeguarding and Contemporary Role of Historic Areas*. Paris, United Nations Educational, Scientific and Cultural Organization.

UNESCO (2003) *Convention for the Safeguarding of the Intangible Cultural Heritage*. Paris, United Nations Educational, Scientific and Cultural Organization.

Zancheti, S.M. and Jokilehto, J. (1997) Values and urban conservation planning: some reflections on principles and definitions. *Journal of Architectural Conservation* 1, March, 37–51.

Chapter 4
Conservation Plans

Introduction

A conservation plan is:

> *a document which sets out what is significant in a place and, consequently, what policies are appropriate to enable that significance to be retained in its future use and development* (Kerr, 2004, p. 1)

The identification of why a place is valuable is, explicitly or implicitly, at the heart of deciding which buildings and sites are worthy of protection but it can, and should, also be at the heart of devising and implementing management strategies and processes. That is, the concept of significance can be the basis of an effective management tool, but it requires a development from a generalised idea that a place is worthy of protection to a position where values are identified, assessed and articulated. As we have already observed, one of the problems in the past has been that what makes a place significant has not always been articulated.

In simple terms, a conservation plan is a tool for managing heritage sites based on the key idea that in order to manage effectively it is vital that an understanding of why the site is significant and how the different elements of that site contribute to that significance are set out, explained and justified. A conservation plan is based on the premise that you cannot protect and manage a site unless you know and can articulate what it is about that site that is important (and why).

The key elements in a conservation plan are:

- An assessment and articulation of cultural significance
- The identification of the extent to which the cultural significance might be vulnerable
- The development and implementation of policies and practices which will mitigate that vulnerability and will protect and enhance cultural significance.

Conservation plans require that significance should be assessed, attributed and compared (through the articulation of relative significance), in a coherent and transparent manner which allows the assessment to be understood and debated.

A conservation plan is also based on the premise that heritage sites will evolve (even if the overarching principle applied to the site is one of preservation). Therefore the challenge, which the conservation plan should address, is how to manage change whilst protecting and enhancing that which is embodied in and represented by the site – that is, its cultural significance. A conservation plan is therefore a tool for managing change based on the understanding that enhancing and protecting significance should drive decisions.

The identification of significance and vulnerability has the potential therefore to be the framework for a coherent management approach which protects and enhances whilst also allowing change. Kerr observes (2004) that 'A clear under-standing of the nature and level of the significance of a place will not only suggest constraints on future action, it will also introduce flexibility by identifying areas which can be adapted or developed with greater freedom'. The conservation plan is essentially a management tool based on developing a management framework and action plan that identifies opportunities and constraints in order to articulate how conservation aims and objectives might be achieved. Inevitably, it embodies the fruits of a significant amount of research that has to be undertaken into the historic building or site. However, once finalised, the conservation plan should have developed into a working document rather than a research study, i.e. the focus is on information gathering for a purpose and not as an end in itself.

A conservation plan is a means by which the site is understood, but this is no real use unless it is used to develop an effective management tool. A conservation plan needs to be understood as, and used as, a dynamic entity which provides a picture of a place at a particular time and which needs to be monitored and reviewed at regular intervals. The plan has to have a single definable goal – the identification and evaluation of the significance of the place so as to facilitate advantageous site management in the future. In order for this to happen the articulation of significance and vulnerability must become the framework and focus and driver for all policies and procedures within the organisation that has responsibility for the place in question. The conservation plan should understand and reflect the implications of this – that is both the idea and its consequences must be accepted and integrated at all levels of the organisation, both vertically and horizontally.

It is sometimes suggested that conservation plans are most useful for 'complex' sites. We believe, however, that significance can, and should, be used as the lynchpin for managing all types of heritage asset, and a conservation plan (or, at the very least, a reduced conservation statement) will always be an ap-propriate tool for its assessment. Many important plans deal with places that are not complex. As but one example, the Australian Antarctic Program's 2001 Conservation Plan for Mawson's Huts at Cape Denison, Commonwealth Bay, Antarctica (http://www.gml.com.au) demonstrates the enormous benefits to be attained in sound management of historic resources at an unusual, but otherwise far from complex, site by establishing guidelines for future care and use based on a thorough assessment of heritage values. Undoubtedly, however, the con-servation plan can prove an invaluable management tool where mixed heritage assets are involved on a single site. A powerful example of this is provided by a fascinating historic property owned by a charitable trust in the west of England.

Example 4.1   Mixed heritage assets on a single site

The trust has owned this site for some 50 years, taking ownership after the death of the last member of the immediate family, which had occupied the estate for over 400 years. The historic house itself is of no more than modest interest, being much reduced from its former glories. Today, it is leased as office accommodation to various public sector organisations. The house is surrounded by around 40 hectares of parkland and 10 hectares of woodland, within which are concealed the traces of a potentially important eighteenth-century pleasure garden, including various somewhat enigmatic garden buildings and structures. With little appreciation of the possible historic significance of the garden, the woodland was leased to a wildlife trust to form a nature reserve around 30 years ago.

The origins of the house and its estate immediately before the English Civil War are unclear, due to the absence of contemporary documentary source material. However, it seems evident that the house was purchased as part of the local manor in the mid-seventeenth century and then occupied by succeeding generations of the same family for 400 years. The estate in its heyday was undoubtedly much larger than it is today. Enforced sales of parcels of land, farmhouses and cottages occurred from around 1800 onwards as the family over-reached itself financially in a bid to nurture and sustain its local standing and as a result of the expensive pursuits of successive profligate heirs. In its prime, the estate was undoubtedly of some regional note and, by the end of the eighteenth century, it appears that two generations of the family had created an important and influential Arcadian landscaped park, which may have influenced the development of others nearby (although undoubtedly itself being influenced by Hoare and Flitcroft's masterwork at Stourhead in Wiltshire).

The problem for the charitable trust as owner of the estate today is that, as a result of leasehold agreements struck when there was little understanding of the importance of the historic landscape, significant parts of the management responsibility for the property lie outside its control. In order to create suitable habitats for particular wildlife, the potentially significant historic gardens have to be kept overgrown. Whilst the historical development and importance of the site are far from clear, it seems possible that modern management of the woodland incorporating the eighteenth century pleasure gardens as a reserve will not prove compatible with the management ethos that needs to be implemented to protect a nationally important historic garden and landscape.

The conservation plan offers the best hope of resolving such conflicts. But, critically in this instance, to be effective the conservation plan must explore, evaluate and reconcile some potentially conflicting disparate aspects of the estate's cultural significance. It seems evident that, although now barely recognised or visible, in their time the historic gardens and parkland were of considerable regional and perhaps even wider importance. Conversely, today, the site is undeniably also of considerable significance as a nature reserve, being designated as a County Wildlife Site because of its indicators of ancient woodland and because it supports a remarkably wide range of habitats. It has over 100 species of fungi and a population of great crested newts: an internationally important species that is also Britain's most strictly protected, but most rapidly declining, native amphibian.

Hopefully, the management dilemma is clear. The site has substantive significance both for its historic and modern environments. Whilst it is all well and good proclaiming that the historic environment forms an intimate and intrinsic part of our modern world, there are times when a profoundly stark management 'fault line' exists between the two. In this instance, it is improbable that a greater management focus on the protection and public interpretation of all or part of the site's historic environment can ever be achieved without

> (*Continued*)
>
> compromising elements of the very particular modern environment that has been nurtured at the site in recent years. For instance, the surviving centuries-old trees in the woodland, which are so crucial to an appreciation of the development of the historic landscape and its use, are of relatively little value to the habitats that are vital to the reserve. It is not in the immediate interests of the wildlife trust to manage the site in ways that specifically perpetuate the survival of this diminishing population of very elderly trees. Instead, reserve management is focused on introducing very different species of trees and some undergrowth that blur and obscure the otherwise crucial eighteenth and early nineteenth century planting regimes. Thus, in one way or another, the site and its significance must be regarded as being extremely vulnerable to compromise or damage from active or passive future management. This is a taxing conservation management dilemma. A robust and holistic conservation plan is the very best management tool for establishing a platform from which sustainable solutions can be reached in this kind of situation.

Kerr (2004, p. 29) suggests that conservation plans provide:

- Ready advice necessary for care and management, or for the preparation of detailed management and master plans
- Appropriate requirements and opportunities to guide the planning of new work
- A basis for assessing proposals to change or further develop the place
- A reassurance to heritage and funding agencies that projects are pointed in the right direction
- A valuable aid in the reduction of conflict – particularly because of the consultation processes built into the preparation of the plan

Genesis of an idea

As we have said, the idea of using significance and vulnerability as a driver and framework is the basis of conservation plans. The conservation plan as it has developed in the UK has, to some extent, been based on the recontextualising of ideas used in the management of natural sites. Here, concepts of environmental capital (what you have got) and environmental capacity have been used as a means of describing and evaluating the value of the asset to its owners, users and wider society. (Environmental capacity is defined as the capacity of the environment to absorb or accommodate activity or change without irreversible or unacceptable damage (English Heritage, 1997).) This assessment of capital and capacity is then used to derive a plan of action. Also, the idea of developing 'management guidelines' – which include an agreement about the relative significance of elements, and were developed as a response to the concerns of owners and investors in listed commercial buildings – helped in driving and consolidating the idea.

However, as we have observed elsewhere, the biggest influence on the development of conservation plans has undoubtedly been The Burra Charter, which was produced by Australia ICOMOS and adopted by them in 1979 (Australia ICOMOS, 1999). The Burra Charter emphasised the importance of identifying the cultural significance of the site and then using this idea as the focus and driver for making management decisions. The book, *The Conservation Plan*, by James Semple Kerr (2004) is an extremely useful reference which takes the basic premise laid out in The Burra Charter and develops both the management concepts and detail.

Organisational drivers

For many organisations with a property portfolio that includes historic buildings, conservation plans are increasingly being seen as an essential tool. Such plans not only provide the basis for the effective management of this stock, but also demonstrate an organisation's commitment to the protection of the public value and interest represented by these sites and places and for which they are responsible. Most heritage organisations are engaged in producing conservation plans for their own buildings and are encouraging others to do so. Likewise, many public bodies are taking a lead in demonstrating 'corporate responsibility' by reflecting the endorsement of the important role of conservation plans by government.

However, in many cases the reason that conservation plans are produced is to fulfil a requirement of either a funding body (such as the Heritage Lottery Fund in the UK), or a statutory consent authority within the context of a development proposal. Some owners of historic sites or places which they intend to develop, will commission a conservation plan as a way of informing what possible further uses might be suitable for the place. Conservation plans have also been initiated as part of environmental impact assessments in large projects, including regeneration schemes. There is clearly a potentially difficult problem when a conservation plan is produced as a reaction to a development proposal, particularly a very detailed one. There is a danger that the establishment of significance will be developed in such a way as to merely reinforce the feasibility of the scheme, resulting in damage to the value of the place. Another possible situation, where there may be a tendency that might restrain or distort the development of an understanding of cultural significance, is where an organisation wants to downplay significance if it is known that its implication for conservation and the future management of the site will be difficult.

It is inevitable that where a proposal for change prompts a conservation plan then this will influence its scope. But, ideally, conservation plans should be produced without such pressures and influences, particularly to the extent that they may adversely affect the time and energy given to key elements such as the measuring of values expressed by the community.

Of course all conservation plans are produced in an environment where constraints and opportunities have to be taken into account, but this reinforces the need to produce plans which ensure that significance is assessed in a rigorous and transparent way and that the policies produced by the plan do not take any constraints implied by the proposal as a given. It is important therefore that the place itself is what sets the agenda through a process which seeks, as a first step, to understand what is important about the site and why.

Format and content of conservation plans

Since every heritage site is unique the standardisation of conservation plans is a possible danger because it might:

- Produce a formulaic approach to determining significance which fails to appreciate, or indeed ignores, information from non-standard sources
- Fail to take into account the particular context of the site and its use
- Fail to maximise the synthesis of the conservation plan policies with the needs and requirements of the organisational culture and policies of the owners and users of the site – leading to it being more likely to be a generalised 'wish list' rather than a focused and practical management tool

Because each site is unique it is important to acknowledge that the detail and contents of a plan should be determined by both the characteristics of the site and its operating context, and therefore the process of creating a conservation plan must not be rigid and formulaic in its approach. Nevertheless it is possible to define an overall framework. The Burra Charter (Australia ICOMOS, 1999) states that the procedure for making decisions must be appropriate to the place and circumstances but that it always involves some key steps:

- Assess cultural significance
- Develop a conservation policy and strategy
- Carry out the strategy

Kerr (2004) suggests that the plan should consist of a two-stage approach: the first stage being that of **understanding the place** through the gathering and analysis of evidence, and the second being that of **developing conservation policies** and evolving strategies for the implementation of those policies.

A key factor in the suggestion of a two-stage approach is the idea that significance should be assessed 'away from extraneous pressures and without regard to those practical requirements which must subsequently be taken into account when developing policies' (Kerr, 2004, p. 3). This clearly makes sense from an 'ethical' point of view, and such an approach will add to a sense of rigour and objectivity in the process. It is also clearly an approach which mirrors good planning practice in other areas where the question, 'Where do we want to be?' is, in the first instance, answered irrespective of any known restraints in order that the plan might be as creative as possible.

In order to be effective, a conservation plan must engage with the constraints and opportunities related to the site and its context, as well as the needs and requirements of the organisation that occupies the place. The two-stage approach ensures that the determination of the significance of the site is not distorted by predetermined outcomes.

It must be remembered that the two stages, though carried out separately, are not independent – in the sense that stage one has no real value (at least in this context) if stage two is not carried out properly, and stage two is operating in a void if it is not derived from the logic and understanding arrived at in stage one. A sense of disconnection is not uncommon in conservation plans, and one of the 'tests' for a good plan is to be able to 'read it backwards' – that is, to be able to easily trace back the processes and policies set out in the second part of the assessment to the evidence of significance in the first part.

A typical step-by-step structure for a plan therefore would be:

Stage 1 – The conservation plan

Step 1 **Understand the site** by drawing together information, including documents and physical evidence, in order to present an overall description of the place and an understanding of how it has developed through time.

Step 2 **Assess the site's significance**, both generally and contextually and in detail for each of its main components. This will include the site's relative significance (to other places), as well as how each part of the site contributes to its overall significance.

Step 3 **Define issues** that are affecting the significance of the site or that have the potential to do so in the future – in other words, assess the site's vulnerability to deleterious change.

Step 4 **Write a conservation statement** – a short accessible summation of what is significant about the site and why (and a description and justification of the sources used and methods adopted in arriving at the assessment).

Stage 2 – The management plan

Step 5 **Develop conservation policies** and processes that will ensure that the significance of the site is respected and retained and, where possible, enhanced in its future management. This will include identifying and appraising options in the light of opportunities and barriers – including the assessment of vulnerability.

Step 6 **Apply the conservation policies and processes** at all levels of the organisation.

Step 7 **Develop and implement policies and processes for monitoring, reviewing and readjusting the management plan.** As with all good practice in planning, there needs to be a monitoring system that asks 'How are we doing?' Therefore a timetable to the action plan is needed which can provide measurable benchmarks. In addition, it is important to acknowledge that conservation plans are time-specific, because circumstances change as do perceptions of significance (new evidence may also emerge that affects the understanding of significance of the place). Even if this were not so, the sense that conservation plans are a management tool – and not a documentation of the past – means that they must be dynamic and therefore reviewed and updated at regular intervals in order to ensure their continuing validity and usefulness.

These steps are not mutually exclusive and the process of developing the conservation plan must be iterative. However, each step does represent a logical progression from the proceeding one. The appropriate range of conservation management policies can only be established once a comprehensive understanding of the site's significance and its vulnerability to change have been developed. This is a large step away from the earlier notion that conservation policies should be automatically focused on minimising intervention with historic fabric at all times, whatever the circumstances and however mundane the material involved.

Although the effectiveness of this approach will ultimately rely on the integrity, sensitivity and skills of those writing (and commissioning) the plan, it does provide a framework which is logical, coherent and robust.

The process of developing a conservation plan is described in Clark (1999, 2001). In Clark (2001, p. 62), the assessment of significance (Step 2 above) is described as using 'the understanding of the site as a basis for a clear statement of the values that make the site important'. This forms the heart of today's approach to conservation management. The value to society of a historic structure or place is not just the amount of historic fabric that it contains. Indeed, this may be entirely irrelevant to the asset's significance.

Who should be consulted?

There are three categories of stakeholders who need to be consulted and involved in the development of a conservation plan (in addition of course to the owners and occupiers):

- Those stakeholders and interested parties who might be affected by the conservation plan and/or who might have an impact on an ability to actually deliver the plan. The range of such stakeholders will vary from site to site and will always include the local community, including: the business community; the local planning authority and other appropriate statutory bodies; advisory bodies, local conservation groups; and possibly, depending on the nature and status of the site, national conservation bodies. In part, such consultation will be necessary because of possible statutory requirements that might affect the delivery of the plan. However, involving stakeholders from the beginning and throughout the development of the plan may also actually be the key to its successful conception and implementation. It will be important therefore to identify the other two categories of stakeholders, which are listed next.
- Those individuals and groups who may have documentary evidence that may help to inform and clarify issues relating to the establishment of significance.
- Those individuals and groups who because of their association and involvement with the place have memories and insights into the place, which are actually part of its significance and which should be assessed in conjunction with the other values of the site (see later).

Who should write the conservation plan?

To a large extent the make-up of the team writing the plan should reflect the intricacies and qualities of the site and the circumstances and specific purposes of the plan itself. For complex sites there is clearly an argument for a multi-disciplinary team, but this should be chosen more on the basis of specific skills and qualities rather than narrow concepts of professional discipline – and particularly so as each site is likely to produce its own specific issues and conundrums. It is important to take account of Kerr's observation (2004, p. 17) that 'the more disciplines and people involved, the more difficult it is to evolve a coherent product'.

To some extent this is an argument about the efficiency of the process. But the more important dilemma is the possible effect on the integrity of the product, particularly because when dealing with the determination of significance we are already addressing a subjective concept. A multi-disciplinary approach has the potential of being more rigorous and objective, and also the team may be better placed to think creatively, or at least more holistically, about how to gather evidence and interpret significance from it. However, if the team is not well managed and cannot work effectively together then there is a danger that the result will be an ill-focused and fragmented document. It is perhaps an obvious point, but there will need to be a clear project leader with skills in people management and interaction. Although the issue of the precise make-up of the team will be determined by the type of site in question, it also, to some extent, reinforces the importance of the client producing a clear brief that identifies the contextual circumstances affecting the site, the reasons for producing the plan, its intended use and therefore the issues to be addressed.

Whether or not the conservation plan is written in-house or by a consultant may be decided solely on an assessment of available skills, but the use of an outside consultant may have value in terms of objectivity and a 'fresh pair of eyes'. This however should be balanced against the value of an in-house team's understanding, (hopefully), the culture and the policies and processes of the organisation owning and/or occupying the site. Whatever the make-up of the team, it is important that all understand the purpose of the plan to ensure that they are all working towards the same goal.

As we have said, the range of skills necessary to write a plan will vary from site to site and will be determined not only by the characteristics of the site but also by its complexity – and other factors such as its completeness. It is important to understand that complexity is not just a characteristic of the age and the amount of development on a site. Very old places with multiple layers of development may still be relatively easy to analyse, whereas some more modern places may represent more complex and perhaps competing values that are challenging to measure and analyse.

Skills and knowledge of construction and structures will be important, not just in terms of understanding the history and therefore the significance of the site but also in determining the present condition of the site. Clearly, at least for Step 1, the team must have good research skills and experience. However, it is also important that the team has the skills and knowledge – and, perhaps crucially, the motivation to engage with and understand the culture, policies and processes of the organisation(s) that own/occupy the place in order that:

- The institutional memory within the organisation might be part of the evidence gathering for the place
- The policies to protect the cultural significance of the place can be made more effective by being synthesised, as far as possible, with the aims of the organisation

Developing the plan

The English Heritage consultation document, *Conservation Principles* (English Heritage, 2007), says that to articulate the significance of a place it is necessary to answer five questions:

1 In what ways is a place or any part of it valued, and by whom?
2 How do particular parts and phases of a place contribute – negatively as well as positively – to those identified values?
3 Are the values of the place enhanced or diminished by its contexts, or are they independent of them?
4 What is the relative contribution of each identified value to the overall significance of the place?
5 How clearly are those values exhibited at the place compared to other places?

Undertaking a conservation plan – understanding the site and assessing significance

Perhaps the first task is to clarify the brief and set out the background and purpose of the plan and how it will be used – that is, why is it being done, what is to be achieved and how will this achievement be measured? Setting out a vision and aims for the site and how it may evolve in both the long and short term are vital in achieving an effective plan.

The second task is to understand the site as it appears today by recording it, and by developing an understanding of some of the general issues that do, and will, affect it. Such issues include the location of the place and its context related to local geography and the surrounding environment, as well as sociopolitical and economic factors. This might include understanding and then describing:

- The wider context in terms of the political, social and economic environment in which the site is operating – and the extent to which these might affect the aims and objectives of the plan both in terms of opportunities and threats.
- How the conservation plan might relate to, or be affected by, other policies and decisions in both the wider context – e.g. planning strategies for other

historic sites – the wider spatial planning issues related to the area, including any regeneration, redevelopment or master planning issues that might involve the site or may have an effect upon it.
- The specific issues that need to be addressed by the conservation plan, for example perhaps in relation to new developments, changes of use, improving facilities and interpretation approaches for visitors.
- And clarifying ownership and interests in the site, how it is managed and the uses to which it is put.

Describing the place – as it is now

This will be a written and visual description of the place as it is at the present time, including its buildings, other structures and its open spaces. The process is an important part of beginning to understand the significance of the site by assessing 'what we have got now'. Much of the information may of course be already available.

The buildings and open spaces should be described in terms of their functional relationships, both holistically (that is how they relate to each other and to the overall function of the site) and as individual elements. The individual elements – both buildings and spaces – should be described in terms of their layout and how they are used.

Contents should be described where they are key to either the function of the space or perhaps more importantly to the architectural style or design of the building – for instance, the furniture in an Arts and Crafts building or artworks such as the Sutherland tapestry in Coventry Cathedral – or some perhaps more intangible aspects of the significance of the space.

The main methods of construction should be noted, as well as their architectural style and the key materials used in their making.

The condition of the physical aspects of the site should be assessed in outline in both general and relative terms. A more detailed assessment may or may not be needed later in order to clarify issues of vulnerability: there may be particular defects which are in urgent need of attention because they may be endangering known and unknown elements of significance.

It would also be useful to carry out an initial assessment of the character in terms of the nature of the quality of the place and the factors that affect its character (e.g. atmosphere, use, activities, etc., as well as architectural qualities, materials, etc.).

The different types of heritage that exist on the site should be described, including, where appropriate, the natural heritage – this would cover buildings, archaeology, collections, historic landscapes and gardens.

The limits of the place should be shown as boundaries of the site and its topography and setting should be described and visualised. Of course the significance of the place may also be tied up with other sites and so an understanding of how plot size has expanded or contracted over time will have a possible effect on understanding the cultural significance of the site. This is an important point because it could affect an understanding not just of the site but also of adjacent sites and structures – that is, there may be a symbiotic relationship which is more than just contextual.

Establishing and analysing the historical development of the place

This is the key part of the conservation plan and is concerned with determining significance through tracing the origins of the site and how it has changed over time. (The previous section will obviously be part of the process, particularly as it will involve some analysis as well as description.)

This section of the plan is concerned with gathering material that informs an understanding of the place and its social, historic and environmental context, as it was and how it has developed, and analysing this information to determine its cultural significance and how this is embodied in and represented by the elements – the buildings, spaces, objects, structures (and their relationships) that constitute the physical manifestation of the place – and by its uses and associations.

It is also important to understand and analyse the geographical context because, as Pearson and Sullivan (1995, p. 103) observe, 'Heritage places exist in two contexts – they are part of the physical landscape and they relate very closely to it . . . factors such as transport, arable land, access to natural resources are important in the placement and pattern of early settlement. A prerequisite for a meaningful survey is a general understanding of the physical landscape and the relationship of the places to it'.

Gathering evidence about significance

> *Conservation of cultural heritage in all its forms and historical periods is rooted in the values attributed to the heritage. Our ability to understand these values depends, in part, on the degree to which information sources about these values may be understood as credible or truthful. Knowledge and understanding of these sources of information, in relation to subsequent characteristics of the cultural heritage and their meaning, is a requisite basis for assessing all aspects of authenticity*
>
> (ICOMOS, 1994)

All the guidance on conservation plans stresses that before the cultural significance of a place is assessed all the evidence relating to its significance needs to be identified, gathered together and analysed. It is essential that sufficient time be allocated for understanding before any assessment of significance is made. For a large and complex site this process can take a significant amount of time and resources.

It is extremely important that all aspects of the site are investigated and that relative importance is not assumed. There is perhaps a feeling that for some (renowned) sites what is significant about them is known and documented and that this part of the process can be either missed or its rigour or breadth and depth curtailed. This is potentially a dangerous assumption for various reasons. It may be that the manner of gathering and interpreting the evidence on long-established sites means that the process of assimilating cumulative material was not carried out effectively. Moreover, new material may have been accepted or rejected (or even sought out) on the basis of whether or not it conformed to the established understanding of the development of the place – or indeed the particular interests of those in receipt of such information. Also the chance to review holistically how the integration of accumulated material might affect perceptions may not have been taken. An overriding point, however, is that, as we have said before, ideas of what is valuable and why is itself subjective and changes with time. There are many examples of where the rigorous, focused and holistic approach adopted by a conservation plan has shown new aspects of significance to places which it was assumed were already well understood.

In gathering information it is obviously important to know where such information might be stored and how it can be accessed. But this should not be confined just to the obvious – lateral and divergent thinking, objectivity and imagination in identifying sources are important.

Information sources include:

all physical, written, oral and figurative sources which make it possible to know the nature, specifities, meaning, and history of the cultural heritage'... Depending on the nature of the cultural heritage, its cultural context, and its evolution through time, authenticity judgements may be linked to the worth of a great variety of sources of information. Aspects of the sources may include form and design, materials and substance, use and function, traditions and techniques, location and setting, and spirit and feeling and other external and external factors   (ICOMOS, 1994)

Evidence gathering will consist of identifying and retrieving the documentary material and carrying out an interpretation of the evidence embodied in and represented by the buildings and structures on the site. Kerr (2004, p. 4) emphasises the importance of paying proper attention to both sources and to their interactions because as he suggests, 'neither can be neglected as each corroborates and complements the other'.

The development of an understanding of the significance of a site should be as objective as possible. It should, however, be borne in mind that it will always be an assessment carried out by a particular of group of people, with particular interests, knowledge and skills, who are operating in a particular cultural context and at a specific point in time. It is therefore important that the process is not only rigorous but is seen to be rigorous, and therefore the methodologies and processes used should be set out and explained. Any areas or aspects of the site that could not be documented should be highlighted and all source material should be referenced.

The guidelines to The Burra Charter (Australia ICOMOS, 1999) suggest that the information that needs to be collected concerns:

(a) the developmental sequence of the place and its relationship to the surviving fabric;
(b) the existence and nature of lost or obliterated fabric;
(c) the rarity and/or technical interest of all or any part of the place;
(d) the functions of the place and its parts;
(e) the relationship of the place and its parts with its setting;
(f) the cultural influences which have affected the form and fabric of the place;
(g) the significance of the place to people who use or have used the place, or descendants of such people;
(h) the historical content of the place with particular reference to the ways in which its fabric has been influenced by historical forces or has itself influenced the course of history;
(i) the scientific or research potential of the place;
(j) the relationship of the place to other places for example in respect of design, technology, use, locality or origin;
(k) any other factor relevant to an understanding of the place.

In addition, Kerr (2004, p. 9) suggests that the following are relevant:

• the reasons for and the context of the changes, including requirements of owners and users;
• comparisons with contemporary developments and similar types of plans.

Research and types of evidence

It is not the place of this book to provide a comprehensive account of all documentary sources or to expand upon research issues and methodologies. It is important, however, to flag up some of the matters that need to be considered in developing conservation plans and assessments of significance.

Location of archival material

Documentary evidence essential for the preparation of conservation plans and related management tools is available from a wide range of sources. Generally, research of this kind will require that careful consideration be given at the start of the study, and throughout the process to the types of information that may exist and the possible archive/record locations that need to be visited and accessed. Even when working in the depths of the provinces, this may require visits to be made to cities far away to access records. Increasingly, much time will also need to be spent using the internet to locate relevant material.

In addition to data held on online databases in the UK, vital archival material may be found in the following:

• National archives – these include:
  – National archives housing state papers in London (Kew), Edinburgh, Cardiff and Belfast
  – The British Library

- National Museums, including the V&A National Art Library
- Land Registry
- Probate Office
- National Monuments Record (English Heritage) which amongst other data has building survey reports, measured drawings and a large photographic collection dating from the 1850s
- Regional and local collections and archives
  - Museums
  - Libraries, including Local Studies' Libraries
  - County Record Offices
  - Diocesan Record Offices (if not the CRO)
  - Archaeological, local, family and natural history societies
- Private collections and archives
  - University libraries and archives
  - Professional organisations and their libraries such as the RIBA Library and Drawings Collections
  - Estate and family records
  - Private collectors

Documentary evidence

Documentary evidence can be taken to mean written or graphic evidence that helps to build a picture of the place and how and why it has developed over time. Depending upon the place and the type and source of the documents, some specialist skills and knowledge may be necessary in identifying, sourcing, reading and interpreting the materials.

There are seen to be two categories of documentary evidence – written/ graphical and oral. Documentary material about a built cultural heritage as- set may be available from a variety of sources. Obviously the quantity, quality and veracity of the available material will be variable depending on a number of factors, including the age and perceived importance or relevance of the site, the record-keeping activities of the different owners and occupiers over time, etc. Some of the material will be primary and some of it will be secondary.

In this context, primary source material can be taken to mean original docu- mentation. It might include the original deeds or grant for a building or land, the original drawings or contract details, or letters between clients, tenants, owners and contractors. Although there is, for some places, a wealth of information that is available in archives stretching back to the medieval period (and before), access may often be restricted to these documents because of their fragility or condition. Some documents only survive in part, due to conditions of storage or subsequent events – for example, many World War I service records, which are now available to researchers in the National Archives at Kew in west London, were damaged in bombing during World War II. In addition, even where material is openly accessible, it is sometimes a skilful task just to decipher the text – even when the reader has knowledge of medieval and church Latin, Norman French or medieval English. Fortunately, many such documents are available as printed copies – and often as translations.

Secondary sources are the books and articles written about the place. They may have been derived from the original material or be based on other secondary writings. There is a great deal of such material around. The Victorians were particularly interested in 'antiquities', and investigating old buildings, including churches and their archives, was a popular activity – as it is today. The results of such investigation and study were, and are, sometimes published by local publishers, interest groups or individuals. Clearly, one problem with using secondary material is the reliance that has to be placed on the quality and thoroughness of the research that underpins it. Unless research has been carried out in a rigorous and objective manner and the fruits of that academic effort have been interpreted and synthesised correctly, the secondary record may be seriously flawed or biased. However, original material can also at times be misleading – for instance, a contemporaneous report may not be a truthful or full account and, as is encountered so many times in practice, a building may not be built exactly as it is shown on a plan or in an illustration. Inevitably, secondary sources are often the starting point because of their immediate availability and accessibility; hopefully, they will draw attention to original documentary sources, including some which may no longer be available.

In conducting research, all material, whether primary or secondary evidence, should be treated initially with a discerning and sceptical eye. Reliance should never be placed on received data – the interpretation of which may prove of great importance – until corroboration from demonstrably correct further sources can be achieved. This is a pitfall for the unwary. Unbridled enthusiasm and an understandable 'desire' that something that is unsubstantiated should prove to be true (simply because it tells a 'good' story or fills in a frustrating 'blank') have often led inexperienced researchers to make very wrong assumptions and jump to seriously flawed conclusions. A legion of instances might be cited from the field of ever-popular family history research. For example, working back from the present day, people have made a 'leap of faith' about lineal descent as a result of studying parish records (especially when dealing with common surnames in densely populated cities), and, thereby, unknowingly have 'changed horses' and begun to explore the family history of someone else's eponymous kinsfolk. It would be heartening to suppose that this kind of error does not blight professional historic research and assessments of significance, but experience suggests otherwise. It is a considerable problem and risk, and a trap that can catch many research 'veterans' in an unguarded moment of 'blind certainty'. The point is, quite often, it only needs one flawed building block to be assumed and used in constructing a 'story' from research, for the whole to be substantively compromised and open to criticism from peers. Management based on the platform of a weak assessment of significance, built off subjective interpretation of data or imperfect research, can be very bad management and may lead to damage to or increased vulnerability of the asset's significance.

As we have already noted, it is not our intention to give a detailed and comprehensive account of the research that may prove necessary in preparing a conservation plan. The following discussion of types of documentary material that may need to be sourced and consulted is undoubtedly partial, but, it is hoped, will provide a flavour and some useful pointers and advice for the inexperienced researcher in the UK.

Primary source material
Illustrations including paintings   These can be extremely useful, although they are often associated with relatively prestigious sites and have been commissioned by wealthy owners, who may not have appreciated the 'warts and all' keen veracity of the artist's eye. As a result, one of the problems with such illustrations is that they may not be accurate representations – obviously, the primary purpose of art is not one of recording. Also, images of buildings (both internally and externally) and landscapes may be incidental to the purpose of the picture and, therefore, rendered inaccurately. For instance, in portraits the focus was generally on the people, or at least the principal subject of the picture, and the building (often part of its interior) would merely form a backdrop where accuracy was either unimportant or needed to be sacrificed in order to present the subject with greater clarity. Alternatively, the building or landscape may have been deliberately changed to enhance the aesthetic or the 'message' of the image (or the status of the owner).

Registrations of births, baptisms, marriages, deaths and burials/cremations   Before 1837 in England and Wales and 1855 in Scotland, registers of baptisms, marriages and burials were kept by the established Church and, in the latter years, some non-conformist religious denominations as well. The amount of information provided by such records varies enormously over time and from place to place. Depending upon the type of record, information may, typically, be gained on parentage, domicile, occupation of father and age, as well as the occupation of the groom, bride or deceased person. Parish records of this kind are generally found in County Record Offices (but occasionally in the parish or at the chapel concerned), although partial transcripts may be found in local libraries (especially in local studies' sections), in the library of the Society of Genealogists, and elsewhere.

From 1837 onwards, civil registration has recorded births, marriages and deaths. These records are available at a variety of locations including libraries, the National Archive and increasingly online from subscription-based and pay-as-you-go commercial services.

Particular pitfalls to be avoided are inaccuracies – often numerous – in transcripts (which are essentially secondary sources of data) and occurring through misinterpretation of handwritten records. It is worth being aware that commercial online services have also suffered occasionally from erroneous transcriptions of data from official but handwritten registers. The subtle difference between birth/baptism and death/burial records can also lead to errors for the uninitiated. Pre-nineteenth century records can be bedevilled by gaps, omissions, lost and damaged registers, and the lack of interest of particular incumbents in keeping accurate or timely records. Sometimes, registers were only filled in from memory and from scrawled notes many months after the relevant event – usually just in advance of the local bishop's visit to the parish.

Registration data of this kind can be important for tracing people associated in one way or another with the heritage asset. Sometimes, this information is directly relevant to the subject of the conservation plan; at other times, understanding relevant dates can be vital for use indirectly in obtaining other information that is pertinent to the study. An example of this will be given later in this section.

Correspondence, reports, minutes of committee meetings, specifications of work, contractor's invoices, etc.   Such evidence might include written material produced by individuals or the organisations who commissioned, designed, built and occupied (and changed) the place over time. Depending on the place and its uses, such evidence may range from official material stored in public authority archives to more personal documentation, such as letters and diaries, possibly held by friends and relatives or given to museums or local societies. Many, particularly public, organisations such as government departments, hospitals, local authorities, etc. will keep records not only of the site and buildings and how they have evolved over the years but they will also have accounts of the factors that drove and influenced the creation of and changes to those buildings. It is important here, as elsewhere, to link the physical evidence – what happened to the building/site – to the organisational and socioeconomic drivers for change and evolution.

The survival of original detailed specifications of work can be very important, but it must never be assumed without further verification that what was specified was actually ordered or built in the way intended. For instance, the survival of the original Bills of Quantities and Specifications for the former Public Record Office in Chancery Lane, London (being archived in the new Public Record Office – now the National Archives – at Kew) proved invaluable in understanding the construction and fixings of rare zinc ceilings found in the reception hall and Round Reading Room during conversion of the empty building to use as a library for King's College, London, in 2001/2002. Those records included letters from the supplier to the architect, explaining the problems that had been experienced during erection of the prefabricated ceiling sections, following their importation from France. This opened up other lines of enquiry that shed more light on the site and its significance. However, the same specification that contained detail of the form and fixings of these ceilings, also dealt with another zinc ceiling which appears never to have been built. All such records require very careful interpretation.

Census returns   Census records exist in a number of countries including the United Kingdom, the United States and Canada. In the UK, detailed, largely complete, decennial census data are available for the years 1884–1901. Partial information is also available for the years 1801, 1811, 1821 and 1831, although this is often not especially useful for family and local historians, including researchers for conservation plans. These data are available as primary evidence through the original enumerators' scheduled returns and microfilms/microfiches of these in the National Archives, and in some County Record Offices and public libraries/local studies' libraries. The same data (give or take!) are also available as secondary source material through transcripts of varying extent, quality and accuracy in libraries and other collections (including that of the Society of Genealogists) and, as with birth/baptism, marriage and death/burial records, increasingly online through searchable subscription-based and pay-as-you-go commercial services. The Church of Jesus Christ of Latter-Day Saints' International Genealogical Index (IGI) – arguably a secondary source using raw primary material – is also available online without charge for access/search. It combines a number of sources including 1880s census and partial (transcribed) parish register data – a useful resource, but patchy and increasingly outdated by online databases developed in the past few years. The uncertain accuracy of transcribed material should be borne in mind at all times.

The information provided in census entries depends upon the year and location. Typically, this might include the address, listings for other occupants living at the same address (giving an idea of the number of rooms or size of the property), make-up of the household, ages, occupations and/or employment information such as the number of people employed by the same person, details of servants and visitors on census day and their place of birth. Official (Government) and unofficial (research) analyses of census returns are also available as secondary sources, giving invaluable statistics and/or insights into demography and employment, amongst other matters.

The potential uses of census evidence are wide, including: mapping change in an area (population, housing densities, employment, occupations, class, construction of new roads and housing, renaming of roads, slum clearance, and so forth); identifying individuals and tracking (some of) their movements and changes of occupation, means etc.; and establishing occupiers of property at given times. Researchers need to bear census data in mind at all times and think laterally about the possibilities that they might offer in any given circumstance. It is strongly advised that, for those unused to accessing and interpreting such data, further reading is undertaken to understand the peculiarities, problems and limitations of using census material (for instance, Herber (2004), as updated).

Trade directories   Commercial and trade directories were, in many ways, the forerunner of telephone directories and the *Yellow Pages*. Although some eighteenth century directories survive for London, most towns and cities (and some rural areas) have some extant coverage from the 1830s and often a good run of annual directories from the 1870s onwards. These are often available in County Record Offices and local studies' libraries, although some university libraries and the British Library also have partial – sometimes good – coverage. A small number of directories are available as scanned images (generally therefore incapable of interrogation) online.

The information contained in commercial and trade directories does vary according to publication and date, but generally commercial occupiers are listed by name and nature of business, and sometimes the names of the heads of household are given for every residential property as well. Some later nineteenth century directories for parts of cities like London give less, not more, information per entry, just because there were so many people and therefore the publishers had to greatly restrict the information that they gathered. Directories also require careful interpretation, partly as a result of this, but also because some relied on out-of-date information from previous years, so that the closure of a business or the move/death of a person did not work through to show on the printed page for several years. Despite these limitations, our experience has been that commercial and trade directories offer an invaluable resource for study in preparing conservation plans and that their potential is often underplayed or entirely unrealised by researchers.

In recent research for a historic area analysis of part of Liverpool, it was found that two important conservation commentators had written that, to paraphrase, 'no direct contemporary evidence could be found to establish the date of construction of ten roads of late 19th century terraced housing' which lay on either side of a reasonably major arterial road and was the subject of regeneration proposals including potential partial clearance. Further study revealed that, while it was correct that no other documentation furnishing this information appeared to survive within the local archive, an incomplete run of commercial and trade directories from 1860 to 1910 in the local studies' library (filled in for the remaining years at the British Library in London) provided firm dating evidence for the first appearance of streets and occupiers of residential and commercial premises. With this knowledge, substantiation could be attained and the story fleshed out by occasional articles that appeared in the contemporary local newspapers for the area. Similarly, a comprehensive record of use of two adjoining properties in Russell Square, London from 1870 to 1968 has been collated from directory entries for use within a conservation statement in recent months – information that had proven difficult to obtain from other sources.

Maps Maps of various places of course go back to at least Roman times. There is a wealth of map-based information available in the UK covering both rural and urban areas, particularly from about 1850 onwards. Often maps from this time onwards were updated at relatively short intervals, which may be particularly useful in tracing the development of a site. Before that time, tithe maps, estate maps and various maps of towns and cities can provide invaluable comparative or specific data, although the purpose for which they were prepared needs to be kept in mind to assist with interpretation.

There are a number of useful sources of information on maps and the location of relevant archives, including sections in Herber (2004) and Beech and Mitchell (2004). The locations of maps will depend upon the subject matter and may include the National Archives, County Record Offices, local libraries, university libraries and private archives.

The technique of map regression is mentioned again briefly in dealing with management tools for heritage assets later in this book. In essence, it is an extremely valuable technique for use in building up an understanding of the origins and changes that have occurred at mapped sites over time. Sequential historic maps for the relevant area (from the earliest available through to the present time) are used to analyse change at the site and in its setting, and link this to interpretive information from other documentary evidence and from an analysis of the built fabric and/or present-day landscape with their 'fossil' traces of previous activity, use and change. Often, overlays to maps can be used to good effect in both analysis and in the presentation of findings/data.

Plans   The Public Health Acts of the 1800s means that there are associated record drawings of buildings showing how they would comply with the Acts, which will also provide information about the building itself. Likewise, plans showing local authority and statutory proposals for the introduction of various services, such as sewerage, gas and electricity to new and existing developments, may be of use in tracing the development of the site (and being able to date the introduction of the services themselves may add important information). Building regulation and planning drawings from more recent times will also provide information of latterday changes, and will also show how the building was at the time of the application.

Photographs and postcards   The increasing use of photography from about 1900 onwards means that photographic evidence can sometimes be quite extensive. Unlike paintings and drawings a photograph (at least in the past) will provide an accurate record to the extent that it is decipherable. But photographers can and will choose what to photograph for various reasons and therefore place emphasis on certain aspects to the exclusion of others. Aerial photographs will often provide valuable evidence as well as clues for further investigation, and are valuable because they obviously provide a particular perspective that is normally not available. Aerial photographs are obviously a product of recent times but are not uncommon from the 1920s onwards. Relatively good coverage has sometimes been driven by particular events – for example, the extensive aerial photography carried out by the Royal Air Force in 1946–1948 in order to assess the extent of bomb damage in World War II.

Surveys   Surveys have been routinely carried out in many urban areas since the second half of the nineteenth century. The purpose of these varied from being a matter of record to design and planning proposals. Such records will vary in detail, scope and accuracy, quality and quantity (as will their survival/availability). The record of development of the site and area will also be in response to such public works as drainage, sewerage, gas and electricity – and in latter times cable television – and may provide more general evidence of development than just these utilities – which themselves will be of value of course in understanding historical developments.

Local newspapers and journals   It can be debated as to whether contemporary newspapers are primary or secondary sources or an amalgam of both. In the end, it might be argued that the distinction hardly matters. For ease, we have included local newspapers here, and alongside these should be placed long-running journals such as *Country Life*, which is useful for architectural reports and commentaries, and *The Builder* – the forerunner of today's *Building* magazine, which provides unrivalled contemporary information on many Victorian construction issues and buildings.

Although some journals were published at a strikingly early date – for instance, the *London Journal* from 1665 – the great age of local newspapers began in the mid-nineteenth century. Many early newspapers were short lived but they often had meteoric impact (some essentially crusading on single issues such as the corruption of a local Poor Law Union) and, for the local historian or property researcher, they contain invaluable information as well as gossip. The trick can be working out which is which.

By 1800, there were around 100 provincial newspapers in the UK. The abolition of stamp duty on newspapers in the 1850s led to a massive growth in numbers. Local newspapers of the age covered meetings, building work, slum clearance, the doings of the Great and Good, the wretchedness of the poor, fires and accidents, murders, deaths, criminal cases, and so forth – the list of topics covered is seemingly endless. As such, they can provide essential direct and indirect evidence that may be vital for the developing an understanding of an asset and of how its significance has changed over the years.

Historic newspapers can be found at local studies' libraries, County Record Offices and the British Library's Newspaper Library at Colindale in north London, where journals such as *The Builder* can also be studied.

Some other primary sources of direct and indirect information on built assets and land are:

- Wills and the evidence of bequests of property
- Fire insurance plans and other documents
- Tithe awards
- Estate records
- Land registration
- Title deeds
- Mortgage deeds
- Leases
- Inland Revenue valuations and surveys
- The National Farm Survey 1941–1943
- Place and field names
- Electoral registers
- Poor Law records, including Settlement examinations and orders
- Glebe terriers
- Records of trades, businesses and professions, including guilds and livery companies
- Licensing of inns and various shops and businesses
- Taxation records, including seventeenth century hearth and seventeenth to nineteenth century window taxes and land tax records
- Civil and Ecclesiastical Courts' records, especially those of the Court of Chancery, Criminal and Magistrate Courts, and Quarter Sessions
- Coroners' records

- Trade catalogues and pattern books (as with others, depending upon circumstance, these may be primary or secondary sources)
- Archaeological excavation and scientific reports
- List descriptions, Register of Parks and Gardens, etc.

It must be stressed that this analysis does not claim to be and is not comprehensive. Further information on sources can be obtained from a number of texts, including Herber (2004) and Porter (1990).

Secondary material

As has already been suggested, secondary material is often the more readily available, but, given that it is based on information that has been 'processed' by others, considerable judgement needs to be applied to its acceptance and use. A list of secondary source material would be long and out of place in this book and hence will not be attempted. Typical sources, however, that might be consulted during research include:

- Books and indexes
- Histories – for instance, the *Victoria County History* series
- Architectural commentaries, including *Pevsner's Buildings of England* series
- Transactions of archaeological societies
- Archaeological and other treatises
- Historic environment records
- Other conservation plans, research and professional reports, dissertations and theses

Research takes time, and good research takes practice. At all times, the researcher needs to be cautious of becoming sidetracked by interesting but, in the great scheme of things, futile facts and discoveries. Good research requires balance and constant objectivity. Too many conservation plans are distorted by imbalance and, as has been pointed out before, this can only lead to skewed assessments of relative significance and, on the back of that, risks poor management decision making in the future.

The researcher also needs to be aware of the inbuilt law of diminishing returns. The conservation plan process does not require – in fact, specifically does not need – everything there is to know about the asset and its associated personalities. There comes a time when further research is unlikely to provide anything of value to the specific objective in hand – which is different to saying that there is no place for comprehensive analysis, for that is patently untrue. There is considerable skill involved in deciding when the appropriate balance of information has been attained. Thereafter, the need for ongoing research into remaining aspects of interest (which, if appropriate balance has been achieved, should be unlikely to impact on the assessment of the asset's significance in any substantive way) can form an important recommendation of the conservation plan itself.

The balance between inadequate, sufficient and excessive research material and data is a delicate one, as Example 4.2 demonstrates.

Example 4.2   A north of England church

A conservation plan was commissioned of a long-redundant church in the north of England to form the backbone of a feasibility study into reuse of the site.

Background research into the history of the site and the wider area was commissioned from a professional researcher who had worked as part of many similar conservation plan teams. The researcher investigated primary source material at the County Record Office relating to the construction of the church in 1835 and its extension in 1858. Surviving records of the Building Committee from 1857/1858 were found, which provided useful information on the architect, contractors and the considerations of the Committee in planning the extension. Unfortunately, no records appeared to survive relating to the original construction of the church only 23 years before. The researcher resorted to comparison with other church and public buildings in the locality in the 1820s and 1830s to make suggestions regarding the identity of the earlier architect and he backed this up with information obtained from a very incomplete series of early trade directories for the area. He did not investigate other available contemporary documentation – especially local newspapers and census records.

The manager of the conservation plan process was slightly concerned about this paucity of contemporary source material about the original church and undertook some very brief research of her own. She looked first in contemporary local newspapers held at the local library. Whilst this provided no information on the completion of the church in 1835, it did turn up a number of articles from the laying of the foundation stone of the extension in 1858 to a report of a service and a tea party held to celebrate the opening of the extended church later that year. These included quotations from the extension's architect in which, contrary to the supposition of the first researcher, he told the congregation that he had designed the original church. Subsequent research of census records and registrations of death revealed that the architect had died in 1863.

Using this information, the plan manager was able to find various newspaper obituaries which filled out information about other local buildings that the architect had designed or worked on. Additionally, examination of newspapers for the 50-year anniversary of the building of the church provided a wealth of information on its design objectives and brief, which had clearly been collated at the time from then extant primary source material that had since been lost.

This illustrates that even experienced professional researchers, however skilled and talented, sometimes get the balance of research wrong. Moreover, it almost certainly highlights another significant, but rarely mentioned, problem. We all come with baggage that tends to distort the sources of information we use. As just one instance of this, a number of academic researchers appear to be suspicious and, to a degree, dismissive of family historians, regarding their work as a debased and poor relation of true academic research. There is a natural inclination in these circumstances to tend not to use primary sources that are regarded as being the province of family historians – for example, decennial census data and contemporary local newspapers. Bias is a risk that confronts us all. The researcher needs to guard against this risk at all times, giving frequent consideration to the developing products of research and considering alternative sources that might be used to fill in vital gaps.

There is a danger in listing possible sources, in that it reinforces the idea of a standard set of information. Clearly there is a danger that in looking for evidence the team only goes to the obvious and usual sources. It is important when searching for evidence to think divergently and to follow other leads and possibilities. Research data should be corroborated from alternative sources, including, where appropriate, the record of the built fabric itself.

In writing up the documentary evidence it is important for reasons of credibility, transparency and accountability that:

- It is made clear what information and evidence was drawn upon, and how it was analysed and interpreted. It should also be shown how competing ideas, contradictory information, etc. was dealt with.
- All sources used in the report are cited with sufficient precision to enable others to locate them.
- All sources consulted are listed, even if not cited.
- All major sources or collections not consulted, but believed to have potential usefulness in establishing cultural significance, should be listed and the reasons why they were not used explained.

Interpreting the building/physical remains

In addition to the use of documentary evidence, an understanding of the historical development of a site can also often be derived from an analysis and interpretation of the physical evidence provided by the buildings, structures and landscape at the site. This is evidence that derives from the place itself – the way that the fabric and layout of the site, its landscape and immediate setting and/or the building(s) and its/their use, have changed over time.

Traditionally, conservationists have placed strong emphasis on the importance of protecting the fabric of significant places and on valuing the evidence of changes in the fabric. In this instance, it must be remembered that, for the purpose of interpretation, fabric may also include the immediate landscape as altered by man, for this can be read too.

As we have pointed out in Chapter 3, conservation principles emphasise the importance of keeping accurate records of how and why changes to the built fabric occur (although generally the equivalent potential of the landscape is sadly overlooked). The reason for such emphasis on record keeping is that historic fabric contains vital archaeological information about the site and its past use and change. If properly interpreted, these physical remains can reveal critical information, not only about architectural and constructional detail of the evolution of the place, but also the wider socioeconomic and cultural story of human habitation, use and interaction with the place and how it has evolved over time. As Kerr (2004, p.7) asserts, the fabric of a place is the most accurate (though often incomplete) document of the history of a place. He suggests that the physical evidence 'tells the story of what actually happened rather than what someone intended should happen or believed did happen'. English Heritage reinforce this by stating that, 'The fabric of any place, however recent is the primary record of its evolution' (English Heritage, 2007, p. 25).

The process of interpreting the historic fabric will involve study of the development of architectural form, layout, construction technique and the materials and services used in construction, along with indications of change held within the accessible fabric in the form of the remnants of redundant elements, vestigial traces of removed structures, straight construction joints and other archaeological evidence. Physical evidence of changing uses and the processes that occurred there should be sought in order to understand the specific functions that took place on the site.

Hopefully, the results of documentary research and physical analysis of the built fabric and/or landscape will complement and reinforce each other, leading to increased confidence in interpretation. Equally, when things work well, positive evidence from the one can often help in filling in gaps in the other. In practice of course, complex sites are rarely so compliant. Therefore, it must be anticipated that study will end up in a developmental history that can be partly read and interpreted, but which contains a number of frustrating lacuna and some bits of documentary or more often physical evidence which cannot be placed with certainty anywhere into the 'jigsaw'.

Reading and interpreting built fabric and landscapes takes time and practice. They are not skills that can be learnt from a book or generally by an individual in isolation. On complex sites, the professional and academic rigours of archaeology, architectural history and/or landscape and garden history need to be combined. It is human nature that many building and landscape analysts believe that they can deliver all such skills on their own. In reality, this is rarely the case – different disciplines require different attributes – especially, different ways of looking at things – and these are not often combined in one person.

This book is not about interpreting fabric and it is therefore not possible to discuss the various techniques and tools that are used in the process. It is worth pointing out, that, in addition to visual analysis, an increasing range of non-destructive analytical tools is now available. These all have strengths and shortcomings, and investment in the hire of equipment or specialist contractors for such work should not be made until the suitability of the method for the purposes intended and the circumstances involved is assured. On occasion, it can be beneficial to follow up visual and non-destructive analysis with targeted and limited opening up of the fabric to clarify critical uncertainties. This approach should never be adopted lightly and without consideration of the impact on the historic fabric and its integrity. If the site carries statutory protection such as listing, prior consent for opening up may be necessary from the relevant authority, depending upon circumstances.

Assessing community values (oral evidence)

Another source of evidence (in addition to documents and the fabric) is the values that the place represents to the community. As we have discussed, local communities need to be involved in the 'conservation plan' because what happens at the site may have a material effect on them. It is important, however, that liaison with the local community is not just a case of keeping them informed about decisions but that it also actually involves them in making decisions – particularly in identifying what is valuable about the site. The community (and, importantly, others who have or have had an association with the place – including those who have or do still work at the site) may be a useful source of written, visual and oral material, which can add to an understanding of the site because they may know how it was used and how it worked. That is, they may be able, because of their first-hand experience, to help to complement the evidence from elsewhere and, in addition, they may be able to explain, interpret and validate the written and visual documentary evidence (or perhaps question its validity). In addition, it is important to acknowledge, and take account of the fact, that people's memories and associations with the site are also an important part of the make-up of what contributes to the cultural significance of the place. In a sense they are effectively the repository of the contemporary social value of the place. That is, the significance of a place essentially resides in how it is valued by people.

Stakeholders therefore need to be identified and involved in the determination of significance. This will include the past and present owners and occupiers of the site and also past and present members of the community who used, or were associated with, or associated themselves with, the place. We are concerned here with those for whom the place has memory or ties because of its physical and/or its symbolic presence. In many cases the insights that are added are related to the 'intangible' aspects of the atmosphere and 'the spirit' of the place.

This is a particularly important aspect of establishing significance, not least because conservation activity is often actually justified on the basis that society chooses to value certain things, whereas in reality 'experts' – and often experts drawn from certain strata in society – have decided what is valuable and why. As Blunstone (2007, p. 67) observes:

> *Getting at the meaning of places should not reside with professionals alone but with the people that use and visit and construct their own meanings out of places.*

Involving people in decision making – as against merely informing them of decisions that have been made – is also one of the benchmarks of sustainability.

It can be argued that the incorporation of stakeholders' memories and associations has been better prioritised in recent years, but it is still an area where much can be done. In part, the problem is related to the 'mindset' or perhaps the willingness, or otherwise, of those involved in the conservation plan (including the client) to engage with stakeholders, but, in part, it is also an issue related to available resources – skills, time and money.

In addition, although worthwhile and important, it is also a quite difficult area to deal with effectively. The sort of issues that arise might include:

- How to identify what constitutes the appropriate community/stakeholders. It is relatively easy to map who will be affected by decisions but less easy to identify (and sometimes contact) those whose memories and associations can contribute to the idea of significance. This is particularly so as communities are more mobile and more dispersed and less homogeneous than they used to be – and meaning is now perhaps more than ever lost between generations.

- The meaning of the place may be important only for a small and politically unsophisticated or disenfranchised group.
- There is of course power in the process of identifying who the stakeholders are, and therefore it is important that this is viewed as holistically and – as the process evolves – as dynamically as possible.
- Mapping and recording and articulating some kind of community vision may also be difficult where it may become necessary to interpret competing memories – or, indeed, conflicting memories.
- How to deal with powerful groups who may distort or dominate the process is sometimes problematic.
- Memories can of course be distorted and 'the truth' filtered through nostalgia, which can cause problems of verification and 'authenticity'. It should however be remembered that the important connection for people to the past is a value that does not necessarily rely on historical accuracy but is important for its symbolism and its sociological and psychological value. The smells, sounds, sights – the atmosphere (and even things that cannot be directly sensed) – are important characteristics which connect people to the place and should be treated as seriously as the more easily 'measured' aspects. Nevertheless, this can present problems where the memories and values of the community contradict or are in tension with the 'fact based' investigation of the site through documentary and physical evidence gathering, and the experts may therefore have to adjust their interpretation of what is important and why.

There can also be an overarching difficulty in relating intangible issues, such as the emotional draw of a place associated with memories, to the physical aspects of the site and therefore to policies in the conservation plan. Indeed, English Heritage 2007, p. 29) have observed that:

> [*Social value*] *can also survive, and may even encourage, replacement of the original structure, so long as its key social and cultural characteristics remain intact…Compared with other heritage values, social values are thus less dependent on the survival of historic fabric.*

There is also a judgement to be made about relative significance, particularly where, perhaps, a recent incident has occurred at a site and the community sees it as being the main reference for significance, rather than seeing it as one aspect, or where the place is in fact an incidental background and the incident, whilst of high impact, is highly temporal. That is, memories may be intense but related to incidents that are not that important in the long term, or which may distort other values now and will anyway be diminished in the minds of the next generation. The opposite problem might occur of course, when some people's memories associated with a place may be painful and unwanted and they are antagonistic to plans to conserve that place. For example, places of hardship associated with poor and/or dangerous employment such as cotton mills or mining. A similar but slightly different issue can arise with more modern buildings, where the social and perhaps the aesthetic values of places, such as post-war social housing estates, might be contested.

Nevertheless, as we have said, this is an important aspect of measuring significance that requires more attention than is usually given to it, particularly as there are examples of where community involvement has not just added to an understanding of significance but has changed the understanding of how significant the place is and what aspects of the site that significance resides in. As Pearson (Pearson and Sullivan, 1995) observes, 'Local communities have a more holistic view of the elements in their environment that they value and they can clearly articulate the contemporary relevance and significance of those elements'.

Assessing significance

The cultural significance of the place will be assessed and determined by an analysis of both the physical and the documentary evidence (including community values) gathered about the site. The analysis will be used to interpret and articulate meaning and significance from the evidence. There is a tendency in some conservation plans to put a substantial amount of effort into gathering the evidence of the history of the place but less into this analytical stage. It is important, therefore, in the evidence gathering stage, that the purpose of the exercise – to understand what is important about the site rather than to produce an exhaustive history – is borne in mind. In the evidence gathering stage it is both inevitable and useful that some analytical work occurs – the process should be seen as an iterative one (which should also always keep the aims and objectives of the exercise in mind). Such interaction will help in focusing and rationalising the evidence gathering and should save time and resources. However, it is important that it does not exclude material relevant to an understanding of significance, nor stifle a divergent approach which seeks out and is open to the validity of a variety of sources. It may well be that the analysis highlights gaps or deficiencies in the material, which may make it necessary to revisit some material and/or expand on its scope.

It is important that the integration and analysis are carried out, as for any type of research project, with rigour, clarity and transparency to ensure that the conservation plan is credible. The methodology used to synthesise and interpret the evidence should be stated and justified. It should be made clear what evidence was drawn upon both directly and indirectly (it should also be properly referenced), how, if necessary, it was weighted and/or how conflicts in evidence were resolved. Any assumptions made should be indicated as such, and the basis on which they were made should be clearly set out. If there were any gaps in the information-gathering stage – evidence that cannot or has not been retrieved and analysed – this should be made clear.

In addition, to this perhaps prosaic explanation, it would be useful to set out the 'philosophical' underpinning used in the assessment. Such rigour is necessary to justify the judgements being made and to allow others to understand, and perhaps challenge, the basis of such judgements.

The assessment of significance should be based on an analysis of the qualities of the site. This assessment should be derived from the evidence and related to the/a range of values (such as those set out in Chapter 3). As we observed in that chapter, it is important as a starting point in the assessment that all these values, where they exist on the site (and it should be assumed they do until shown otherwise), are treated as having equal importance. However, as the process of analysis develops it will probably become clear that some values are more relevant/important than others for the particular place (and of course some may not exist in the place). Also because the value categories are relatively broadly defined it may be useful to break them down into subsets, both in order to analyse them more clearly and also to help explain and illustrate them.

Vulnerability

Once the site has been understood and its cultural significance assessed, it is important, before policies are developed to protect and enhance that significance, that there should be an assessment of what factors might possibly damage or detract from that significance. That is, it is important to understand the extent to which the values inherent in the site are at risk now or in the future. The conservation plan needs to 'set out the issues facing the heritage and the problems that need to be solved to find a long term sustainable future for it' (Heritage Lottery Fund, undated, p. 13).

The way in which a site and its values may be vulnerable may be multifaceted; some of the factors may be intertwined and relatively complex to address. Others, such as a lack of financial resources, may be simple to identify but extremely difficult to address adequately.

It is important to understand that, although the plan may be reviewed at regular intervals, it should itself be a relatively visionary document and therefore the anticipation of possible threats should look at the medium and long term as well as issues that may cause immediate problems. This may not determine priorities of course, as something which is potentially a threat that will not be realised for say 5 years may still have to be addressed straight away.

Examples of factors that might affect the vulnerability of the site and will need to be addressed by the plan might include, for example:

- The poor physical condition of the place (which may require funds but might also be related to poor maintenance management)
- Management of the site generally
- Lack of financial resources and/or lack of certainty, to the extent that there is little ability to plan effectively
- Socioeconomic factors that affect the viability of the site, which might mean that there will be a need to find new uses for the site
- Traffic volumes producing levels of atmospheric pollution that will cause unacceptable levels of deterioration of the fabric
- Changes to the natural environment (flood levels, coastal erosion, etc.)

- Loss of context and meaning to the site because of developments taking place which detract from an understanding of and/or the aesthetic value of the place
- Vandalism
- Tourism levels, which are unsustainable because of physical degradation or because of damage to the atmosphere and a sense of place
- Insufficient access (generally and for specific groups, such as the disabled)
- Lack of development land for expansion (perhaps to deal with a need to increase visitor numbers or provide for better interpretation facilities)
- Incompatible policies or actions of the users which do or may detract from the significance of the place

Developing policies

The definition of sound conservation policies for the asset is the fundamental objective of the conservation plan process. Too often, the policies section of a plan appears to have been added as an afterthought – almost literally tacked on at the end after the 'interesting bit' (the academic research and telling the story of the place) has been finished. This reflects the discomfort that many in the conservation world feel with the notion of 'management'. It is, after all, only a few short years since the process of conservation has been more widely acknowledged to be one of management of change rather than one of skilful repair.

Since effective management is the focus of the conservation plan, drafting of conservation management policies needs to be undertaken with care. Appropriate time must be dedicated to the process – again, it should not be a rushed afterthought. Policies need to be tailor-made for the asset and for its management organisation. They should not be taken off the shelf or cobbled together from work done previously for very different assets or, worse, for very different management situations. It should go without saying that, if policies need to reflect the capacity and capability of the management organisation that will implement them, those responsible for drafting the policies in the first place need to have an intimate understanding of that organisation, its culture and its limitations. Surprisingly few conservation plan teams take the time to gain this understanding. The result must be the potential for dislocation between intent and actual implementation of the conservation management policies. That may well prove to be an inherent weakness in the management that is delivered off the conservation plan platform.

Policies should be tightly drawn and unambiguous. All policies must be practical and capable of implementation. Policies should flow from the assessment of significance, and especially the evaluation of vulnerability and issues that might potentially affect the asset and its significance. The temptation to throw in 'general' or arbitrary policies on the basis that it would be 'good for the organisation' should be avoided. If the policy does not flow logically from the assessments of significance and vulnerability, its place in the conservation plan is open to challenge and that weakens the logic and conceptual basis of the whole plan. Management organisations and individuals within organisations will not take ownership of policies if they cannot see the logical basis for their adoption and implementation. Each policy should be supported by a simple and lucid explanation of the rationale that lies behind it. The corollary to ensuring that all policies flow from the assessments of significance and vulnerability is also important. Every aspect of vulnerability raised within the conservation plan should either lead to a policy for its mitigation or risk management, or to a statement explaining why this is not considered necessary. Again, maintenance of the internal logic of the plan process is vital in winning over the hearts and minds of the sceptical owner or experience-hardened manager (to mention but two crucial stakeholders).

Policies are not generally well drafted by committee. Experience suggests that they are best developed by one or two people intimately associated with the conservation plan process, after initial consultation with managers and before circulation of a draft for consideration and discussion. Policy development should be an iterative process. In our opinion and experience, it is unlikely that all policies can be developed and drafted successfully in a single phase. If the first draft of policies passes through the consultation process without challenge and debate, there is a strong chance that those who will be responsible thereafter for adopting and managing their implementation have no ownership of the process and the policies, and perhaps no intention of putting them into practice in any meaningful way. If that is the case, rigorous efforts must be made to re-engage the managers in the whole process – otherwise the effort and funding put into development of the conservation plan will have been wasted.

The significance of the foregoing should be recognised. The conservation plan does not deliver a comprehensive management plan – this is why the term 'conservation management plan' is ambiguous and, in our view, potentially dangerous. The conservation plan delivers a set of conservation management policies that seek to address vulnerability and other issues of potential risk that need to be carefully managed. The conservation plan – with its policies – can than be used as a platform for developing other management tools, including a comprehensive management plan for the asset. It is not possible to manage every aspect of a complex place on the basis of the conservation policies contained in the conservation plan alone. Therefore, the conservation plan should not try to wear the guise of a management plan. This is why policies in the conservation plan should address issues raised in the plan and step no further – otherwise, there is a serious risk that it will 'fall between two stools', having neither the conceptual strength that flows from the step-by-step logic of a conservation plan nor the rigour or depth of a fully developed management plan. It must be stressed again that one of the principal failings of conservation plans to date in the UK has been the lack of ownership in the process by those who will take on the day-to-day implementation of its recommendations. Unless ownership can be cascaded to all those who have a hand in management (and all those who are subsequently given that responsibility but were not part of the conservation plan development process), the benefits flowing from investment in the plan will be very limited and most likely of very short duration. Significance-based management can only work when those who manage understand, respect and approve of the purpose and product of the conservation plan. That is a major challenge. Engagement in policy drafting can help, but, by itself, will never provide the level of common ownership of the process that is essential if conservation management is to be effective.

Having said that policies should be written to suit the specific circumstances, it would be illogical at this juncture to set down a series of typical policies. Nonetheless, it is useful to review the typical coverage of policies that appear in conservation plans. This should not be taken as being comprehensive or used as a guide for policy drafting, for, as we have already observed, policies must flow logically from the unique assessment of significance and issues of risk and vulnerability that each conservation plan contains. With that in mind, typical policy areas found within conservation plans include:

- **Use and management of the asset**, e.g.:
  - retention in current use to safeguard its status
  - development and review of the management plan for the asset
  - development of other management tools such as historic area appraisals
  - revision of management structure to improve protection of significance
  - conservation safeguards in contracts and tenders
  - development of risk-based resource allocation plan
  - maintenance of the balance between needs of different users
  - acquisitions, disposals and leasing strategies
  - environmental management policies and actions

- **Records**, e.g.:
  - development of a comprehensive database of accurate architectural records (for example, site plan, floor plans, elevations, sections, rectified photographs of interiors, building archaeological survey)
  - maintenance of the archive of the site's historical development
  - creation of a permanent and accessible written record of all interventions in historic fabric
  - development of a catalogue of important contents/collections

- **Conservation principles and the management of change**, e.g.:
  - adoption of standard principles as an approach to different parts of the asset: benchmark standards; maintenance standards to be applied
  - ongoing review and revision of the conservation plan
  - maintenance of heritage values and significance
  - restrictions and potential for change across the asset or on an elemental basis
  - protection of the asset's setting
  - training of staff and contractors in conservation approach
  - dissemination of the findings of the conservation plan to site users and others
  - management of the buried and building's archaeology
  - management of flora and fauna
  - establishment of monitoring procedures to identify effects of change on the asset and its significance

- **Maintenance management**, e.g.:
  - implementation of a planned maintenance regime
  - development of long-term and annual maintenance plans
  - implementation of periodic condition surveys of the asset
  - development of a detailed work's history record

- **Disaster management**, e.g.:
  - commissioning of disaster and safety audits
  - implementation of new regime
  - training of staff and emergency services, etc.
  - development of a disaster plan for the asset
  - review of security arrangements
  - training of salvage team

- **People management**, e.g.:
  - upgrading of orientation and signage
  - improvement of facilities
  - resolution of conflicts between the needs of different users
  - improvements in access for all people to the site

- **Communication, education and interpretation**, e.g.:
  - improved dissemination of information regarding asset
  - encouragement of outreach through wider use of the internet
  - upgrading of interpretation
  - involvement of local communities in the asset's future
  - establishment of community and stakeholder forums and development of an engagement policy
  - exploration of the potential of strategic partnerships

Once the iterative process of drafting, refining and amplifying policies has been taken as far as is practicable and meaningful within the context of the conservation plan, the plan itself should be ready for its final round of consultation and, in due course, adoption by the management organisation and/or key interested parties. We are aware of a number of instances where consultation has been restricted by the responsible management organisation to the pre-policy draft of the conservation plan on the basis that external oversight of and intervention with its policies would be unacceptable. Whilst such insularity and determined control are – to a degree – understandable in certain circumstances, this management approach flatly contradicts the notion that the significance and value of heritage assets transcend simple property ownership patterns. Owners and managers are guardians of heritage assets for the nation as a whole as well as for future generations.

In most cases, formal adoption of a conservation plan by the asset's owner(s), manager(s) and/or other key parties is critically important – it is not just an administrative nicety. On the one hand, it signals a positive and transparent intent to manage the asset on a day-to-day basis in accordance with the evaluation of significance and vulnerability and the thrust of conservation management policies that have been defined within the plan. It also triggers implementation of the plan's policies – establishing a clear starting date from which a change of management approach should be perceivable to all and can be monitored for impact and effectiveness. Formal adoption can also be an important component in the vital strategy of ensuring that ownership of and a willingness to comply with the plan's conservation management policies are cascaded throughout the organisation to reach those involved in taking and/or implementing day-to-day site management decisions. This issue has already been referred to earlier in this chapter, where it was noted that, whilst broad engagement in policy drafting can help, this alone will not engender the degree of common ownership of the process that is essential if conservation management is to be effective. Once the management organisation has formally adopted the conservation plan, steps need to be taken to begin to nurture and, thereafter, safeguard this common ownership, so that the significance-based management approach becomes second nature to everyone involved in the care of the asset. This is a major challenge. Interest and, as a consequence, conceptual ownership tend to diminish in management organisations towards lower levels in the line management hierarchy. Equally, ongoing staff changes over time will dilute recognition of the existence and importance of the conservation plan, unless rigorous procedures are set in place to ensure appropriate training of new recruits to the workforce and occasional training updates for all. Internal review cycles for conservation plans can be used as an opportunity to involve staff afresh in the plan's content and recommendations, although this is a process that needs to be actively planned and managed if it is to be of real benefit.

This brings us to the final key point that needs to be made about conservation plans. Our knowledge base about the historic environment changes over time – sometimes dramatically within short periods due to new research opportunities or the re-discovery of additional sources of information. Ongoing management action may inadvertently or intentionally change the cultural significance of an asset, as may transformations in society as a whole. The vulnerability of an asset and/or its significance may increase or lessen markedly with variation in external causal factors. Conservation management policies, through their positive and successful implementation, may sooner or later become redundant (or, at the very least, come to be in need of redefinition). No conservation plan should be regarded as being fixed in stone forever – or even for a long time. For good reasons, as a general rule of thumb, it is normally suggested that conservation plans should be reviewed quinquennially – but this advice should not be adopted blindly. In some circumstances more rapid review is desirable, even essential; in other cases, little disadvantage will occur through carrying out a major review after say seven years rather than five. Yet at all times, managers must bear in mind that taking management decisions on the basis of out-of-date information and policies is a counterproductive and potentially damaging matter. The concept permeating this book is that asset management without the platform that is provided by an understanding of significance and vulnerability introduces increased risk of compromise and permanent reduction in the asset's value. The corollary is that management decisions and action fashioned around outdated assessments of significance, vulnerability and conservation management policies can be equally harmful. Ongoing change in the asset and its wider context needs to be monitored and understood so that satisfactory cycles for review of the conservation plan can be established.

With the adoption of the conservation plan and its conservation management policies, attention can be turned to the next steps in significance-based management – use of the plan as a platform for the development of other co-ordinated management tools, which together are to be used as the foundation for logical and sustainable decision-making. The next chapter looks at the raft of management tools that can be built from the conservation plan's significance-based platform.

References

Australia ICOMOS (1999) *The Burra Charter – The Australia ICOMOS Charter for Places of Cultural Significance*. Australia ICOMOS Inc.

Beech, G. and Mitchell, R. (2004) *Maps for Family and Local History*. Richmond, Surrey, The National Archives.

Blunstone, D. (2000) Challenges for heritage conservation and the role of research on values. In: *Values and Heritage Conservation, Research Report* (eds E. Avrami, R. Mason and M. de la Torre). Los Angeles, The Getty Conservation Institute.

Clark, K. (1999) Conservation plans in action. *Proceedings of the Oxford Conference. Conservation Plans for Historic Places*, 27–28 March 1998, Oxford. English Heritage.

Clark, K. (2001) *Informed Conservation*. London, English Heritage.

English Heritage (1997) *Sustaining the Historic Environment*. London, English Heritage.

English Heritage (2007) *Conservation Principles, Policies and Guidance for the Sustainable Management of the Historic Environment*. London, English Heritage.

Herber, M.D. (2004) *Ancestral Trails: The Complete Guide to British Genealogy and Family History* (2nd edn). Stroud, Sutton.

Heritage Lottery Fund (undated) Accessed via the website at http://www.hlf.org.uk/English/

ICOMOS (1994) *The Nara Document on Authenticity*. Available online at: www.international.icomos.org/charters.htm

Kerr, J.S. (2004) *The Conservation Plan* (6th edn). J.S. Kerr on behalf of The National Trust of Australia, Sydney.

Pearson, M. and Sullivan, S. (1995) *Looking After Heritage Places*. Melbourne University Publishing.

Porter, S. (1990) *Exploring Urban History: Sources for Local Historians*. London, Batsford.

Chapter 5
Managing Use and Change

The management plan

As we have emphasised in Chapter 4, a conservation plan, in order to be effective, needs to be accompanied by a second stage – the 'management plan'. The management plan should be carried out separately for the reasons previously discussed. The final two-stage document, however, must read as one entity, as neither part has any real value unless both are completed in an integrated manner. It may seem an obvious point, but at the end of the management plan it should be possible to easily follow a detailed trail backwards through the policies and procedures to the detailed articulation of the significance of the place.

The management plan is concerned with determining what is required on the site by focusing on significance, thinking about how the place should and can develop, and determining the key management issues related to this and how they will be addressed. That is, there is a need to move from a vision to general policies to specific guidelines and actions.

It is important that the main thrust of the management plan is the development of clear integrated policies, strategies and procedures, which are focused on the protection and enhancement of the cultural significance of the place as identified in the conservation plan – including, of course, the mitigation of vulnerability. The policies, rather than conforming to a predetermined set of headings, should come from the site and the statement of significance and an understanding of the threats to that significance. It is also the case that these need to be integrated with other issues, including the needs and aspirations of the owners and occupiers of the site. Pearson and Sullivan (1995, p. 189) observe that 'significance assessment alone does not and cannot dictate management decisions, which are constrained by a whole range of factors, such as conflicting land use options, financial considerations, technical conservation problems or legislative or social concerns'.

The sequence of undertaking the management plan might be to:

- Reaffirm the statement of significance
- Consider what actions need to be taken to mitigate vulnerability

- Consider opportunities and constraints in relation to the place itself, its setting and its sociopolitical and economic context
- Develop policies to protect and enhance significance and mitigate vulnerability
- Identify and appraise possible strategy options for the implementation of policies
- Develop and implement an action plan that links policies and strategies to procedures and processes, and which:
  - sets out a timescale and sequencing related to requirements, priorities, generation and availability of resources
  - sets out how the plan will be implemented, and by whom
  - develops and implements procedures for monitoring and review

The management plan must also address issues related to tensions and contradictions.

Pearson and Sullivan (1995) suggest that the management plan should (among other things):

- Articulate the implications of the statement of significance
- Be able to be implemented by the owner authority that controls the place
- Pay due attention to the needs and desires of the community, and especially those with a special interest in the place
- Be financially feasible and economically viable
- Be technically feasible and appropriate
- Provide a long-term management framework
- Be sufficiently flexible to allow review, improvement or alteration

A conventional approach to developing a plan such as this might include asking:

- Where do we want to be?
- How are we going to get there?
- Where are we now?

And once the plan is implemented, asking:

- How are we doing?

Requirements, opportunities and barriers

These need to be considered before policies are developed. Some of the constraints would of course have been identified in the assessment of vulnerability.
The issues to be addressed might include:

- Cultural values vs. other values on or around the site (this may be an opportunity and a constraint, and of course may raise issues of trade-offs between heritage values and other (say, socioeconomic) benefits

- Requirements and aspirations of the owner (again may be an opportunity and a constraint)
- Resources – financial and skills and knowledge (a constraint perhaps, but also may be an opportunity – the production of the plan may provide access to grants/funds or identify development opportunities)
- Physical or environmental issues (difficulties in reducing vulnerability related to, say, poor condition, overuse, vandalism, pollution and natural risks such as flooding, erosion, etc.)

A SWOT (Strengths, Weaknesses, Opportunities, Threats) analysis or similar tool might be a useful way to approach this analysis. Pearson and Sullivan (1995, p. 215) suggest that such a process has the advantage, in that it 'brings home to key people the real situation at the place and perhaps they can then provide vital support in its improvement'. We would also suggest that such an exercise can be a vehicle to involve a relatively wide constituency from inside and outside the organisation, and will highlight their perceptions of the place and its value – which may itself be an opportunity and/or a barrier.

The question of the knock-on effect of certain actions not being achieved – or certain policies not being effective (i.e. what are the key and/or crucial activities) – should be addressed.

The client and organisational culture

Although the protection and enhancement of significance is the focus for the conservation plan, this, as we have said, needs to be grounded in the reality of resources and organisational needs, particularly as the best theoretical plan will be no good in the face of organisational intransigence, apathy or antagonism. In developing a management plan it is therefore extremely important that there is a thorough understanding of the nature and culture of the organisation that owns and occupies the site and of its existing policies and procedures (generally, as well as those that are specifically related to 'property management'). This will be necessary to ensure the best fit between existing policies and procedures and those that it will be either desirable or necessary to introduce as a result of the assessment of significance.

As Pearson and Sullivan (1995, p. 198) observe:

> *the ideal course of action based only on a consideration of the place is often in conflict with management constraints and limitations... Alternatively assessment of the significance might point to a clear and unequivocal need to conserve the place in a certain way reducing options for use, interpretation and other aspects of management.*

It will also of course be necessary to consider owners' and occupiers' requirements and their aspirations for the site. That is, it is important that the asset has a functional value that it will be necessary to maintain. For non-heritage organisations it will be a function that is probably unrelated to the cultural significance of the place. Indeed, it may be in tension with it – although it may be that there is some kudos for the organisation in owning or occupying a building of cultural significance which they already set off against various issues, such as possible restrictions on development and use.

The management plan will also have to take into account the aspirations that the organisation has for the place. Some of these issues may have already been identified as contributing to vulnerability – indeed in some cases they are the main threat – but for other aspirations it may be more a matter of synchronising them to work with cultural values.

There needs to be an assessment that considers how, and the extent to which, the organisation's culture, management structure, policies procedures and practices might:

- Enhance and protect significance
- Have little or no effect on significance
- Have had, or might have in the future, a detrimental effect on significance

Understanding the existing organisational culture as well as both policies and procedures should allow an assessment of what detail the plan needs to go into in order to ensure the protection, and where possible enhancement, of significance. There is no point in having policies that are in conflict with procedures that remain unchanged; for example, with maintenance management procedures that do not focus decision making around an understanding of relative significance and/or which allow 'salami-slicing' to occur – where fabric and character are lost in small increments.

However, a perceived need to influence detail in processes has to be balanced against being seen to intervene with the professional judgement, and possibly the competing objectives, of the organisation and its managers. The key to addressing this dilemma is involving people from the organisation at an early stage – and ensuring that this involvement includes a range of people at different levels and from all the appropriate areas, such as visitor management, property management and maintenance management. Clearly this is important because they will be useful in identifying requirements, opportunities and barriers and then later helping to analyse the options for delivering the policies and ensuring the development, where necessary, of new practices and procedures. Conversely, if people throughout the organisation do not understand or accept the premise of the management plan (or indeed the conservation plan) there is a danger that they may feel resentful and work against it either passively or actively. Put bluntly, the conservation plan and the management plan will not work effectively if the organisation at all levels is not committed to making it do so.

In addition, there will be a need to consider the resources that are or may be available for implementing the plan. This will obviously include financial resources (including how and when they are available), but it will also involve resources such as people – with appropriate skills and knowledge.

Condition of the place

A condition survey of the place should be undertaken which considers the physical state of the fabric of the buildings and structures (and, where appropriate, their contents).

Some suggest that because the purpose of the assessment of condition is to inform policy then a detailed survey is not necessary. This may well depend on circumstances – including the assessment of vulnerability – but it may be appropriate to carry out a new strategic condition survey (see later section) as a baseline for future surveys, in order to align this key activity with the review process. Such a survey should look in detail at the fabric in order to ascertain relative condition and to develop priorities for maintenance and repair. It should also state a time period for action to be taken – but with re-inspection being seen as a key action. The survey should take into account the analysis of significance and consider the impact of various factors on the elements of the building in the light of this assessment. For example, are elements of importance being damaged through wear and tear which could be avoided, or by say, a change of function, or the way in which that function is carried out?

Integrity of the place

In assessing vulnerability we may have looked at a number of factors but there may also be the possibility of addressing negative impacts of a lesser nature, which may then improve the integrity and the cohesiveness of the place and which will serve to protect and enhance its cultural significance.

Pearson and Marshall (2005, p. 57) define integrity in this sense as meaning 'the degree to which a place or component of a place retains the form and completeness of its physical fabric, historical associations, use or social attachments that give the place its cultural significance'.

Examples of this include a consideration of the appropriateness and the impact of functional operations and activities in respect of their interaction with the cultural significance, which might then lead to a consideration of whether those functions could be performed in other areas within or without the site. For example:

- Does a particular function detract from the atmosphere of a particular place, or part of it, through perhaps:
  - the noises associated with that function, the equipment necessary to perform it or the intensity of use associated with it – for example, the type of equipment or the way it is laid out detracts from the visual understanding or appreciation of a room. Apart from what we might call noise pollution, there may also be incidences of odour pollution and light pollution that may detract from the significance of the place.
  - the incompatibility of the spiritual or emotional significance of the place and the activity taking place there?

- Does the impact of the function, including the number of people using the place, have an avoidable effect in terms of wear and tear on the fabric, which could be mitigated through changing function or controls on use?

- Does the way that services have been added to the buildings, internally and externally, have a detrimental impact on cultural significance, either in respect of the fabric or in their visual impact? Could this have been handled in a different way, for example through re-routing, using different designs or materials, or by minimising their impact by avoiding more culturally sensitive areas (including changing the function of certain spaces)?

- Are activities and uses, including temporary ones, appropriate to the cultural significance of the place? An example might be corporate parties or events which work against the sense of place (weighed against the income generation).

- Are the designs of recent buildings or structures appropriate – do they add to or detract from the understanding and/or the atmosphere of the place for example?

- What is the impact on integrity of vehicular access, circulation and parking? These factors may have an important impact on the atmosphere of the place, but they may also exacerbate deterioration rates in significant materials (for example through wear and tear, danger of impact, the visual effect of their presence and the possible effect of their emissions on the fabric – e.g. from oil spills or increased damage to stonework or other materials).

Conservation

There should be a clear framework for showing how decisions about physical interventions in the fabric of the place will be made, and the basis on which this should be done. In essence, it should show how conservation principles (see Chapter 3) are to be interpreted and then integrated and applied within the significance-based management of the place and all processes and procedures in relation to the fabric in respect of:

- Maintenance
- Repair
- Alteration and additions
- Reconstruction and restoration

Management responsibilities and processes

This would address such issues as the clarity of the management and decision-making structure in relation to the built cultural heritage structures, and how this relates to decision making and management of all aspects of the organisation. The extent to which current structures and lines of responsibility might be appropriate is important — some aspects may have to change. A consideration of such factors clearly needs sensitivity, needs to understand about best fit and requires the backing of key people in the organisation as there will often be pragmatic and cultural reasons to resist change.

Maintenance

Given its key role in protecting significance it is important that maintenance management should be at the heart of a proactive management of the place rather than being a reactive provision. There may need to be specific policies for the protection and treatment of specific parts of the place, including fabric, spaces, fittings and surfaces. Maintenance management is discussed further in the second section of this chapter.

Interpretation and promotion of heritage values

This will relate (mainly) to heritage organisations – as well as to other sites that allow or indeed encourage visitors – and is concerned with how the organisation is going to interpret the place in relation to its values, and how visitor understanding is to be enhanced. It should also consider the effect of visitors on the place in relation to visitor numbers and their impact on the:

- Physical fabric
- Atmosphere of the place
- Maintenance and repair processes (and, conversely, the impact on the visitor experience of maintenance and repair processes)

Attention should be paid to the visitor experience, including facilities and encouraging access for all – e.g. the disabled and other groups who might be excluded (including for social reasons). This might take into account, amongst other things:

- Trends in numbers – this may be financially critical and therefore a strategy may be needed to provide better access, more 'attractions', car parks, etc. – which may impact on significance.
- A need to deal with issues such as access to more fragile elements and any possible tensions with, say, education, enjoyment and understanding (and possibly income generation).
- A desire to attract visitors from a wider social constituency.

Property management strategies

Various strategies may be needed to cover dealing with leases, appropriate uses, acquisitions and disposal in the light of the identification of cultural significance. There may be opportunities on larger sites to review the relationship between functional use and cultural significance and to relocate functions to various buildings or spaces in order to achieve a better fit that protects and enhances significance. The management plan should be an opportunity to reflect on this and also, for instance, to consider whether more areas, or more significantly important areas, of the place can be made available for access to the public (through, for example, moving administrative offices out of significant areas).

New uses, new buildings

There should be a consideration of the appropriateness of current uses in the light of the assessment of cultural significance and the development of a framework for guiding decisions about new uses.

New uses may be part of the natural development of the site, or finding them may be essential to securing its future and therefore safeguarding the cultural significance that it represents. It is important that proposals for adapting existing buildings, developing new buildings – or even demolishing existing ones – is based on a proper understanding of the relative significance of the main elements of the site and of each building on the site. For new buildings, the plan should provide a framework for decisions about siting, function and design. The design should consider such issues of massing, scale, rhythm, use of materials, etc. It should also bear in mind conservation principles which generally suggest that the new building should respect the existing but be clearly a modern design – 'of its time' – and therefore adds to the 'story' of the development of the place rather than attempting to copy or provide a pastiche.

Obviously this will be a key issue where the driver for the conservation plan has been a particular development proposal. But even if this is not the case it will be necessary to consider the appropriateness of potential uses in the light of the assessment of significance, and taking into account the medium- and long-term financial (and cultural) viability of the site. Clearly the possible uses should be measured against their likely impact upon the cultural significance of the place. Of course, the possible uses may change over time, not only because the assessment of significance may change but also because the social, economic, financial and spatial planning context within which the site operates may change (such factors should have been taken into account as far as possible in the assessment of vulnerability).

From a perspective of cultural significance, the issue will often be in relation to an assessment of the impact of new uses on either the fabric or the atmosphere of the place (or both of course). Relative significance will be an important factor here because, for example, you could have a new use that does not interfere with or damage the fabric but which damages understanding and interpretation, or detracts from the atmosphere or the 'spirit of place'. It is generally felt that the original and/or traditional use will always be the most appropriate. Often, however, the 'original' use in its modern guise may be less compatible than other sympathetic uses because, for instance, of modern functional requirements (open plan offices or the need for extensive sight lines because of security issues, for example).

Pearson and Sullivan (1995, p. 207) distinguish between 'compatible use' and 'most appropriate use'. Compatible use being the use that will not damage the place or the cultural significance of the place, whilst a most appropriate use will be one that is not only compatible but will actually reinforce and maximise the understanding of the cultural significance of a place.

Clearly when considering new uses, financial viability will be a big influence but sometimes the implications of a new more financially viable use may be a serious erosion of cultural significance. The interaction between retaining and enhancing cultural significance, the need to find a viable use and perhaps max-imising income generation, can sometimes lead to situations where the building is retained but its significance is lost almost completely.

Setting

This should include, where appropriate, the setting of the site and its relation to significance. On a large site of heritage and non-heritage buildings the setting may include the wider site itself in relation to the heritage elements. It might cover:

- Views into and out from the site
- Spaces between buildings – both formal and informal
- Hard and soft landscapes
- Natural and built means of enclosure
- Boundaries, definition and way finding
- 'Street' furniture

But this can also be seen in terms of senses other than the visual and may relate to noise, smells and activity that effect a sense of place. Noise and smells may detract from significance, but may of course add to it or indeed be essential to it.

Statutory compliance, health and safety, security

This considers the interaction between compliance with statutory obligations – and the good management practices associated with them – and the protection of cultural significance. Particular care is, perhaps, needed to comply with statutory obligations regarding:

- Disabled access
- Energy
- Fire protection

The issue of disabled access is clearly an ethical as well as a statutory compliance issue, and therefore, to some extent, should also be addressed in the context of widening opportunities for all sections of society to access, enjoy and benefit from a shared cultured heritage.

The issue of reducing energy use is similar to fire and access issues, in the sense that there is perhaps some tension between compliance with statutory obligations and the protection of cultural significance. However, there is, as with disabled access, an ethical issue here related to the greater social good of reducing impacts on the environment. This can be seen as an interesting juxtaposition, which raises a more general 'sustainability' issue of trade-offs between environmental impact and the social value of the built cultural heritage. There is also the issue of the embodied energy in the existing building and its energy consumption now. It is therefore important that there is a detailed understanding of the actual energy performance of the buildings and, irrespective of the issue of statutory compliance, that there is perhaps a policy on, say, mixed estates (heritage and non-heritage) of energy trade-offs between the built cultural heritage buildings and the others.

Fire precautions work at a number of levels of course. They are there primarily to protect life, and they do this through trying to ensure effective means of escape and through a consideration of the performance of the fabric in the event of a fire, in tandem with active fire precautions (there can be trade-offs between these active and passive precautions). In protecting the fabric, the fire precautions also help protect the functional and financial asset that the building represents. In the case of the built cultural heritage they also protect the cultural significance of the building. Where there is a conflict between fire protection and cultural significance it is important to take a holistic view of the performance of the building in fire, and to relate this to approaches such as 'fire engineering'. It is also important to link the options to the assessment of significance, and therefore consider the extent to which the value of the building will actually be undermined by interference with the fabric and/or the aesthetics of the place.

Use of expert skills and advice

The management plan should ensure that the necessary built cultural heritage skills are either sought or developed in relation to planning, management and processes associated with work to be undertaken on historic fabric. There should also be proper provision for ensuring that consultants and contractors – through their briefing, through contract and specifications and through their terms and conditions – understand the implications for policy and practice and their service delivery on the cultural significance of the place.

Training and awareness raising

There should be programmes for staff at all levels related to organisational understanding of cultural value, the purpose and intent of the conservation plan and the management plan and how it impacts on them and their role (and vice versa). This should clearly go beyond just those staff who deal directly with the fabric, and is part of a process of bringing all levels of the organisation 'on board'.

Recording

As we have emphasised elsewhere, all actions related to the place should be recorded. This should detail not only what has been done but also the reasoning behind the action. Recording is both an important management process and, as pointed out in Chapter 3, a key conservation principle. It is of course, as pointed out in Chapter 4, also part of the research process for establishing cultural significance. There should be a clear framework and process that identifies responsibility for and methods of recording decisions and the consequent actions (including work that is altered or removed – whatever its significance).

Incorporating community perspectives and liaison with the community

Developing and delivering a common vision for the place will include the aspirations and concerns of the organisation, but it should also continue to involve other stakeholders.

The views of the local community and others associated with the place will already have been taken into account in assessing significance. However, it is important, particularly with intangible or relatively intangible aspects of significance, that it is clear how such individuals and groups will continue to be involved in decisions about protecting and enhancing significance – and what are the management processes that are going to ensure that this happens. It will be necessary to have a policy and a process for liaising with the community and other stakeholders to ensure that they understand the basis and the implications of management decisions and actions, and that they are given an opportunity for their views and insights to continue to be taken into account.

Although there may be constraints depending on the site and the organisation, community involvement is essentially about an ethical approach. It is also of course concerned with minimising conflict.

Monitoring the plan

As we have observed elsewhere, there needs to be a process set in place to monitor how the plan is working through an assessment of how well the policies are being applied (to the appropriate time-scale) and therefore there will need to be targets which have to be reviewed. These targets should be based around policies that are set out to enhance and protect cultural significance and should therefore primarily be drawn from the assessment of significance and the assessment of vulnerability.

This may mean that new performance indicators need to be developed or existing ones adjusted. These should fit into and complement the organisation's overall management and property management benchmarks, but they should be derived from a perspective which monitors issues of cultural significance protection and enhancement (rather than concentrating on, for example, such things as financial expenditure).

Reviewing the plan

It is important to ensure that the policies, strategies and actions are reviewed. A conservation plan and its management plan should be seen as dynamic. Not only does there need to be a robust method for ensuring that objectives are being met, but it will also be necessary to review whether they are the right objectives in the light of changing circumstances. It clearly makes sense to synchronise the review of the conservation plan and management plan with the strategic planning cycle of the organisation. Although three-year or five-year periods are quite common, there may be reasons why it should be shorter or longer, including perhaps where major changes are envisaged to the place or to its management. It is important that the conservation plan is included in the review in order to ensure that changes to the understanding or perception of significance, or more likely relative significance, which may occur for various reasons – including of course because of the changes to the site that the plan envisages – are taken into account.

Maintenance management

Introduction

The idea that effective maintenance of the building fabric is a fundamentally important activity goes back to the writings of John Ruskin and William Morris along with other early pioneers of the conservation movement. Ruskin (1989) exhorted people to 'Take proper care of your monuments and you will not need to restore them', and Morris (1877) called upon those who deal with monuments to 'put Protection in the place of Restoration, to stave off decay by daily care'.

This historic emphasis is reinforced in the current SPAB document '*SPAB's Purpose*'. This document states that regular maintenance is 'the most practical and economical form of preservation'.

James Semple Kerr's observation that 'Maintenance is the single most important conservation process, whether the place is architectural, mechanical or botanical, prevention is better than cure' (Kerr, 1996) is echoed in many of the international guidelines, which emphasise the importance of an effective maintenance programme in protecting the significance embodied in and represented by the fabric of buildings. In addition, the British Standard, BS 7913 (British Standards Institute, 1998), *Guide to the Principles for the Conservation of Historic Buildings* states that 'systematic care based on good housekeeping is both cost effective and fundamental to good conservation'.

The British Standard on building maintenance, BS 8210 (British Standards Institute, 1986), describes maintenance as a 'combination of any actions carried out to retain an item in or restore it to an acceptable condition'. However, it is important to note that, whilst for the maintenance of the majority of buildings, the distinction between repair, restoration and improvement will not be conceptually important, for the built cultural heritage these definitions, and the actions which are implied, are of fundamental importance. The phrase 'As much as necessary as little as possible' is a maxim in The Burra Charter (Australia

ICOMOS, 1999) which encapsulates a key overarching theme for the care of historic buildings and echoes the conservation principle of minimum intervention. The Burra Charter refers to maintenance as 'the continuous protective care of the fabric', and goes on to say that it should be distinguished from repair. Obviously repair works will become necessary for historic buildings and, when carried out properly and judiciously, they will prolong the life of an element and the building. Good repairs are important for the long-term protection of cultural significance, but it is important that it is understood that they are an intervention that will, in most cases, involve some level of damage or loss to the fabric – they are in a sense inevitably either restoration or reconstruction. Brereton (1991) makes the point that any unnecessary replacement of fabric is likely to diminish its authenticity and thus its historical/cultural value. The balance therefore between preventative maintenance and repair is important, not just in relation to the conservation of fabric, but also because of cultural significance. As Clark (2001, p. 56) points out, sensitive repair and management does not merely involve specifying appropriate materials and techniques, it also requires an understanding of site significance, how this is manifested in the fabric, and the effects that any repair action might have.

Feilden (1994) suggests a hierarchy of interventions, which implicitly puts some actions in order of least harm to the fabric:

- The prevention of deterioration
- Protective measures
- Consolidation
- Repair

This hierarchy reinforces the previous point about the need to distinguish between maintenance and repair when dealing with historic buildings, as repair can be seen as a 'point of failure' because, as mentioned, it will usually involve damage to and/or replacement of historic fabric. Feilden's explanation of a hierarchy of intervention is a useful way of considering maintenance activity from the perspective of emphasising the need to protect and enhance the cultural significance represented by the fabric. In order to ensure this, he suggests that the degree of intervention should be informed by conservation principles. This should include, in particular, the notion that 'Conservation is based on a respect for the existing fabric and should involve the least possible intervention. It should not distort the evidence provided by the fabric' (Australia ICOMOS, 1999).

Maintenance then can be seen as the primary activity supporting the key building conservation principles of retaining the maximum embodied cultural significance through a process of minimal intervention in the fabric of historic buildings.

A strategic perspective

The notion of strategic maintenance management suggests that the overall medium- to long-term aims of an organisation should inform policy, tactics and day-to-day activities. There should also be clarity about where the maintenance function resides in the organisational structure, what other functions and processes it interacts with, and how and why this occurs. This is important because maintenance management generally, and within corporate contexts particularly, has a low status and is seen as non-strategic. Even within 'estates departments', maintenance management generally lacks kudos. This seems to the case even in organisations whose *raison d'être* is the care of historic buildings (Feilden, 1982). One consequence of this is to produce a reactive maintenance provision, which, because it is not integrated into the property or wider organisational strategies, does not have a strategic perspective and does not think in terms of organisational goals.

Whether we are considering heritage or non-heritage organisations, the essential aim of maintenance should be related to the protection and use of the physical asset. In turn, this asset should be conceived as a resource that can be managed proactively in order to help deliver corporate goals via processes which focus on the needs and requirements of the users, customers and stakeholders. Effective maintenance will be one of the processes that can maximise the potential of the built resource by protecting and enhancing the asset, but to do so the maintenance management culture and activities will need to be strategic, proactive and integrated in nature.

The objectives of most maintenance programmes will include retention of continuity of function, protection of the capital asset represented by the buildings, protection of the comfort and convenience of users, reinforcement of image and, increasingly, meeting statutory obligations (related to such matters as fire, health and safety, disabled access, etc.). For most organisations there will be specific drivers and emphasis which might prioritise certain activities because of the nature of the corporate goals and/or the key activities. For example, for a health service, the possible impact of building condition on a range of issues, from infection control to the psychological impact on patients' feelings of well-being, should be taken into account.

With historic buildings, irrespective of both ownership and wider organisational goals, the specific driver for maintenance should be that it is the fabric itself that is important because of its significance – and not just because of its function. As The Burra Charter observes: 'the cultural significance of a place is embodied in its fabric, its setting and its contents'. That is, the 'historic' building itself is an artefact, and it is the value represented by and embodied in such buildings or sites which should be the focus for maintenance strategies and process. It follows that the maintenance management of the built cultural heritage requires the development of a plan for maintenance which integrates it into the wider strategy for the management of the property portfolio, but all within the context of an assessment of cultural significance and vulnerability that provides a framework and reference point for maintenance and which drives its strategy, processes and actions.

For what we might term 'heritage organisations' – that is those organisations for whom the protection of the built cultural heritage is their core business (for example, the National Trust) – such a focus is easily adoptable for their maintenance strategies/policies because the protection and enhancement of the physical estate, or rather the cultural significance represented by it, is (part of) their 'core business'. However, for most organisations with a property portfolio, the length of interest in their property is usually determined by the length of tenure, which is, in turn, linked to organisational goals and other functional requirements (as discussed in Wordsworth, 2001). Hence, for non-heritage organisations the emphasis tends to be on functional life (which could be very short for dynamic, fast-changing businesses), and the importance of the physical life of the fabric is related to the effect that it has on function. For organisations with 'mixed' estates (that is, organisations whose business is not 'heritage' but who nevertheless own or use some historic buildings), the justification for expenditure is likely to be in relation to functional life and a 'core business' which is separate from the buildings. The problem in such organisations might be that the maintenance of their historic buildings may tend to be driven solely, or at least mainly, by a statutory compliance requirement culture, not by a sense of obligation to protect a cultural asset. This may be particularly so in decision-making processes involving the reconciliation of a number of competing organisational priorities. There could also be an issue in situations where the organisation sees the primary value that ownership of a historic building contributes is related mainly to the image they wish to project. In such a situation there is the danger that the priority for maintenance activity is focused more on retaining the aesthetic appearance of the building and less on protecting its cultural significance, which could lead to inappropriate priorities and early intervention. It is important therefore that for all estates where historic buildings are part of the portfolio, a culture and system is created that acknowledges, understands and contextualises conservation principles, and which links these to an understanding and use of cultural significance as a driver for strategic and operational activities. This should help to ensure that any decision on the protection of the built cultural heritage is not (mainly) based on bureaucratic and pragmatic criteria – particularly in those organisations where historic buildings are seen as a burden – but on the development of an approach which protects and enhances that significance.

As discussed above, in order to be effective, maintenance management must be related to the overall goals of the organisation and integrated with the corporate strategy, and this should then inform policy, tactics and day-to-day activities. Property management generally and maintenance management in particular, have long been criticised for lacking a strategic approach. Without strategic awareness and data (on significance and vulnerability) there is a danger that a non-integrated approach will develop between the maintenance activity, other property management functions and other organisational interests that interact with the fabric (for example, visitor interpretation in a heritage organisation). This can result in maintenance activity being undertaken and prioritised in isolation. There is the danger of the maintenance function adopting an inward-looking logic of its own where efficiency of the process is measured rather than how effective it is in serving organisational objectives, and this may work contrary to the principle of minimum intervention.

Rather than comprising a series of individual elements, the maintenance management operation should be a coherent, integrated system. This system should be driven fundamentally by the concepts of cultural significance and minimal intervention through to an inception of the policies, programmes, management and practices derived from those concepts. It follows therefore that a strategy for maintenance cannot be truly effective unless the organisation has a clear understanding of the cultural significance of the historic buildings within its care, and a commitment to protecting and enhancing it over and above that which is a requirement of statute. Such an understanding needs to permeate the organisation and this, along with minimum intervention, should be the focus and driver.

Given the importance of maintenance for buildings, an overarching strategic plan for heritage organisations should provide a clear indication of how maintenance is to be managed. In addition, the plan should explain where and how it integrates with the organisation's overall structure as well as its asset management function.

By implication, this reinforces the need, in mixed estates as well as heritage organisations, for comprehensive and rigorous conservation planning in the form of a conservation plan and management plan (or other appropriate tool), which is based upon conservation principles and addresses issues of significance and vulnerability. This should then be followed up by integrated management plans that make the vertical and horizontal connections through all activities, including the operationalising of maintenance. Conservation plans should identify what aspects of the fabric are important and why, and from this there should be some sense of recontextualisation and prioritisation by the maintenance organisation in order to operationalise this idea of relative significance for the functions/processes that they carry out.

The idea of maintenance management implies a context that involves notions of time, the gathering and use of data and the generation, manipulation and allocation of resources (finance, expertise, materials). For all organisations, whether heritage or non-heritage, a balance will need to be struck between performance and resource inputs, which implies that maintenance management involves determining a series of relative priorities. This emphasises the requirement for setting standards appropriate to the needs of the building, and also to the objectives of the organisations – something that must permeate through both strategy and tactics. As we have observed, in some organisations maintenance management tends to be driven by process, or rather optimising the efficiency of the process, rather than a clear articulation about what that process is serving. The tendency is for aspects of maintenance management orthodoxy to be imported from elsewhere without recontextualising them for the needs of historic buildings. For example, whilst planned maintenance programmes can provide cost savings, they may, without the proper focus, work against the principle of minimum intervention. Maintenance programmes should therefore be set within the context of rigorous policies focused on minimum intervention and the need to retain and enhance cultural significance, and they must use these concepts as the context and drivers for management decisions and processes. Working within the context of a conservation plan, the maintenance plan will take this overview of the historic stock and must reflect the identification of significance, how and the extent to which it is represented by and embodied in the fabric, along with the identification of the relative significance of different parts of the fabric. The maintenance plan should show how decisions based around significance and relative priority will affect the organisation of maintenance and how it is carried out. This will include reference to how conservation principles (such as minimum intervention, honest repairs, etc. – see Chapter 3) are to be interpreted by the organisation.

These issues and connections might be articulated through a maintenance manual containing:

- Extracts from the conservation plan showing how the identification of cultural significance has been recontextualised and synthesised with conservation principles, and how these inform and direct maintenance objectives and processes.
- A breakdown of the elements of the site building showing relative significance (of the various buildings and the elements and components of each building).

This should be supplemented by:

- Plans and elevations showing the site and buildings
- An architectural historical account
- A description of the building's construction materials
- An identification of vulnerable points and areas of risk from a cultural and a functional perspective – and an analysis of the interaction between the two
- Information on condition, at both a broad brush (i.e. condition A) and a detailed level which is updated by the surveys and inspection

Both the Government Historic Buildings Advisory Unit (1998) and BS 7913 (British Standards Institute, 1998) also recommend the use of logbooks. The British Standard characterises these as current information on key persons and managers and concise instructions on maintenance and inspection routines, and recommends that completed logbooks should be kept as part of the permanent record of the building.

Recording

Records are likely to be a combination of drawings and text and will both describe the fabric and record interventions (and the reasons for making them).

Good information and records are vital for the effective maintenance management of listed buildings. The recording of maintenance processes and actions is important in terms of developing management information and informing decisions (for example, on cost of works carried out). But for historic buildings, the keeping of proper records of decisions made, their context and the reasoning behind them is an important conservation principle as the maintenance and repair of the fabric is part of the story of the historical development of the site or building. Clearly, decisions made now, and the reasoning behind a decision, will also give future generations an insight into the conservation consciousness of current times.

There is some evidence of an interesting blind spot here, even amongst heritage organisations. Although they will acknowledge the importance of records as management information documents, often they will not conceive modern records as important archival documents, which are part of the history and therefore the cultural significance of the building, even though they treasure the equivalent documents of the past.

Programmes

Feilden and Jokilehto (1993, p. 41) suggest that preventative maintenance is 'the highest form of conservation', and comment on maintenance programming:

> *The maintenance programme is aimed at keeping the cultural resources in a manner that will prevent loss of any part of them. It concerns all practical and technical measures that should be taken to maintain the site in proper order. This is a continuous process not a product.*

Clearly the maintenance strategy needs to be delivered through a coherent and cohesive set of processes and actions, and which will operationalise maintenance in a way that reflects the aims of the strategy. As we have said, for historic buildings, maintenance needs will be driven by an understanding of the cultural significance of the fabric. However, this driver also needs to be related to the proper functioning of the asset and to be synthesised with insurance requirements, health and safety considerations and other statutory obligations. There also needs to be set in place a process which identifies what maintenance and repair work is to be carried out, and how and when it is to be done – particularly taking into consideration the continuing functionality of the building (including for heritage organisations, the visitor experience). The question of how work is to be prioritised and on what basis is also of fundamental importance.

Wordsworth (2001, p. 98) defines programming as 'scheduling the manner in which maintenance work will be carried out'. He emphasises different timescales for programmes: long-term programmes (an expression of policy rather than a detailed scheduling of tasks); medium-term programmes (on an annual basis) and short-term programmes (daily, weekly and monthly tasks). Similarly, the importance of scheduled, but flexible, routines of daily, monthly, annual and quinquennial maintenance tasks is emphasised by Feilden (1982) and Feilden and Jokilehto (1993).

It is usual to make a distinction between two broad types of maintenance action:

- **Reactive** – day-to-day, or corrective – This is usually seen as a response to a problem or failure, and an intervention that is usually initiated by the building user.

- **Preventative** – This is a planned approach that maintains buildings through a rationalised programme formulated through knowledge of condition and identified priorities and predictive assessments. It creates benefits associated with economies of scale and simpler management arrangements. Although a focus on economies of scale can work against the notion of minimum intervention, generally problems identified and dealt with in the early stages can minimise the need for more intervention and costly repairs later on, and therefore this approach is seen as functionally and financially effective. Planned maintenance may also play a role in ensuring that the buildings project the right image for the organisation, in protecting the visual impression that 'well-maintained' buildings give to occupiers and the public at large.

Holmes (1994) suggests that planned maintenance can be divided into 'condition independent' and 'condition dependent'. Condition-independent maintenance, which is often called 'cyclical maintenance', requires no pre-inspection and tends to be work that is undertaken at regular intervals – work such as external painting, annual safety checks, clearing gutters, lubricating moving parts, removing plant growth and bird droppings, painting and testing, etc. (some of which might relate to statutory or insurance requirements). Condition-dependent maintenance occurs when an element or component is assessed through an inspection or a condition survey and the action to repair or maintain it is subsequently prioritised. Where such intervention is carried out in time to avoid failure it could be termed 'planned preventative' maintenance. In practice, however, intervention/condition surveys also identify immediate remedial work that is necessary as a result of deterioration/failure that has already occurred.

Clearly a management system based around condition-dependent maintenance is the more complicated and resource dependent, as it requires monitoring of the condition of the fabric, effective information collection and management, and the development of an approach that involves decision making informed by a system based on relative priorities.

Even with an efficient planned maintenance programme, some form of user-initiated reactive ('response' or 'day-to-day') maintenance is inevitable. This needs to be considered at both the strategic and operational stages, in terms of establishing response criteria, timing, procurement and recording. An over-reliance on response maintenance is costly, not just in terms of financial costs, but also with regard to the loss of function, the resultant disruption and management efficiency. Good practice guidance in the public sector (see for example: HEFCE, 1998; Audit Commission, 2002) advocates that – for reasons of equity, efficiency and effectiveness – the majority of the maintenance budget should be spent on planned maintenance, with a lesser amount on response maintenance. Criticism of this approach (Williams, 1994; Wood, 2003) contends that it may appear economic in the long term, but, if the wider organisational and political context is one of uncertainty, then the use of risk analysis and a focus on the short term (response maintenance) can reduce immediate costs, give greater flexibility and should have the additional advantage of immediate 'customer' (user) satisfaction (Wordsworth, 2001). For the built cultural heritage, however, planned maintenance should be the overwhelmingly dominant approach, mainly because of the need for a minimal intervention ethos (rather than for budgetary control,

as might be the reason in other building types) and the fact that reactive maintenance by definition allows a failure to occur – and therefore entails the possible
loss of historic fabric. Clearly some reactive maintenance will be necessary to deal
with emergencies and also in terms of 'customer service'. It should, however, be
kept to an absolute minimum, because it allows failure to occur.

Prioritisation

Making decisions about relative and competing priorities is an important maintenance management process. Prioritising work will be important from a functional perspective and a cost perspective in all organisations. But it should also
take wider organisational issues into account – such as the impact that condition
has on the overall performance of the particular asset (energy for example) or the
overarching property strategy of the organisation (corporate image for example).

Of course statutory concerns will drive priorities – particularly issues related
to health and safety, fire, disabled access, etc. – but problems exist where aspects of such legislation are in conflict with the statutory provision for historic
buildings and/or conservation principles. (In some instances the statutory framework for historic buildings is in conflict, or at least at odds, with conservation
principles.) There can be a tendency for aspects of the maintenance management
process to be imported from elsewhere without re-contextualising them for the
needs of historic buildings. It is important therefore to avoid a situation where
the approach to maintenance management tends to be driven by process, especially one that emphasises optimising the efficiency of the process, rather than by
a clear strategy about what that process is serving. In the case of historic buildings therefore it will be important to prioritise with cultural significance and,
importantly, relative significance as a driver for decision making. Prioritisation
should take the assessment of cultural significance of the elements/components
and their vulnerability as a starting point, and link this to functional performance
and cost issues, and to the practicalities of carrying out the work. Planned maintenance programmes can provide cost savings, but they may work against the
principle of minimal intervention where they develop a logic and momentum of
their own, which may work contrary to the principle of minimum intervention.
For example:

- By its nature, repair and maintenance work consists of a number of small
  jobs. Batching them for economic reasons or other management priorities
  may result in repair work being undertaken too early or maintenance work
  being undertaken too late.
- Where access costs (scaffolding, etc.) are high, both financially and also in
  terms of loss of function or even image (or for heritage organisations a reduction, say, in the quality of the visitor experience). This may lead to work
  being undertaken that will involve unnecessary damage to the original fabric,
  through repair work undertaken early whilst the scaffolding is in place.

In addition to being possibly at odds with cost and programming concerns,
minimum intervention can also be in tension with both a 'let's do something'

(a)

(b)

Figure 5.1(a),(b)   The cost of items, such as scaffolding, which are necessary to gain access and work effectively on roofs, spires and walls, etc. may have an effect on decisions about such issues as 'minimum intervention'.

attitude, a culture of spending fixed budgets and, in some circumstances, issues of health and safety.

Another aspect of prioritisation comes more directly from the issue of relative priorities. The logic of a conservation plan is that relative significance is attributed to the physical elements of the building or site. It follows that repair decisions should not only take into account the functional and technical issues, but also a consideration of where one element might be sacrificed in order to ensure the protection of another of greater cultural value. For example, a lead roof covering might be replaced or repaired earlier than might be absolutely necessary because its functional role includes the protection of a stone exterior wall or a plaster ceiling which is considered more important culturally. This (rather obvious) notion raises interesting questions that need to be addressed in both the conservation plan and the management plan. For example, the question of whether in a traditional timber-framed building the infill panels are as culturally important as the frame may not need to be considered until a situation arises where the presence of one is damaging the other – perhaps through damp retention and/or expansion problems related to a brick panel. A proper repair will involve an understanding of the technical and functional issues related to the cause and effect of the processes of deterioration occurring here (water penetration, timber pest, timber detail and distortion of the frame and panel, for example) and the physical interaction between the frame and the panel. But a solution should also be based around notions of relative cultural significance of the elements. A similar issue arises around the question of whether to improve technical performance by altering details. For example, altering the detail around, say, a window on a sleek modernist building in order to improve the shedding of rainwater and therefore protect the fabric, judged against the detrimental effect on the significance of the architectural integrity of the building.

Prioritisation should also be linked, particularly in heritage organisations, to policies regarding such activities as visitor management and interpretation. This connection raises various issues – for example, access, timing of repairs, presentation of the building/site – as all of these interactions will be affected by the implementation of conservation principles such as minimum intervention and honest repair as well as the carrying out of a maintenance regime.

Condition surveys

An exhaustive guide to the art and science of carrying out condition surveys of the built heritage will not be presented here. Instead, we will examine the conservation planning and management issues that impact or interface with the condition survey as a management tool.

An essential element in any management process is the collection, analysis and use of information. Effective management can only develop from a basis of knowledge of the asset, its problems, needs and life expectancy.

In a maintenance management system the important information is the state of the fabric, and the collection of such data is normally carried out through

(a)

(b)

Figure 5.2(a),(b) The idea of relative significance may affect decisions about prioritising repair work if it becomes necessary to protect the building by altering an element or replacing it earlier than necessary.

Figure 5.3   The question of whether approaches to repair using principles such as honesty and minimum intervention are easily applied to (or indeed appropriate for) more recent buildings is an interesting one. (Image shows the Rietveld–Schröder House in Utrecht.)

condition surveys. A condition survey is a snapshot that will provide information on the physical condition of the stock. Such surveys involve the systematic inspection of the fabric of a building in order to produce accurate information on its condition and an assessment of the extent and timing of future work. A condition survey is the foundation for decisions on future planned maintenance programmes, as well as the opportunity to consider the effectiveness of previous programmes. A good condition survey informs the site manager about the materials that are present in the built fabric; about their condition, rate of degradation and remaining serviceable life; about the asset's vulnerability (whether, for instance, to the elements, vandalism, mismanagement or to other causal factors of decline); and about its critical needs in the foreseeable future in terms of maintenance, protection, repair, adaptation and investment. Condition surveys thus lie at the heart of the proper management of use and change in built historic assets (as indeed they do for every kind of asset).

All this may seem perfectly obvious to us today, but it must be recognised that it has only been in very recent decades that the desirability of conducting regular detailed condition audits has been recognised for even the most culturally significant assets. In 2000, English Heritage published *Power of Place*, in which it was still deemed necessary to urge that, 'There should be a shift from cure to prevention, by encouraging regular condition surveys and planned maintenance'.

What we all say seems obvious is not always what transpires on the ground in practice. Even today in the UK, within professional heritage management organisations that look after some of our most major historic sites and which have adopted policies that promise to conduct or commission regular condition surveys on all their principal assets, there remains the strong possibility that reliable up-to-date condition data are not available for many sites or buildings. Programming, funding and organising condition audits on a cyclical basis is a fundamental management task, yet it is easily overlooked and, like maintenance management, readily put off until another time when funds are less tight. This is bad economics and poor management.

It is important that the organisation is clear about what information it wants to obtain from a condition survey. There is a common tendency to collect too much information without being clear about purpose and this can be a waste of resources, but more importantly it can disturb clarity and inhibit decision making. In addition, the organisation also needs to be clear about:

- The level of detail required
- The format in which the information is to be collected and expressed
- The use(s) to which the information is to be put
- The manner in which it is to be stored, retrieved and analysed
- The nature and detail of the other management information that informs, and is informed by, the surveys

These issues will be discussed further in due course.

Experience has shown that, for assets of any substance, condition surveys should be conducted every four or five years (respectively, quadrennial and quinquennial inspections). Best practice would undoubtedly be to programme detailed surveys at these intervals, with annual updates being undertaken in between. Indeed, a five-yearly survey is recommended in BS 7913 (British Standards Institute, 1998), and the British Standard BS 8210 on building maintenance (British Standards Institute, 1986) refers to full inspection of the building fabric at no more than a five-year interval. The quinquennial model is nearly 50 years old, originating in the *Inspection of Churches Measures 1955*, which was the first statutory recognition of the need to inspect historic buildings. Its successor remains the only statutory requirement to inspect historic buildings. However, in practice, it seems that few organisations have the luxury of the availability of resources and funding to make such cycles work satisfactorily. Most, if not all, heritage management organisations in the UK have been unable to strictly maintain five-yearly periodic condition survey programmes across their complete estate. Instead, they have resorted either to prioritising which buildings/sites will be resurveyed to comply with their intended cycles or have allowed the whole programme to slip – sometimes in effect tacitly tolerating decennial or even more extended survey cycles. Survey programmes that are unrealistic, whether because of restricted availability of resources or the prevailing management culture of the organisation, are extremely dangerous. They bring the process into disrepute; they fail to deliver to operational managers' expectations and needs; and they form a millstone around the maintenance manager's neck. In short, an ill-judged, over-optimistic programme of cyclical survey may well undermine sound decision making instead of providing the fundamentals for informed management. Within reason, it is better to establish a longer cycle for survey inspections that suits the management organisation than to adopt a short cycle that cannot be delivered reliably. However, this has particular problems for historic buildings, since it leaves fabric, which contributes to or forms the mainstay of cultural significance, exposed to perhaps unknown levels of risk. This places greater emphasis and importance on the need for annual update inspections. Unfortunately, the record of implementation of these across estates is woefully poor. This is a problem to which management organisations need to give consideration – performance generally across the sector has to be improved dramatically.

Outside of the condition survey cycle, the presence of non-technical staff and other users and visitors on a daily basis can provide the maintenance management function with vital information regarding condition, which would otherwise wait until a subsequent inspection cycle (or until failure becomes impossible to ignore). Whilst users will doubtless report those defects that are causing a functional breakdown which directly affects them, their presence could also be used in a more proactive way to highlight factors that might lead to failure. A number of maintenance management texts refer to the value of using building users as an informal source of information on building condition. Feilden (1982) and Feilden and Jokilehto (1993) emphasise the importance of making use of staff (for example, cleaners) and building users' informal observations of building condition, although they recognise the need for a co-ordinated strategy to collect, process and store these observations so that they may inform action. Anecdotal evidence would suggest that this aspect of information gathering is either ignored or not carried out very effectively, with little thought being given to collecting and integrating users' observations in a way that can actually inform decision making and action. It should be considered, however, that listening to and reacting to occupiers' observations has value over and above the effect that this might have on the condition of the built fabric because of the way it includes people, values their experience and invites them to make a positive contribution to the protection of 'their' cultural asset. This is an important way of helping to develop widespread ownership of built cultural heritage and its significance. Conversely, the management organisation needs to develop ways of assessing and managing this input. In a case we have recently seen, a heritage management organisation was potentially over-relying on the observations and interpretation of potential defects to significant high-level fabric on a historic building by a steeplejack/mason, who though skilled at his own job was less sound on defect analysis and building pathology. The encouragement of user participation in defect/failure reporting must not be allowed to dilute professional interpretation and management decision making.

It has been said in introduction that the condition survey is a snapshot in time, providing vital information on the physical condition of the built stock. If designed, conducted and written up properly, cyclical condition survey reports build up a history of snapshot images of the state and vulnerability of an asset that can often prove extremely valuable. The National Trust's guidance on quinquennial inspections requires the building surveyor to report on significant changes in the condition of built elements since the last survey, and also upon the success in implementing the principal recommendations made in the preceding inspection report over the intervening years. This provides a useful check both on increasing or changing vulnerability of parts of the asset and on the organisation's own asset management and work planning performance.

Frequently, in-house site managers express reservations about disclosing previous survey material to surveyors who are about to conduct a new condition survey. (Hereafter, the terms 'surveyor' and 'building surveyor' will be used generically to include any qualified practitioner undertaking condition surveys whatever his/her professional background.) This fallacious notion presumably reflects concern that the findings of the inspection process may be coloured or skewed by the existence of the previous survey report. If it does, the fault lies in the choice of building surveyor whose task must always be to provide an independent professional assessment of condition at the time of inspection. However, the surveyor's understanding may well be greatly enriched by the provision of data from one or more earlier surveys. This highlights the need for condition audits to be carefully planned. Often, a limited investment in background research to inform the survey process pays dividends. A condition survey of the Wellington Monument in Somerset for the National Trust in 2005, provides a suitable example (Example 5.1).

Example 5.1 (see Figure 5.4)

The survey inspection, conducted using a 62-metre high, mobile access platform ('cherry picker' in common parlance, Figure 5.4) revealed, amongst other things, long but narrow vertical fractures close to the blades of the triangular sectioned shaft of the obelisk. It also revealed newly bulging panels of ashlar, where courses of individual stones had seemingly been drilled for dowelled repairs and refilled at some time in the past. Whatever interpretation might have been reached in isolation about these apparently relatively modest defects, the surveyor's comprehension was significantly improved by background research, which revealed that identical failures had iteratively been seen and subsequently repaired approximately every ten to fifteen years over the preceding sixty years. Clearly, the reappearance of these striking defects was a matter of some considerable importance and meaning – a fundamental point that would not and could not have been appreciated if access to previous survey material had been restricted by the National Trust.

The foregoing demonstrates the importance of providing copies of previous survey reports and associated data to the building surveyor. The heritage manager should also provide other information as part of the condition survey briefing process (it should be remembered that this is as critical for in-house building

Figure 5.4   A 'cherry picker' being used to inspect The Wellington Monument.

surveyors as for consultants). Ideally, material provided as part of the survey brief should include:

- Previous survey data
- History of major repairs for the preceding 10+ years
- Maintenance history since last condition survey was undertaken
- Maintenance plan
- Site plan
- Accurate floor and roof plans
- Elevational drawings and sections, if available
- A conservation plan, conservation statement, statement of significance or other assessment of the cultural value and special interest of the site (and the wider area, if applicable)
- The current management plan, or, if this does not exist, the specific conservation policies that the management organisation or building manager applies to the place

- A health and safety plan, identifying known or perceived risks relating to the site of which the building surveyor should be aware
- Copies of access, fire safety or any other current assessments of the site in use
- Ecological data on the known presence of protected or otherwise vulnerable species that may be disturbed or damaged during the conduct of the survey inspection

As has already been said, this is not a comprehensive guide to condition surveys of heritage assets, but a number of the preceding items do need explanation or expansion.

The provision and use of maintenance and repair data requires little further comment. Such information can prove critical if the building surveyor is to interpret signs of failure correctly and with appropriate balance in respect of severity, urgency of action and long-term ramifications. Provision of the maintenance plan enables the surveyor to appreciate the asset's current condition within the context of the manager's wider intentions for care. Responsible managers will wish the building surveyor to comment, for better or worse, on the appropriateness and success of the maintenance plan, given his/her findings about the state of the place, as well as evidence which highlights the level of adherence to the maintenance plan that is being achieved by the management regime.

Equally, the provision of drawn records of the site and individual structures to the surveyor should need no detailed explanation. At the most basic, the surveyor must understand without ambiguity precisely what is in ownership and who has responsibility for the maintenance of elements such as boundaries. Floor and roof plans are essential for planning the survey work, let alone as a means of helping to identify and record survey findings. All the drawn record data identified in the list of documentation above is integral to developing an understanding of the site before and during the inspection process. Deplorably, as we note elsewhere, the availability of accurate record information of this kind is often woefully poor, even where major heritage management organisations and/or nationally significant heritage assets are concerned. This is a problem that the conservation sector needs to address urgently.

The inclusion of the conservation plan, statement of significance or other assessment of cultural value on the list brings us to the heart of the matter. Regrettably, many will find it peculiar that it is there. Why does the building surveyor need to understand the values enshrined within a site and the relative significance of its elements and fabric merely to assess its condition? Hopefully, within the context of our argument, the answer is obvious. The building surveyor cannot advise on priorities for action unless he or she has an intimate grasp of these matters. To be effective, a condition survey report needs to dovetail into the management organisation's policies and wider priorities for action. These should be built around some form of evaluation of the asset's significance. Equally, a good survey report must be able to challenge such aspects of the prevailing management culture, if it has been built upon weak or partial analysis. These are necessary checks and balances in striving to achieve proper management and care. As has already been seen, a key component of the conservation plan is an assessment of the vulnerability of the place and its significance to causal factors of potentially deleterious effect. Many such factors will fall within the ambit of the detailed condition survey. The building surveyor needs to understand how the built fabric and the wider site are perceived to be vulnerable in order to produce a balanced interpretation of survey findings. Conversely, the building surveyor in undertaking a detailed assessment of condition should be well placed to advise on how the exposition of vulnerability could be finessed. The surveyor can contribute, accordingly, to the essential ongoing review of the conservation plan or assessment of significance and the conservation management policies that flow from these.

The most pressing yet simplest reason why the building surveyor needs sight of the conservation plan or equivalent has been left to last. Such documents, if well prepared, are likely to give the best oversight available of the history of development of the heritage asset. Once again, the building surveyor cannot hope to interpret properly unless he or she understands this history and, where relevant, places observed issues and defects into this context. The Wellington Monument once more can be used to illustrate this point. When conceived in 1817/18, the Monument was not intended to be the 53.6-m (175 feet) high obelisk we see today, but a 36-m (118 feet) triangular column surmounted by a 10-m (32 feet) cast iron statue of the Iron Duke. That was how it was constructed. The triangular column was completed in the 1820s to its full height, but finance dried up and the statue of Wellington was never cast. The incomplete Monument, in a severely dilapidated state, was only extended and transformed into obeliscal form after the Duke's death in 1882. Remarkably, externally this is simply not apparent – the monument appears to be of a single build (although admittedly some evidence is to be found in the tight unlit internal spiral staircase at the junction between the two phases some 36 metres above ground level). Crucially for the building surveyor, many of the most significant external defects up the shaft that were identified in the 2005 condition survey were concentrated immediately above the join between the repaired head of the original column and the 1850s upwards extension. The reasons for this do not need to detain us here; the fundamental point is that satisfactory interpretation of the cluster of defects two-thirds the way up the obelisk was entirely reliant upon the building surveyor comprehending the development and repair histories of the structure. This is another area where the conservation plan or equivalent has so much to offer the surveyor.

For all these reasons, the provision of a conservation plan or other assessment of significance should be a key component of every condition survey briefing on heritage assets of any substance. Unfortunately, at the present time, many sites in the UK are lacking this crucial documentation, although this position is beginning to change rapidly. Regrettably, some conservation plan commissions incorporate the preparation of a detailed condition survey as an integral task. Admittedly, the availability of an up-to-date condition survey is so important to sound asset care that, in the event that this is absent, it is desirable to have one prepared as soon as it can be funded and undertaken. An understanding of condition is also essential to appreciating certain aspects of a site's vulnerability to compromise and damage. Nonetheless, in an ideal world, the conservation plan should come first to aid interpretation of the survey findings and the setting of priorities for repair. English Heritage's 2006 Standard for Periodic Condition Surveys and Reports (of its own properties) puts this simply and succinctly: 'Conservation Statements or Plans shall identify significance and are a prerequisite for all condition surveys' (English Heritage, 2006a).

Experience shows that inadequate attention is paid by most heritage asset managers to the preferred format for their condition surveys and to the level of data that their reports should contain. These matters can be of considerable consequence to the usefulness of condition survey reports, to their cost and hence to the value for money that they provide.

Survey report formats tend to fall into three groups:

- Free text description and reporting on an elemental basis
- Spreadsheet summaries
- Hybrids of the two, based around or tending towards either free text or spreadsheet formats

The implications of these differing formats need to be understood before a sound decision can be made on the appropriate one to be adapted to suit the asset and the management organisation or individual concerned.

Free text formats tend to be preferred by 'lay' readers, since they permit a full 'story' of the site and each principal element to be told, describing what is there, the problems that exist, their cause and effect and any pertinent issues regarding remedial action, ongoing performance of the structure and fabric, and so forth. Illustrative photographs can be incorporated within the text or as an appendix at the end of the report (depending upon numbers and ease of use) to improve the narrative and the general reader's comprehension. However, for sites of some size or complexity, free text reports tend to become unwieldy, repetitive, lacking in balance and depressing to read, consisting of a litany of problems, failures and hazards. Although they may tell the 'story' well and in a logical fashion, with so many words, rapid extraction of relevant information in the future by the manager is extremely difficult. Equally, the free text format does not facilitate reliable interrogation by computer or creation of a forward maintenance plan from the survey data. Thus, it is not particularly user-friendly for the maintenance or management professional.

In many ways, the use of a spreadsheet format represents the antithesis of the free text approach to reporting. The spreadsheet is excellent for recording the identification and location of different materials around the site; for summarising the condition of principal elements (or even of each individual component); flagging up priorities for remedial action and further inspection needs; and for ready comprehension of long-term repair and maintenance expenditure profiles. It can be interrogated readily (if sufficient preparatory time is spent in structuring the report properly) and can be used to sort information electronically by, say, priority, condition or material. On the other hand, lay users generally find it more difficult to understand and interpret information presented in this way. Proper use of the data requires a certain level of aptitude in computing generally, and with spreadsheets in particular. This format is unsatisfactory for telling the full story about a problem; and, practically, photographs can only be incorporated as an appendix or, more usefully perhaps, in a separate volume of the report. Offsetting these disadvantages, for the maintenance manager the spreadsheet format makes production of a forward maintenance plan from the data a considerably easier task than when attempting to transcribe free text for this purpose.

So, free text and spreadsheet formats both have particular strengths and weaknesses as a reporting medium. To a degree, some inherent weaknesses of each can be ameliorated, as described, by creating a customised hybrid of the two approaches. An example of a well-tested successful hybrid is the quinquennial inspection format used by the National Trust. This supplements a free text-based report (which is often written in note form to reduce the word count, whilst retaining sense) with tabular presentation of forward maintenance and repair needs. This overcomes some weaknesses of free text condition reports, but inevitably has particular shortcomings of its own. Reading numerous pages of text in note form can be unrewarding and irritating. The tabular summary of future expenditure needs is very generalised and does not allow for sorting or interrogating data by material, element, condition, repair type or the like. In terms of facilitating the production of a long-term maintenance plan, this kind of hybrid is slightly better than a textual report, but far inferior to the full spreadsheet format. Hybrids can also be created to make the spreadsheet report approach more appealing to the general reader. Free text explanations of particular problems and issues can be inserted in an appendix, or as a subsection within a text-based introduction to the survey report and cross-referenced at appropriate places in the 'comments' field/column of the spreadsheet against the relevant entries. This is slightly cumbersome, but does help to tell the 'story' of the condition of the asset in a better way than is possible within individual cells of a spreadsheet.

There are a couple of additional matters that need to be considered when selecting an appropriate format for the condition survey report, if it is to constitute an effective management tool for the heritage asset. A number of heritage and large property management organisations have used condition surveys to feed data directly into asset management registers or plans. To be comprehensive – and there is little point taking this route if the coverage is not total – this approach requires the building surveyor to record and report upon the location and nature of every element and each and every occurrence of different materials. Instead of reporting, by exception, on items that are defective or at risk of failure, the condition – good or bad – of every element or material occurrence needs to be recorded. Significant management benefits can flow from creating and maintaining this database of record information on the nature and condition of the asset – for instance, it is possible to flag up the presence of inappropriate materials used in past repair which can then be tackled in programmed packages of work. However, data collection is a labour-intensive and hence expensive process that tends to skew or overwhelm the conduct of the condition survey. Generally, data collection and onward manipulation is most efficiently managed using pre-programmed 'palm top' or other computer hardware that can be used by the building surveyor out on site. Almost without exception, the future use of the data dictates that a spreadsheet or database format is adopted for reporting purposes. This approach can work well when dealing with relatively simple modern structures. It has been less successful, so far, in application on major heritage assets, primarily because efficient data collection and handling requires the asset record to be based around a predetermined hierarchy of simple elemental descriptions (for example, elevation/window/casement/glazing). Devising a meaningful hierarchy of this type for complex historic sites is problematic, as extension of the example to encompass varieties of historic glass, lead cames, ferramenta and so forth, as well as the condition of each and every material readily demonstrates. Historic places are often valued specifically for their individuality and idiosyncrasies. Fitting these into a simple, intelligible hierarchy for this use is bound to be challenging. Allow free text to define the unusual and the manager's ability to interrogate the asset register or condition survey is compromised immediately. This does not mean that the holistic asset management approach has no place in managing portfolios containing or consisting solely of heritage assets. Far from it, but to be manageable the approach almost certainly must be adapted and the compromises and weaknesses that this introduces must be appreciated by managers and kept in check. In the nightmare scenario, the manager wanting detailed asset data is frustrated by the dilution of a clear and simple interrogative elemental hierarchy through innumerable free text special entries, whilst the building/maintenance specialist regards the value and clarity of essential condition data as being degraded as a result of the process being 'hijacked' for a wider purpose. Equally, we have seen several instances where complex elemental hierarchies and reporting formats have been developed and adopted for condition surveys to fulfil the needs of global approaches to asset management, only for the condition survey record to be restricted to 'by exception' defect reporting so as to make the survey process less cumbersome and more affordable. This serves neither purpose particularly well.

The question is often asked as to whether condition surveys of heritage assets differ substantively from the process applied to their modern counterparts. Intellectually and practically, however it is viewed, the answer must be a resounding 'yes'. Indirectly, some of the reasons have already been mentioned. Appropriate repairs and the prioritisation of remedial action cannot be determined in isolation when dealing with heritage assets – such decisions have to be taken within the context established by a site's wider cultural significance and vulnerability to diminution. Correct interpretation of the evidence of failure in the fabric is often dependent upon an appreciation of the developmental history of the site in a way that is rarely the case with modern structures and estates. Historic places are frequently individual and idiosyncratic. Conservation philosophy seeks to retain historic fabric that can be repaired, sometimes irrespective of cost. That often demands inventiveness and flexibility of approach, fundamentally influencing recommendations for care and repair in the condition survey.

Traditionally, condition surveys tend to result in the need for repairs being identified based, broadly speaking, on concerns about functional performance, aesthetic considerations and cost (including the cost efficiencies to be made by packaging works together). Therefore, they often identify repairs as being urgent or specify a period within which they should ideally be carried out based on estimates of remaining life. The danger with this approach to the survey of historic buildings is that it may well operate contrary to the philosophical concept of minimum intervention, as it aims to set up a near-automatic process where a rate of deterioration is predicted, a prioritisation for action is set accordingly (in other words, the task of future repair is allocated to a particular year in the maintenance plan) and then acted upon at that future date, whether or not it is strictly necessary at that time. Put another way, the 'normal' conceptual approach to surveys is that, once a defect has been identified by inspection, repair will be carried out involving some kind of intervention into the built fabric. Such an 'automatic' approach does not necessarily make economic sense for any kind of building, but, when dealing with built cultural heritage, it increases the risk of historic fabric being removed or 'lost' unnecessarily. For historic stock, the concept of 'just in time' or 'little and often' maintenance is frequently determined to be the most appropriate way to manage this risk of premature degradation of the significance encapsulated within the built fabric. In best application, this concept minimises intervention by initiating a second tier of survey through focused re-inspection of non-critically defective or deteriorating fabric that has been identified in the previous periodic condition survey. By this process, it is intended that essential repairs or replacements are deferred until unavoidable, whilst ensuring that consequential damage to surrounding fabric and elements is not allowed to occur. The incorporation of second-tier survey work helps target precious (and often limited resources) and, in our view, should be a prominent planned feature of recommendations made in condition surveys of heritage assets.

Undoubtedly, this list of the differences between the survey of heritage and other built stock could be extended far further. However, in essence, condition surveys of built heritage assets require a different skill set and attitude of mind from those on modern assets. If the building surveyor does not realise this, the survey findings will be seriously compromised.

In considering the conduct of condition surveys, experience shows that there are three characteristics of historic structures that more frequently than any other baffle or are undervalued by surveyors more versed to inspecting simple modern buildings. These are:

- The identification and functional properties of both natural and traditionally used materials
- Decorative ornament and features
- The form and material properties of fixings used with the above

It is true that indirectly the surveyor of, say, a rectangular, steel-framed light industrial 'shed' needs to give consideration to the material properties of its elements, such as its external profiled metal sheet cladding and concrete block walls. However, it is unlikely that analysis of these materials and their fixings is going to dominate the thinking behind and findings of the condition survey report in a way that is all too possible with a historic structure. Again, the example that we have considered throughout this section, the Wellington Monument, can be used to illustrate this point simply. There, the iterative appearance of long vertical fractures close to the blades of the obelisk's shaft and repeated bulging of large panels of ashlar on its faces were found to be intimately linked to the nature, thickness and properties of the selected stone (extremely thin, local calcareous grit ashlar) and, given the innate characteristics of this ashlar facing, over-reliance on bedding mortar to hold stone to stone and each stone to the solid mortar and chert core behind.

This is not the place to wax lyrical about the importance of the notion of the 'breathability' of traditionally used materials such as lime, soft brick and stone to the durability and longevity of historic buildings, grand and modest. There is now a wealth of readily available material on this subject on various websites, as well as in recent publications. The point for us here is that the building surveyor analysing the performance of the built asset and the manager taking on the surveyor's findings and reaching decisions about how and when to repair need to understand that historic and modern structures tend to function in different, almost mutually exclusive, ways. Traditional buildings the world over depend upon the breathability of materials – or put another way, the absorption and subsequent evaporation of moisture – to work and survive, whilst most structures built in the last 100 years keep dry and sound through the use of impervious barriers – damp-proof courses and membranes and cementitious renders. Mix one approach with the other and, for traditional buildings at least, disaster is just around the corner. Arguably, more damage has been occasioned to historic buildings in the UK by ill-judged attempts at care and repair by the insertion or use of impervious materials to form a barrier to damp ingress than by any single other factor. This places a massive responsibility upon building surveyors carrying out condition surveys of historic assets.

The presence of decorative ornament or features – such as pinnacles, finials and crockets – is another pitfall for the unwary surveyor. With justification, good inspection practice tends to focus the surveyor's mind from the very start of his or her training on certain principal issues, especially the stability, integrity and adequacy of the structural elements of the building and the soundness and weather-tightness of its external envelope. Modern structures are generally barren of applied decorative ornament; larger or more complex historic buildings are sometimes extremely rich in it. Ornament frequently forms a significant part of the defining character of historic building exteriors. Often, especially with Gothic architecture, much of the external ornament is at high level and the adage 'out of sight, out of mind' may permeate the incautious surveyor's approach to the condition survey inspection. Experience highlights that ornament barely impinges upon a mindset that concentrates heavily upon structural elements and the external envelope. Yet, such ornament holds particular dangers for the building surveyor and the building manager. Small, three-dimensional and at high level, it is almost impossible to assess the condition of such ornamental elements from ground level, even using binoculars. Applied to the face

Figure 5.5   Taylor's 1890s wing of the former Public Record Office (also known as the Rolls Estate) in Chancery Lane, London.

of turrets, towers and walls, carved ornament is extremely vulnerable to degradation by the elements; iron and other fixings employed to attach it to the main building fabric are especially liable to corrode or fail. Concentrated for effect around the visible perimeter of historic structures, debris from failed ornament represents a particular health and safety risk to building users and passers-by. On many larger buildings, similar ornamental components – such as pinnacles and finials – are used repeatedly and, typically, close inspection will reveal multiple failures of the same kind affecting these elements. Lastly, in terms of repair, access and labour costs to ornament tend to be very high and, where renewal is necessary, carving of replacement sections is expensive. One example will suffice to make the point. In a recent repair programme to the external stone fabric of the former Public Record Office in London – a Gothic building of 1855–1901 with a mixture of limestone and sandstone ashlar elevations and extensive, often replicated, Portland stone carved ornament above parapet level and to turrets and towers – the access and essential repair costs to the high-level ornament were some ten times higher than expenditure required to the principal structural elevations. This is not atypical. So why does ornament receive disproportionately little attention in so many condition surveys of buildings where it is present, and why are such survey inspections so often conducted without the use of appropriate means of achieving close access to the ornament (for instance, by 'cherry picker')?

One final issue remains to be mentioned in this discussion of the condition survey as a fundamental management tool in sustainable conservation of our built heritage. This is the problem of ensuring consistency of approach in multiple surveys across a historic estate, or from one cycle of periodic survey to the next, or where one survey of a single asset or site is undertaken by a team of several surveyors. Issues of consistency permeate and bedevil the condition survey process from beginning to end. Different individuals do not necessarily see the same thing as being a 'defect'. They may not interpret the cause and severity of a defect in the same way. They may use different terminology to describe or define the element they are looking at and its state of defectiveness. They may interpret the impact of the site's assessment of significance and the management organisation's conservation policies on the condition survey process and recommendations in starkly different ways. They may hold diametrically opposed views on the appropriate remedial action for a particular defect, as well as the relative priorities for action across the site as a whole. It is the involvement of individuals that makes condition surveying an art not a precise science! Yet lack of consistency puts at risk all subsequent management decision making and action that is based upon the findings and recommendations of a condition survey.

In the end, improving consistency rather than achieving it as an absolute is probably a more realistic goal. This demands good, carefully co-ordinated briefing, training, planning and team management. It must involve the site manager as much as the survey team manager.

As a conduit to improved consistency, the best condition survey briefs set out definitions for key terminology that may be used. English Heritage's 2006 (2006a) standard brief refers the surveyor generally to 'national norms and standards', including two relevant British Standards (BS 8210:1986 *Guide to Building Maintenance Management* and BS 7913:1998 *Guide to the Principles of the Conservation of Historic Buildings*), and sets out in a detailed way definitions of 'alteration', 'asset', 'backlog', 'benchmark', 'breakdown maintenance', 'conservation', 'fabric', 'intervention', 'maintenance', 'planned maintenance', 'preservation', 'repair', 'restoration' and last, but by no means least, the meaning of 'surveyor' itself. Either within the survey brief or within the pre-inspection team planning and briefing process (or even better as part of both), it is essential that the definition of all elemental descriptors and the elemental hierarchy that is to be used are established unambiguously.

It is perhaps worth reviewing what has been said and implied about consistency in the survey and reporting processes and the ramifications of its absence in order to emphasise the key part that it plays:

- Regular accurate cyclical condition surveys are crucial to the proper management of use and change in and around heritage assets.
- Effective management decision making has to be based upon sound and reliable knowledge of the asset, its problems, needs and life expectancy.
- Inconsistency in condition survey data, findings and recommendations will undermine the site manager's confidence in the process and in the survey output.

- Consistency needs to be achieved:
  - across multiple surveys where an estate or a dispersed portfolio of separate assets is involved;
  - through time, between successive cyclical surveys of the same site or property;
  - within a single survey where two or more surveyors undertake the inspection and prepare the report as a team.
- Among other things, inconsistency may occur in the use of terminology, in the identification of what is a defect, in its interpretation, in assessment of its severity and consequence, and in fulminating recommended action and its relative priority.
- Management based on patchy data and analysis is likely to result in bad decision making.
- Improved levels of consistency will only be achieved by a concerted and co-ordinated approach being taken to briefing, training, planning and team management by the client and service provider throughout the process. At the present time, this is rarely attempted and almost never delivered.

Financial management

Planned maintenance programmes allow for greater financial control and accountability. In such systems money tends to be allocated to work identified as belonging to a number of categories such as:

- Cyclical maintenance
- Maintenance and repair work identified through inspections
- Unforeseen work – i.e. reactive maintenance

Although budgeting for maintenance works needs to take account of the likely resources available, it should be established on the basis of an assessment of the maintenance need and should reflect and be informed by the maintenance policy. Some sense of certainty about budgets over at least the medium term is important for effective management.

There are a number of factors in the way that budgets are often set, divided up and spent, which can work against the idea of minimum intervention and the protection and enhancement of cultural significance. One of these, which can have negative effects irrespective of whether historic stock is involved or not, is the tendency for budgets to be set and finalised on an annual basis – a situation which will work against the idea of a strategic approach to maintenance. A situation where an organisation has developed, say, a five-year programme but only has budget certainty of 12 months or less, produces an uncertainty which leads to inappropriate decisions being made. Ideally, at the least, there should be medium-term budgets for maintenance, which allow for some certainty in planning work based on clear priorities. In addition, and perhaps just as importantly, particularly for historic buildings, a medium-term budget may prevent unnecessary work being carried out, or necessary work being carried out too soon. Such problems may occur with an annual budget cycle particularly when there is uncertainty about the level of maintenance funding for the next year (or a regime where next year's budget is reduced if this year's is not spent). This situation will tend to encourage managers to ensure that the budget is spent. For historic buildings, a decision to spend money on repairs because it will be lost in the future can have a negative impact if the intervention is not necessary at that time. Of course, one might suggest that the frequent re-prioritisation of planned maintenance may have the effect of producing a minimal intervention approach by default, but this is un-likely – and certainly does not constitute good stewardship of a cultural artefact.

For the historic stock it is important that the budget for cyclical maintenance is 'ring fenced'.

Information management

The most important point about management information is to ensure that the right sort of information at the right level of detail is collected, that it is sufficient to allow clear judgements to be made – but that information is not collected just because it can be. In addition, there needs to be a system for analysing and disseminating information which will inform the decision-making process. Systems that manage such information should also make provision for feedback and monitoring.

Potentially huge quantities of information can be produced by the operation of a maintenance function (condition surveys, user feedback, the execution of the maintenance programme, building and service records, etc.), but the informa-tion, by its very nature, tends to be unstructured. That is, it is drawn from many different sources and in practice there is often no agreement about a common structure or levels of detail. Because the nature and form of information pro-duced and required by maintenance activity is extremely diverse, maintenance information should be stored on an integrated database. The information stored should be easily retrievable and should be in a format, and at a level of detail, to enable it to be easily manipulated so as to inform both tactical and strategic decision making. Information also needs to be in a form and a level of detail that allows it to be integrated into the wider property management role, both at a tactical and strategic level. In other words, there needs to be coherence be-tween business strategy, maintenance strategy/policy, financial management and maintenance implementation.

Some traditional formats for condition surveys highlight some of the prob-lems with information management. In some heritage organisations, for example, condition surveys tend towards a lengthy textual format. To some extent this is partly a cultural 'affectation', but it is also a valuable approach as it can pro-vide detailed assessment of historical development to be interposed with data on condition and repair needs. It can, however, produce information which is relatively inaccessible and inflexible and therefore difficult to analyse and use in terms of management; for example, it often cannot deal with 'what if?' en-quiries or, perhaps more basically, does not easily inform the development of work programmes.

Performance indicators

In the public sector, in particular, key performance indicators have become a common tool for monitoring past performance and for allocating future budgets. These performance indicators have certain characteristics in common: in particular, they are relatively easy to measure and they tend to be mainly associated with financial and budgetary information. Hence, indicators for maintenance that are often used are: the amount of backlog; costs per metre squared (or per user); and the speed of response (for reactive maintenance). There is also commonly an indicator for the amount of stock in a particular condition. The problem with this is that important, more qualitative issues are potentially overlooked if politically the maintenance organisation is driven to work towards quantitative targets rather than seeing such benchmarks as (partial) management information. There have been some attempts to measure more qualitative issues, but the overwhelming majority of indicators tend to the quantitative. Whatever the arguments regarding the usefulness and relative importance of such performance measures, some feedback mechanism for management and other interested parties should be regarded as an essential part of a review process which considers whether maintenance strategies and policies are being successfully implemented.

Risk management

A number of factors have led to an increase in the use of risk management techniques for the management of built assets generally: these include greater accountability (to stakeholders or shareholders) and the resultant requirement to create greater transparency. In using ideas of risk management to inform maintenance practices, the emphasis usually involves a focus on the effect of a potential fabric failure on the objectives of the organisation and not simply the effects on the fabric itself (Wordsworth, 2001). The risk management process is also important in terms of legal liability and, in some cases, insurance and links to the effect of the fabric condition on building users and wider corporate goals. Of course, for historic buildings the effect on the fabric becomes the primary concern.

The idea of risk management gives greater emphasis to some of the conservation principles, such as the need for accurate and appropriate records. The recognition of risks associated with component failure has resulted in published component life data, but this is, necessarily, generic. Hence, there is recognition that local knowledge of component lives exists within the particular buildings, and is more useful and more appropriate in informing decision making for repair and replacement in older buildings with materials that have not been 'manufactured.'

The remaining life of a component will clearly be influenced by the nature and quality of the maintenance regime, but in conservation terms the key risk, apart from non-compliance with statutory requirements and issues of health and safety, is the damage to cultural significance posed by undertaking too little or too much maintenance. This factor has to be balanced against the risk of technical failure through insufficient maintenance or where functional failure or health and safety problems arise because, for instance, an intervention is delayed in an attempt to minimise loss of cultural fabric. There may also be a risk of loss of cultural significance in tensions between an archaeological and architectural integrity – which again reinforces the need to identify not only cultural significance but also relative significance and where that significance resides.

Risk management should involve a consideration of the effect of deficiencies in management review and measurement systems that emphasise efficiency over effectiveness, and also what the result may be in reinforcing an inappropriate culture. An example may be where financial input and other quantitative measures are the main measurement of performance, and/or where performance indicators measure generic maintenance factors but not cultural ones.

The interaction between risk and health and safety issues is an important area. In addition to the need to comply with statutory requirements, the risks attached to, for example, inappropriate fire precautions, may include possible harm to cultural significance where fire precaution installations damage fabric and/or aesthetics. This has of course to be measured against the need to protect life and property, but should also take into account that the property is a cultural artefact whose significance may be irretrievable in the event of a fire. A similar situation would arise around decisions about how to deal with worn stone treads on a staircase. The wearing away may be considered to show the 'marks of time' (and the stairs are therefore to be valued because of this), but a decision to not repair them would have to be measured against the risk of injury to users and/or reduced access for the disabled.

A conservation plan can be regarded partly as a risk management exercise, not only in its identification of vulnerability but also in its considerations of options and the assessment of the consequences of not taking particular actions. The danger of using risk management for the maintenance of listed buildings in a situation where there is no articulation of significance is that it could focus maintenance attention onto other risks, to the exclusion of risk to cultural significance. Because of this, where risk management techniques are applied more strategically, that is to the whole property management side of an organisation, there could be less investment and concern to carry out maintenance generally. In order for risk management to be translated into a useful management tool for the maintenance of historic buildings, the development and use of assessments of cultural significance through a conservation management plan becomes critical.

Management tools for historic areas

We have observed in Chapter 2 that historic areas of cities, towns and villages tend to comprise numerous properties – many in the separate ownership of individuals, companies and other organisations – and public areas and spaces which are likely to be managed by the local authority on behalf of the wider community. The only statutory protection available for historic areas in the UK is as a designated conservation area – defined in law as an 'area of special architectural or historic interest, the character or appearance of which it is desirable to preserve or enhance'. The legislation requires local authorities to identify and designate such areas. Unfortunately, by implication, this suggests that undesignated historic areas are not deemed by the relevant local authority to be of sufficient historic interest to warrant preservation or enhancement of their character and appearance. In unprotected historic areas, the right of the owner to make changes to his/her property, irrespective of the impact upon the wider area, is fettered only in so far as the extent to which the alteration work requires planning permission. If the property itself is statutorily protected, then the owner requires listed building consent for those changes that may materially affect the character of the site. Where the historic area has been designated a conservation area, the only additional layer of protection is the requirement for conservation area consent for works involving demolition – unless the local planning authority has issued a specific 'Article 4' Direction removing certain permitted development rights in order to prevent a large number of incremental alterations from changing the essential character of the area.

As Historic Scotland notes in the introduction to its 2004 *Planning Advice Note 71: Conservation Area Management*:

> *effective management of conservation areas requires support and input from [all] stakeholders [in the area]... The management strategy for each conservation area should have shared ownership, involving all the stakeholders in an open and inclusive way.*

Indeed, this is true of any historic area whether designated or not, if its essential character makes a positive contribution to the life of the community. Pickard and de Thyse (2001, p. 290) concluded that sustainable management of historic centres must:

- *respect community life;*
- *improve the quality of life;*
- *maintain identity, diversity and vitality;*
- *minimise the depletion of non-renewable heritage assets;*
- *change attitudes and perceptions – the process of managing change involves wider interests and should involve different actors from the public and private sectors; property owners, investors, residents, and other community and voluntary interests. In other words, the process should become part of everyone's conscience;*
- *empower community action and responsibility through involvement;*
- *provide a suitable policy framework for integrating conservation objectives with the aims of sustainable development;*
- *define the capacity by which the historic centre can permit change.*

Maintaining identity, minimising the depletion of non-renewable assets and defining the capacity by which a historic area can change, all presuppose that an accurate, detailed and up-to-date understanding exists of the character and interest of the area. Without this, sustainable management of the area is not possible.

A number of tools are available that can be used to analyse the character and special interest of an area, but we intend to concentrate upon just three – the conservation plan; historic area appraisals; and characterisation.

The conservation plan

We examined the nature and use of conservation plans in some detail in Chapter 4, and much of that discussion centred around conservation plans for individual sites. However, the conservation plan approach and structure are equally suited for use on historic areas. The same logical process needs to be applied whatever the place. The evaluation of a historic area may of necessity involve extra layers of development history and will undoubtedly introduce different cultural values.

Nonetheless, as a platform for sustainable management of a historic area, the conservation plan offers the same ability to develop policy in a structured way built off an understanding of the locality, its significance and vulnerability to deleterious change. A conservation plan prepared in 2005 for the St Katharine Docks area immediately to the east of the Tower of London adopted the typical four-step structure of understanding, significance, vulnerability/issues and policies. Unusually, however, it contained a major focus on modern townscape character and strategic views into and out of the area, for these were recognised to be key values within the area and particularly susceptible to rapid compromise through development pressures. Thus, embedded within the conservation plan was a historic area appraisal (an analytical tool which we will discuss in more detail shortly). This illustrates usefully a general point that should be made about conservation planning and associated management tools. Such things should not be treated inflexibly. The best means of analysis needs to be fashioned to suit the particular circumstances and issues that are involved. One conservation professional, who was a consultee on the draft St Katharine Docks conservation plan, reacted negatively to the amalgamation of the historic area appraisal within the conservation plan. In our view, it was a fitting approach in the prevailing circumstances and considerably enhanced the analysis of significance and vulnerability and the development of appropriate conservation management policies for the area. In that instance, lateral thinking about values strengthened the output and impact of the conservation plan.

Historic area appraisals

There is no set structure for a historic area appraisal – indeed, a number of different approaches have been adopted in various circumstances within the UK and internationally. However, a certain degree of commonality exists to most appraisal methods. In our opinion, with more than a nod in the direction of value-based conservation planning, it is possible to set out a representative appraisal structure that, with intelligent individual adaptation, will meet most needs. Just as with a conservation plan, we believe that the principal objectives of a historic area appraisal are to understand why the area is as it is, to:

- Define what makes it special, what makes it 'tick'
- Assess what is truly significant and of value about the area to society at large
- Establish how the area has changed and fared positively or negatively in recent decades under the existing management regime
- Surmise how it is likely to continue to develop, and to understand the prevailing driving forces for change and specific influences that together will shape its future
- Generate management approaches that will protect what is of value yet is vulnerable, and
- Target regenerative action or improvements on elements that do not work well in order to optimise the benefit gained to all from the area

Almost inevitably, the area appraisal process is going to involve input from three interrelated activities, which may commence in a self-contained way, but eventually must come together through an iterative dynamic process of analysis and synthesis. The three activities from which the appraisal will be built are: desk and archival study; site evaluation; and public engagement and consultation. As with conservation plans, historic area appraisals require people to think laterally and 'outside the box'. Sticking rigidly to a set range of disciplines and approaches to analysis is an assured way to deliver a flawed appraisal. Compromises of this kind can only lead to poor management decision making and subsequent action.

With appropriate adaptation to take account of particular circumstances, including whether the historic area is statutorily protected in any way, an area appraisal might comprise the following:

Section 1:   Introduction to background
- Background to appraisal
- Purpose and scope of study
- Key dates and milestones
- Methodology
- Contributions

Section 2:   Context and overview of area today
- General identity including summary of the area's character and significance
- General context to wider settlement, landscape and historic environment
- Location and study area maps
- Climate
- Modern land use and ownership patterns
- Economic circumstances and key data
- Demography

- Management arrangements
- Planning context
- Nature and level of statutory protection/designations affecting area, including individual structures, landscapes, species, etc. within and close by

Section 3:   Origins, historical development and archaeology
- Underlying natural factors and characteristics, including landscape setting, geology and soil types
- Origins of settlement
- Reasons for location
- Overview of history and principal events affecting area and wider context; growth, change and their causes
- Historic land use patterns and changes
- Early plan form and subsequent development
- Historical development of wider setting – the local historic environment
- Review of archaeological evidence for any and all of the above
- Assessment of archaeological potential within area and immediate setting

Section 4:   Defining the place today
Area-wide overview:

- Modern plan form, street pattern, built density and urban grain, highlighting survivals of earlier forms
- Balance between and interrelationship of built form and spaces
- Overview of definable distinct character zones
- Building typology, typical architectural style(s) and detailing, materials
- General contribution of public and private spaces, and of vegetation
- Key vistas into, across and out from area

The area in use

- Concentrations of activity and relationship to modern land use and other factors
- People and vehicular movement patterns
- Places of inactivity, seclusion, relaxation and privacy
- Variations (24/7/52)
    – over the day
    – by days of week
    – by months of year/seasons
- Accessibility
- The visitor experience

Character – zone-by-zone analysis:

- Distinctive characteristics of zone
- Sense of place and intangible qualities, including sounds and smells

- Planned streetscapes and landscapes
- Key protected buildings
- Key unprotected buildings
- Qualities of buildings in zone and their contribution
- Key spaces
- Qualities of all spaces in zone and their contribution
- Trees and planting
- Highways and byways
- Contribution of surface materials, signage, street furniture; the effect of night-time lighting
- Aspects of neutral contribution
- Damaging and negative contributions

Section 5:   Significance of the historic area
- Values
- Relative significance of the area
- Significance of constituent parts, including character zones and key spaces and places

Section 6:   Issues facing the area
Needs to be assessed for the area itself, but might cover:

- Effectiveness of current management regime
- Impact of negative contributions
- Condition of buildings, spatial elements, etc.
- Development and infrastructure pressures, including those in wider setting with capability of impacting on the historic area
- Manmade and environmental hazards
- Economic drivers and the changing needs of the community
- Tourism and other 'people pressures'
- Demographic change
- Political pressures
- Disaster management issues
- Capacity to absorb changes without damage to its special interest; specific 'pinch' points of concern

Section 7:   Conservation strategy flowing from appraisal's findings
Again, this must be assessed and structured to suit the particular circumstances, but the strategy should look beyond the immediate future and might include:

- Cross-referral to relevant policies and their application to and within the historic area
- Identification of the various needs for change, for related guidance and development briefing

- Proposals for improved management performance to increase protection of vulnerable elements
- A strategy of planning enforcement
- Resource requirements, including manpower and funding
- Linkage to appropriate regeneration initiatives and other strategic aspirations of potential value to the area
- A methodology for monitoring and review, including key performance measures

Section 8:   Recommendations
- Specific management improvements, including preparation/revision of management plan; need for adjustments to management strategy for area
- Requirement for specific policies to reflect conservation strategy (Section 7) so as to influence future change
- Need for additional statutory protection for the area or constituent parts or changes to existing designations
- Opportunities for regeneration, beneficial development and improvement, and enhancement
- Need for imposition of protective controls on wider setting to area or for strategic views in, across or out of area
- Requirements for further study
- Monitoring and review mechanisms
- Need for preparations and dissemination of care and design or other guidance to individual property owners

Section 9:   Record information
- Schedule of documentary and research sources
- Extensive photographic record for future comparative use to demonstrate ongoing change and effectiveness of management regime

Looking over the model framework for a historic area analysis as set out above, it can be seen how its structure shadows that of the typical conservation plan. Setting aside introductory material, Sections 2–4 equate to the development of an understanding of the place in a conservation plan; Section 5 evaluates its significance; Section 6 explores the area's vulnerability to pressure and change; whilst Sections 7 and 8 use that platform to define essential and desirable management policies for effective, beneficial and benign future care.

The appraisal framework is as beneficial for establishing cultural value and guiding change in small rural settlements (irrespective of whether they are designated) as it is for historic market towns facing considerable development pressures and large or complex urban quarters as might be found in, say, Vienna or Amsterdam. It is also appropriate as a tool for use in multi-layered, historically rich sub-regions. An instance of this kind of application is to be found within a heritage and tourism master plan for Mtskheta in Georgia, produced in

2003 by UNESCO in association with the United Nation's Development Program (UNDP). Mtskheta, a World Heritage Site, was the ancient capital of Georgia and today, still being its spiritual heart, is of enormous religious and cultural importance for all Georgians. With the collapse of the Soviet Union and its influence over Eastern Europe in 1989, Mtskheta became profoundly at risk – firstly from economic decline, and thereafter from the threat of ill-planned new developments targeted at stabilising and turning around the region's economy. The master plan was developed to help in the process of managing beneficial and benign change – thus acting as a catalyst to economic revitalisation. It was built on the platform provided by a sub-regional appraisal – covering both the city and its wider environmental and rural contexts and linkages – that, to all intents and purposes, mirrored our own outline framework above.

In developing historic area appraisals, the character and significance of a place should not be confused. Significance is essentially a hierarchical concept assessed in ascending levels of value. It is a very different concept to character (although, clearly, there may be some overlap). Significance is about social and cultural value. Character is 'the combination of qualities or features that distinguishes one place from another'. The character of a place may form part of its wider holistic value to society, but an assessment of significance is a far broader and deeper concept.

The development of a conservation management strategy (Section 7 in our framework above) and implementation of recommendations such as those outlined in Section 8 of the framework (for instance, the need for additional statutory protection – such as Article 4 Directions – or the generation of bespoke design and care guidance for building owners, developers and architects) are crucial to effecting responsible and sustainable improvements in the management of a historic area. However, ensuring common ownership of strategies and policy direction is equally vital if management is to deliver its objectives successfully. Undoubtedly this demands planned but transparent consultation and briefing on the appraisal's outcome, but, just as importantly, it requires real engagement by the community in the appraisal process itself. This is rarely attempted – let alone achieved – by those responsible for the planning and commissioning of appraisal projects.

Characterisation

The term 'historic environment' is used to represent 'all aspects of the environment resulting from the interaction between people and places through time, including all surviving physical remains of past human activity, whether visible or buried, and deliberately planted or managed flora' (English Heritage, 2007). The kinship between this definition and that for the cultural landscape – whether Sauer's (1925), 'The cultural landscape is fashioned from a natural landscape by a culture group. Culture is the agent, the natural area is the medium, the cultural landscape the result', or, as we have put it, '[the] vital interaction between mankind and the natural environment (or perhaps more accurately the pre-existing cultural environments) over time' – is obvious. English Heritage (2004) has also stated that the historic environment:

- *knows no chronological limits...;*
- *knows no thematic limits, covering everything from an individual site or building to the whole historic landscape...;*
- *knows no geographic limits, being applicable in town and country alike;*
- *knows no limits to its scale, the locally-distinctive now being recognised as equally worthy of consideration, in own its way, as the internationally significant;*
- *knows no limits of culture or ethnicity.*

Characterisation is an analytical tool that was developed initially for use on rural landscapes, but it is rapidly being promoted as invaluable in managing change throughout the historic environment. Indeed, in a review of the application of historic landscape characterisation published by English Heritage and Lancashire County Council in 2004, it was emphasised that 'some of the most innovative [characterisation] work at present concerns the past – industrial towns of Cornwall and Lancashire, the great conurbations such as Merseyside, and the ambitious regeneration programmes of the London–Stanstead–Cambridge and Thames Gateway Growth Areas'.

As that same review makes clear, the development of characterisation as a process was intimately linked to that of the historic area appraisal, for it was built from 'the concept of "character" articulated in 1967 Conservation Area legislation' (e.g. Civic Amenities Act 1967, Section 69 ff (MHLG, 1967)). As will become clear, the two approaches are closely related but they should not be confused. Characterisation incorporates a focus on mapping that makes it distinct from the usual historic area appraisal and, most specifically, it concentrates on landscapes (rural or urban) rather than sites (or as the English Heritage/Lancashire County Council 2004 review puts it, characterisation is 'concerned with area not point data'). This is consciously different from the standard historic area appraisal, which (whilst producing an assessment of the area as a coherent place) reads it, at least partially, as being built up of individual buildings and spaces which each make a positive, neutral or negative contribution to the character of the whole. Characterisation does not deny that contribution, but provides a tool for exploring an area, and demonstrating it as a landscape resulting from many years (often centuries) of enriching growth, development and change – the dynamic ebb and flow of life. From this vantage point the problem, such as it is, with the historic area appraisal is the same conceptual shortcoming that has permeated our thinking in the UK (as well as much of the rest of the 'western' world) over the past century about heritage, and which, for the moment, continues to define our legislative approach towards its protection. Until recently, our notion of heritage has centred not on the all-encompassing holism that is the historic environment, but on individual 'jewels' of historic interest that are worthy of reverence and protection scattered in a 'sea of mediocrity' (that, by definition, does not warrant protection and can be repeatedly recycled for reuse). To a degree, an injudiciously prepared historic area appraisal risks repli-cating this attitude; for, in seeing the area as being built up of 'good' and 'bad' things, it risks drawing protective 'red lines' around the good whilst offering up the remainder for recycling. This is not what significance-based sustainable management should be about. At any one time, the local historic environment represents the present summation of accretive cultural change to the underlying natural landscape (and see here the immediate correlation and convergence with the concept of the cultural landscape). As the English Heritage and Lancashire County Council review of characterisation observes, 'if we celebrate the result of past changes, we must logically accept further change'. Once we have made that challenging philosophical leap of faith we must then be prepared to sanction, and perhaps occasionally even encourage, planned change to the 'good' as well as the 'bad' in the interests of sustainable management of the whole. That is where reactionary protective 'red-lining' breaks down.

As an analytical process, characterisation 'helps to manage change in the historic environment by tracing the imprint of history... It builds up area-based pictures of how places in town and country have developed over time. It shows how the past [survives] within today's world' (English Heritage website: http://www.english-heritage.org.uk/server/show/nav.1292). Critically, however, characterisation studies the present-day world. It does not simply focus on areas of special architectural or historic interest; it does not ignore the mod-ern as part of the landscape; it is just as much about the everyday ordi-nary places that predominate in the world as about the exceptional or the distinctive.

GIS (Geographic Information System)-based mapping usually lies at the heart of characterisation. However, despite the generally perceived exactitude of GIS-based data, characterisation is, in essence, a broad-brush interpretive approach to analysis. One of the principles laid down by Clark et al. (2004) is that character-isation 'is a matter of interpretation not record, perception not facts; understand "landscape" as an idea, not purely as an objective thing'. English Heritage's 2004 *Conservation Bulletin Issue 47*, dedicated to characterisation, described it as providing a dynamic and fluid yet provisional 'big picture' of a place (which might be a whole county as much as say a market town), a 'frame into which others can add their perceptions and views'. It went on to pinpoint the primary objective of characterisation as being:

> to understand better the complex intertwining roads of past decisions, ac-tions and inactions that have led to the present day's historic environment, to our world, whether we like it or not. We can map the trajectory of a place's evolution and chart possible future directions... This ability to set out choices – to preserve or manage, to create or leave well alone – is why characterisation is a tool for the future.

In some ways, there is 'nothing new in the world' in respect of the evaluation of assets and places. Just as with other analytical management tools we have already examined, characterisation involves a combination of desk-based and archival study, field survey, community engagement and synthesis. Indeed, what separates one analytical tool from another might be regarded as being simply gradation and emphasis. However, circumstances and objectives vary, and each process has its strengths and best uses. Characterisation builds from systematic identification of prevailing characteristics within the 'landscape' or place that is under study. As has already been noted, it deals with areas, not with individual sites, it concentrates on mappable patterns and attributes. Maps are used extensively, both for the purposes of map regression analysis (the detailed comparison of chronologically sequential historic maps to develop an understanding of change) and as the primary medium for presenting findings and recommendations from the process.

Characterisation explores the 'time-depth' that gives character and sense of place to an area or landscape. It analyses past change and land usage. It establishes the survival and pattern of meaningful historic elements in the present-day environment through map regression and rapid field survey. A typical example in the town might be substantive traces of former burgage holdings within the urban grain; in the countryside, the continued presence of medieval field systems as part of the modern landscape. Communities must be engaged to integrate collective 'lay' perceptions of the place alongside the analysis of detached specialists.

Characterisation practitioners see their approach to study falling into two distinct sections, which might loosely be thought of as: creating the 'story' of the area, and consideration of its future, based on that interpretation of its present. Characterisation is seen as being a 'vital tool' for management planning rather than an intellectually fulfilling end in its own right. It is perhaps no coincidence then that, by seeing the process as a two-stage one, its proponents place greater emphasis on consideration of the future as an integral component than in the typically four-step conservation plan where far too often, the final step feels to have been 'bolted on' as an afterthought rather than being the principal objective at the outset. Perhaps this is why, to date, over-emphasis has been placed upon the conservation plan process as a self-contained entity of value (in every respect!), instead of its use as a platform for day-to-day site or area management.

In the characterisation process 'creating the story' involves data gathering, analysis, mapping and interpretation. It must be stressed that, in characterisation, much of the presentation of the 'story' of the area's character development takes place pictorially/diagrammatically with considerable emphasis on layered maps. As Clark et al. (2004, p. 12) have observed, characterisation 'provides a context for existing data', demonstrating that 'the historic landscape has importance as a whole – the sum of all its parts'. By the end of its first stage, characterisation should paint a picture for area managers or those involved in planning change, interpreting the present-day environment in a way that reveals it to be the summation of the underlying natural world and subsequent change through its history. Again, this reinforces the notion that the historic environment is everything about us, and also connects back to the developing idea that urban and rural landscapes are different guises of the same entity – the cultural landscape.

The second stage in the characterisation process – consideration of the area's future based on the picture that has been painted of its present – involves making judgements about how to manage, even encourage, further change in a way that sustains character, local diversity and value.

Hopefully, the message from this brief analysis of three management tools for historic areas shines through with clarity. In most circumstances, conservation has moved away from seeking to inhibit or prevent change to historic assets. Instead, it has taken on board what should have been self-evident all along. Urban or rural, the landscape is not made up of a small number of heritage jewels scattered in a sea of mediocrity. The world around us is the cumulative result of all historic change to the underlying natural environment. Some of that change has, and continues to, come about through the impact of the climate and other natural forces; much, though, is change – purposeful or incidental – brought about by mankind. To quote Clark et al. once more, 'if we celebrate the result of past changes, we must logically accept further change'. The task at hand, therefore, is not how to suppress ongoing change, but how to shape it so that we continue to derive precious benefit from the historic environment and its vital sense of place, whilst investing in its development in a way that optimises the cultural value of both the old and the new for society at large. That, for want of any better phrase, is conservation planning and management. Arguably, it is the only satisfactory way we have to manage our world and its cultural heritage resources sustainability.

Heritage impact assessments

As its name implies, this procedure looks in detail at the possible impact of a particular action or actions upon the cultural significance of a place. Essentially, it is the same concept as the environmental impact assessments used routinely in the wider land planning context. Clark (2001) categorises them as being 'about risk assessments for historic buildings and their landscapes'. A heritage impact assessment (HIA) procedure will be appropriate for all places and buildings (and indeed objects), irrespective of their size or complexity. On a complex site, which already has a conservation plan and a management plan, it should be a normal and integral part of the management processes that are put in place to protect and enhance significance. For such sites, the framework for making a judgement on the likely impact should have been developed through the management plan and should be in place, as should, at least, the contextual information relating to significance. Clearly it is important that the HIA is consistent with the plan. However, depending on the amount of detail on significance contained within the conservation plan and the particulars of the proposal, it may/often will be necessary to seek more information about the significance of the items or elements affected.

In a sense, HIAs are a test of the rigour and clarity of the conservation plan with regard to both its management processes and its assessment of significance, relative significance and sensitivity to change. For a place without a conservation plan or a statement of significance, an HIA will necessitate an investigation and articulation of the significance of the element or item in question. It is important that all involved understand that proposals that will generate the need for an HIA are not just those that may have an effect on the physical fabric, and that interventions which have an effect on, for example, a 'sense of place' – perhaps on views in and out or on atmosphere – should be subject to an HIA.

Whether or not the HIA is generated within the context of an already established statement of significance or a conservation plan, it is important to understand that a relatively small action or intervention can have a relatively large impact on the significance of a place; and certainly that a number of small interventions with a 'salami slicing' effect can be particularly damaging. Therefore the trigger for an HIA cannot be based simply around notions of the size of the intervention.

The heritage impact assessment process

The HIA system that is set up should:

- Clarify the nature, purpose, detail and timing of the proposal, the reasons for it, and the benefits to the organisation/individual owner – or indeed the wider community.
- Clarify what aspects of significance are possibly affected, directly or indirectly, now or in the future, and the ways in which those effects will be, or may be, manifested. Some impacts may be easily 'measured' or identified. However, others may be a possible problem and/or add to the potential vulnerability of the element, but it is difficult to determine the exact effect – and therefore issues of risk assessment are important.
- Clarify what information is required to judge the impact of the proposal.
- Make a judgement about the effect on significance of that proposal.
- Make a decision on whether the proposal should be accepted, rejected or amended, and on how to mitigate its potential impact on significance and on the historic integrity of the asset.

As with other management activities it should be clear as to what triggers the need for an HIA. But there should also be clarity and transparency about the information-collecting and decision-making process.

Clearly some proposals may not be a potential threat to the heritage because they are neutral in their impact. Where amendments to the proposal are necessary, or action needs to be taken to protect vulnerable aspects of the site, to mitigate damage to significance, this may involve, for example:

- Technical issues – for instance, in requiring a different approach to repair or the provision of site-specific protection to guard against impact or other damage during implementation of building works
- Architectural/aesthetic issues – for instance, alterations to a design

or:

- Use issues – for instance, suggesting that a new use on a site should be integrated into another part of the site where there will be a less negative impact on significance

The emphasis should be not on preventing change but on finding alternative ways of achieving change without damaging significance – although the question of what will be the outcome if nothing is done will always be a useful one to consider.

In some cases the impact may be positive, in that the intervention is intended to, or may contain the possibility to, further protect and enhance significance. It may well be that any amendments in these cases are intended to maximise potential heritage benefits, or ensure that opportunities are not lost. Therefore, in some instances, the outcome of an HIA may be about increasing the scope of the work rather than restricting or redirecting it.

The heart of a heritage impact assessment may well comprise a tabular analysis of the building or site, broken down into appropriate constituent parts: setting out relevant aspects of significance; the nature of the proposed works or changes to each part; their potential impact; and intended mitigation. This table should be introduced by a commentary dealing with the kinds of issues discussed above, and supported by drawings and schedules specifying methods of providing physical protection or other methods of mitigating known risks.

Table 5.1 (p. 196) shows an extract from a tabular presentation of an HIA for a project involving the upgrading of building services and various repairs to the structure and fabric of a large historic house. Under 'Specific mitigation requirements', the impact assessment refers out to a general mitigation statement ('General Mitigation Procedure 1') and to various scheduled mitigation arrangements (for example, 'Special Protection Procedure 3') that have been designed individually to suit particular circumstances. The general mitigation statement for this specific project might include the following:

> *The works have been designed specifically to mitigate, as far as reasonably and safely possible, the quantity and degree of intrusion into previously undisturbed historic fabric. Throughout implementation of the proposed scheme, emphasis will be placed on minimising the impact on historic fabric and decoration, whilst also minimising disturbance to previously disturbed areas.*
>
> *New power, lighting and fire alarm fittings and fixtures will be installed with the utmost care to avoid excessive damage to the building fabric. Any debris and dust created by the works will be carefully controlled to avoid damaging the contents of sensitive rooms and spaces, including those adjacent to the works and along access routes for delivery of materials to the working area.*
>
> *Where feasible, replacement fittings will re-use existing fixing points to avoid further loss of historic fabric. Any new fixing points will be selected*

with care and consideration for the building fabric and decoration. Where electrical fittings are to be rewired, existing cable and conduit routes will be reused to avoid impacting upon undisturbed historic fabric. Where sections of new wiring are to be created for points/outlets in new locations, these will utilise existing cable and conduit routes, so far as is possible, and make full use of existing access points to floor and ceiling voids.

Floorboards requiring temporary removal for access will be recorded and numbered where taken up in sufficient quantities; otherwise, they will be kept adjacent to their location for ease of refixing in their original position. All floorboards will be carefully removed to avoid damage and will be refixed through their original fixing points.

The appointed Contractor will be provided with a 'tool box' talk prior to the commencement of the project and all contractor's staff and any subcontractors will be required to be briefed on the need for the utmost sensitivity and attention to detail in their work prior to commencing work on site.

The situation-specific special protection measures might include matters such as:

- Careful erection of temporary plywood casings to walls, balustrades, architraves and other vulnerable elements along access routes to and within working areas
- Plywood boxing around vulnerable fire surrounds which must be left in situ during conduct of the works
- Procedures for working in spaces known to be used by protected species such as bats; and
- Propping of delicate plasterwork to ceilings

Local management agreements

In *Streamlining listed building consent*, a research report produced by the Paul Drury Partnership with the Environmental Project Consulting Group for English Heritage in 2003, management guidelines or agreements are described as:

Informal memoranda of understanding between the owners and managers of listed buildings, the local planning authority and (usually) English Heritage.

To make this applicable to the breadth of built cultural heritage assets covered within this book, we need to expand this concept to cover situations that lie outside England and its legislative framework. Management agreements are generally made between the party or parties that own or manage a cultural heritage asset and those responsible for the administration of relevant statutory planning and protective powers. The asset may be a building, site, estate, historic

Table 5.1 Extract from a heritage impact assessment for a historic house.

Room number	History and significance	Proposed work	Potential impact	Specific mitigation requirements
	FIRST FLOOR (Drawing References 1363/FF1 & 1363/FF2)			
FF01	Building phase: 1740s **2005 plan: Dolls' House Room** (public area)	New smoke detector in room and additional detector in Dolls' House display cabinet.	Fixing points in ceiling and wiring through ceiling void for smoke detectors.	See General Mitigation Procedure 1.
	1954 plan: not named			Additional protective measures (Special Protection Procedure 11) for temporary relocation of Dolls' House once removed from display cabinet for duration of works in room to be agreed with curatorial section.
	Previous works: not known			
	Significance: (i) Rare survival of dolls' house belonging to elder daughter of first Earl; figures and artefacts within house include French pieces belonging to 'Revolutionary' period (1790–91); (ii) Family 'story' that Isobel, the third Earl's third daughter, was locked up in room for three years until her death as punishment for dropping Chinese vase beloved of her dead grandmother.			
FF02	Building phase: 1740s **2005 plan: Hall** (public area)	Replacement of existing smoke detector and 'break glass' call point.	Negligible	See General Mitigation Procedure 1.
	1954 plan: Housemaid's Closet Previous works: not known			
	Significance: None beyond surviving historic fabric and as component part of second major post-medieval development phase of Hall.			

Room number	History and significance	Proposed work	Potential impact	Specific mitigation requirements
FF03	Building phase: 1620s 2005 plan: Leather Gallery (public area) 1954 plan: The Gallery Previous works: Repairs to timber ceiling joists, truss ends, wall plates and lintels in 1980s due to long-term water ingress from flat lead roof above and consequential fungal decay; some poor resin repairs; moulded cornice to ceiling reinstated (untidily); other interventions suspected from uneven line of plaster but cannot be identified from documentary evidence Significance: (i) Part of first major expansion of medieval Hall (1620s) which reflected the growing political importance of the family and established the national significance of the Hall (ii) Survival of part of original 17th century ornate plaster ceiling (iii) Extremely rare 17th century Spanish leather hangings mounted on walls; known to have been hung in this room since 1703 (and possibly before)	(a) Removal of unsatisfactory 1980s work to cornice and ceiling to permit inspection and rectification of failed resin repairs to structural timbers; (b) Insertion of new aspirating smoke detection pipework through modern replacement ceiling plaster, routed through void above; (c) Replacement of 2no existing power sockets and 2no light switches. Replacement of existing light fitting.	**Generally** High risk of damage to leather hangings from all works from dust, impact from debris or accidental contact by site operatives. *NB These hangings will remain in place throughout as they are considered too fragile to demount and move.* **Additionally:** *Specific risks* (a) Destabilising/loosening, collapse or impact damage to 17th century ceiling plaster; (b) as (a); also potential for weakening of undersized historic ceiling joists if	(i) Special 'tool box' training at commencement of works for site operatives to emphasise sensitivity of working area and risks; daily reminder by site foreman (to be registered on daily log kept in site hut and initialled by foreman); (ii) Special Protection Procedure 3 to be implemented by curatorial section to erect/secure robust dustproof protective casing around leather hangings; (iii) Temporary ceiling propping with padding to be erected and kept in place during works (a) and (b) – see drawing ref 1363/17 and Special Protection Procedure 4; (iv) No access to roof void

Table 5.1 (*continued*)

Room number	History and significance	Proposed work	Potential impact	Specific mitigation requirements
			notched or otherwise cut to facilitate routing of pipework for smoke detection installation; also note presence of protected species of bats in roof void over FF03 – see entry for Roof Void RV05 and its significance; risk from (c) as replacing existing units.	without prior approval of ecologist and without attendance of registered bat handler; timing of works within void and associated areas must be restricted as set out in Special Protection Procedure 10 and in accordance with ecological policy 02 of site management plan; (v) For all works, General Mitigation Procedure 1.
FF04	Building phase: 1620s and 1740s **2005 plan: 3rd Earl's Room** (showroom from barriers in door openings, but no public access) 1954 plan: Damask Room (then used as private living room) Previous works: *Mid-18th century* – chimney piece and joinery *1896* – papered and painted *Post-1957* – damask removed, room furnished as a bedroom. Current wallpaper (1997) is a copy of	Lifting of all floor boards to provide access to void below as part of installation of aspirating pipework for very early smoke detection installation to main public rooms below.	(a) Damage to 18th century floor boards and adjacent surfaces and joinery; (b) Impact damage to chimney piece; (c) Impact damage to wallpaper, decorations and furnishings;	(i) For all works, see General Mitigation Procedure 1, including numbering, etc. of lifted boards; (ii) Lifting of boards to be supervised by foreman. Temporary storage arrangements for boards to be agreed prior to commencement of work

Room number	History and significance	Proposed work	Potential impact	Specific mitigation requirements
	the late-19th century paper, from a sample found during the room's renovation.			with contract administrator and curatorial section;
	Significance: (i) Important in illustrating changing requirements of early 18th century family, by extension of principal room from previous phase;		(d) Damage to showroom contents.	(iii) Chimney piece to be protected by plywood-faced timber-framed boxing as specified in Special Protection Procedure 2.
	(ii) Good example of mid-18th century chimney piece;			(iv) Room to be cleared of all furnishings, moveable contents, etc. by curatorial section prior to commencement of works;
	(iii) Otherwise none beyond surviving historic fabric;			(v) Decorations to be protected by plywood sheeting as set out in Special Protection Procedure 1.
	(iv) Especial importance to visitors as the 'haunted' room.			

area or cultural landscape. Often it may carry some form of statutory protection, although this does not necessarily have to be the case. To be successful, it is probable that the various parties to the agreement will have the shared objective of ensuring, through the agreement, the adoption of an appropriate management regime for the asset that will lead to more effective, efficient and sustainable day-to-day decision making.

The 2003 research report goes on to note that:

> *Management agreements or guidelines tend to be brief documents that provide a structured framework for decision-making by informed professionals, not (unlike a conservation management plan) an assessment of the significance and vulnerability of all elements of the building fabric at the outset.*

Within the context and objectives of the report, this was a reasonable assertion to make about the form of the local management agreement. However, it is our contention that significance, or value-based local management agreements, have enormous potential to offer in ensuring that sustainable and effective management practices are adopted by local managers of heritage assets – be they individuals or organisations of one kind or another. Again, it is vital to recognise that, although often such agreements relate to a single building, the concept is appropriate for application to any definable coherent or integral entity within the historic environment. In England, local area agreements are being promoted as being 'of increasing importance in determining the future of a local area. The historic environment must be a part of this process, both as an asset in its own right and for the wider contributions it can make to community goals' (English Heritage, 2006b).

In 1995, English Heritage introduced into England the concept of local management guidelines for historic or architecturally important listed buildings in its guidance note *Developing Guidelines for the Management of Listed Buildings*. The 1995 guidance was built upon experience gained in the development of a seminal one-off agreement three years earlier between English Heritage, Ipswich Borough Council and the owners of the Willis Faber building in Ipswich, which was designed by Foster Associates in 1970 and had been listed as Grade I in 1991. As with most subsequent local management agreements, the primary objective of the Willis Faber agreement was 'to provide clarification as to what proposals for the building may not require listed building consent and/or planning permission'. However, it should be stressed that this is not the only benefit to be gained from, or catalyst to the development of, local management guidelines for built cultural heritage assets. Other agreements, as the 2003 report cites, have been aimed at agreeing management principles for the care of the asset and its significance, establishing a framework and positive environment for the resolution of differences of opinion on proposed management action, and optimising management efficiency and costs by creating a structure for informed decision making.

Figure 5.6 Hampton Court Palace. Historic Royal Palaces developed what was, in effect, a local management agreement with English Heritage which applied to all five of the palaces in its care.

The 1995 guidance note envisaged that local management agreements would be suitable and beneficial where large and complex assets were involved. Initially, the guidance was aimed at large commercial and industrial sites, shopping precincts, institutional complexes and housing schemes listed for their 'group value' (or contribution as an unified assemblage) to the local historic environment.

Prior to this development of the concept of local management agreements, a handful of one-off quasi local management agreements had been used to improve management effectiveness in specific situations – some far removed from the kind of context for which they later became known. One example will suffice. In 1991/1992, a form of local management agreement was negotiated between English Heritage (acting as agent for the then Department of National Heritage in its role as the administrator responsible for scheduled ancient monument matters) and Historic Royal Palaces. At the time, the latter was a government agency, established in 1989 to care for five English palaces, which, to all intents and purposes, were no longer occupied by members of the Royal Family. This estate included Hampton Court Palace and the Tower of London.

Although little more than two years old at the time, Historic Royal Palaces had built up a strong and experienced conservation-aware staff. The Agency's brief was to manage and improve its nationally important estate with a strong commercial focus, whilst delivering uncompromised 'best practice' conservation. This meant that rapid and extensive change was being planned at the Palaces.

In practical terms, neither English Heritage nor the Department of National Heritage had sufficient spare resources to administer and determine the enormous volume of applications that would be required under the relevant legislation, if it were to be applied strictly. It was recognised that the most effective management solution would be to negotiate and agree a list of works which could be carried out at the Palaces by Historic Royal Palaces without the need for further discussion and the submission of applications for consent. This agreed list then became the subject of an annual Scheduled Monument Consent and could be monitored retrospectively for compliance, allowing the Department of National Heritage to terminate the arrangement if it was advised by English Heritage that the letter or spirit of the local management agreement was being flouted or compromised. A system of quarterly review meetings agreement was also built into the agreement to allow for regular monitoring of the implementation and impact of the arrangement.

This demonstrates that the concept of the local management agreement can be readily extended to address very specific needs and circumstances. Such flexibility can involve risk – particularly of damage being 'sanctioned' to the significance of the heritage asset. This risk can and must be managed through regular monitoring, review meetings and feedback. This and the consequential power to rescind the agreement and/or impose other penalties have to be active components of any successful local management agreement. Bluntly, if this risk management cannot be effectively delivered, the situation is not suitable for using a local management agreement.

It is worth exploring some other ways in which local management agreements can be applied to the benefit of all parties and to the care of the particular asset. The objective of the 2003 English Heritage research report was to learn the lessons from the use of management agreements and to apply those to 'streamlining listed building consent' (that is, statutory protection) arrangements. The report concluded that 'Management agreements have considerable potential to contribute to streamlining the listed building consent process by making it more transparent, consistent and therefore predictable. . . and they can bring about a net saving of resources for all involved'. Since then, further consideration has been given to whether parts of a revised statutory designation process for England might be built around significance-based local management agreements. In effect, this approach might one day lead to the 'self-certification' of a range of pre-agreed work types by 'conservation-intelligent' heritage asset management organisations (a typical example in England being the National Trust). This would simplify both sides of the application/consent process and, it has been suggested, make conservation management more efficient.

In a very different way, the local management agreement can be extended to assist in situations of varying kinds, where day-to-day management responsibility, for one or more heritage assets, is to be divorced temporarily from the ownership interest. In these circumstances, a significance-based local management agreement can help in bringing clarity to the tenancy or contractual responsibilities and establish a mutually agreed sound management platform. The potential of this approach can be illustrated by Example 5.2.

Example 5.2

In 2002, a charitable trust decided to let one of its estate properties in Somerset – a large former yeoman's farmhouse – to an individual on a long lease. It was concerned to ensure that the significance and historic integrity of the asset were protected, such that, when it reverted to the trust's direct management control on expiration of the lease term, it would be in sound condition and undiminished in its state and significance from when the leasehold interest had commenced.

A conservation plan for the site was prepared, and, using this assessment of significance and vulnerability, essential and desirable conservation management policies were defined. These policies were developed into specific guidelines for the care of the property, including its future maintenance and the management of its use and change. This document then became the core of a significance-based local management agreement between the charitable trust and the prospective tenant, which was embedded within the legal leasehold contract itself.

By extension, local management agreements of this nature, based upon a conservation plan or other assessment of cultural value, have considerable potential for use wherever asset management functions are to be divided from property ownership. This might include subsequent sub-letting, as in Example 5.2 above, or even contracting out of some management functions – for instance, where facilities' management or some elements of estate management are being purchased for a fixed period of years from a private sector contracting organisation. So far, this application for significance-based local management agreements is largely unexplored, but it has much to offer in improving sound management of potentially vulnerable heritage assets.

A general framework for a local management agreement might include:

- Definition of the parties involved in the agreement and their roles.
- Identification of the asset(s) covered by the agreement and a brief description of each, including definition of the curtilage of the asset.
- Description of the management arrangements in place to care for the/each asset.
- Details of the nature of the agreement, including its duration and any limitations on its application.
- Establishment of a review mechanism of implementation or performance of the agreement, including a structure for regular meetings between the parties.
- A summary of the/each asset's significance, including emphasis on the range of cultural values that are present.
- A summary of the vulnerability of and issues that might affect the/each asset and its significance.
- Definition of the management approach to be adopted towards the/each asset.
- Identification of general and specific management policies to be set in place and implemented to care for the/each asset and the cultural values that are present.
- Definition of works, or categories of works, or other changes that can be undertaken without reference back to, or the need for, prior consent from

the relevant statutory authority (who should be one of the parties to the agreement).

- Definition of works, or categories of works, or other changes that must not be commenced without reference back to, or granting of, prior consent by the relevant statutory authority.
- Practical guidelines for sustainable care of the asset(s), including management of use and change.
- Establishment of a framework for resolution of disagreements resulting from implementation of the local management agreement.

Care, design and quality standards guidance

A core part of the effective management of historic areas – urban or rural – has to be the dissemination of user-friendly guidance, setting out fundamental requirements for the responsible care of buildings and the design of appropriate alterations and additions to structures, streetscape and the like. The provision of good guidance can minimise conflict and inadvertent damage to the character and/or significance of individual properties, as well as the area at large. It can also reduce the burden of production of very detailed heritage impact assessments, by providing direct or indirect mitigation advice in advance of design development and more subtly influencing wants and expectations.

A myriad of design guidance has already been produced in recent decades – much by or through local planning authorities – encouraging appropriate design of extensions and alterations both to listed buildings and unprotected buildings in conservation areas. Some of this guidance has been sound and extremely focused; a large amount has been over-generalised, and has failed to deliver the anticipated improvements in the quality of applications for planning permission and listed building consent and in the final construction work. Curiously, rather less care and quality standards' guidance has been produced – yet it is often through poor maintenance or the selection of unsuitable mortar mixes or surface coatings that the most marked piecemeal degradation of the character of historic areas occurs.

The development of the concept of value/significance-based management has provided a powerful platform for the production of targeted guidance of this kind. On the back of an assessment of significance and vulnerability – most probably developed as part of a conservation plan or statement, or as a historic area appraisal (depending upon circumstance) – the guidance can be developed to tackle the day-to-day issues that are likely to affect the area and to diminish its value and potential.

As has already been implied, typically, guidance of this sort can be divided into three distinct categories, although sometimes two or even all three may be amalgamated within a single published document, depending upon circumstance. The growth in the use of the internet has made web-based dissemination extremely popular, cost-efficient and effective. These three categories are:

Care guidance – provides advice to building or landscape owners, occupiers or managers on the basics of good protective maintenance. Some of this advice will simply reflect common good practice (for instance, the need for regular inspection and cleaning of gutters and rainwater downpipes) and will thus be of a generalised nature. However, structured on sound assessments of significance and of character (and, again, these should not be confused), the opportunity exists to explain what is considered to be of particular value about the asset and its component parts and, specifically, how such value can be protected and enhanced by care and maintenance actions.

Design guidance – can be targeted at the same owners, occupiers and managers of buildings or landscapes. Additionally, it can be directed towards: public sector employees who determine applications relating to development in the historic area/asset or who are responsible for the maintenance and upkeep of public spaces and streetscapes; professional practitioners who design and specify alterations or new elements or structures within the area/asset; and contractors who implement those designs and specifications. Within historic urban areas and rural settlements, it is often design issues in the public realm (especially, the selection of materials for the construction and repair of pavements and road surfaces and the design and positioning of street furniture, including signage) that cause the most damage to character and significance. Strangely, this type of damage is frequently only perceived subliminally and is therefore the most overlooked area requiring guidance. Design guidance can cover a wide range of matters, depending upon circumstance and need, including detailing, size, massing, proportion, use, density, location of change, availability and selection of materials, ease of maintenance, accessibility, character, craftsmanship, species of planting, distribution of elements, vistas, and so forth.

Quality standards guidance – is related to both care and design advice. But it is being used increasingly to inform regeneration agencies, local authority administrators and professional practitioners about particular standards that need to be achieved in working in a historic area in order to safeguard both character and significance. An example of adoption of this approach in England was the joint commissioning in 2005 by English Heritage, the Heritage Lottery Fund (HLF) and the regional regeneration agency, Elevate, of quality standard guidance to be adopted for group repair of nineteenth century terraced housing in every conservation area in East Lancashire where HLF grant funding was being provided. The guidance in that instance concentrated on the exteriors of the buildings and the wider streetscape and provided appropriate advice for care, maintenance, repair and renewal of roof coverings, chimneys, rainwater goods, external walling (including coatings and finishes), windows and doors, decorative detailing, boundary walls and railings, external yard areas, and the streets and pavements.

Figure 5.7   Nineteenth century terraced housing in East Lancashire – unlisted but deserving of proper care steered by value-based quality standards guidance.

The content of care, design and quality standards guidance needs to be very carefully honed to each case's specific needs. This makes identification of suitable content impossible. However, in a very general sense, a framework for such guidance notes might cover:

- Explanation of the purpose of the guidance
- Identification of the target audience(s)
- Identification of the asset(s) covered by the guidance
- Description of the management arrangements, statutory protection and planning policies in place to care for the asset (be it an area, estate, landscape, or other multi-property asset)
- An explanation of the structure and content of the guidance
- The date of production of the guidance and any limitations on its application
- An outline of the history of the asset and its development to the present day
- A summary of the character of the asset, where relevant
- A summary of the significance of the asset, including emphasis on the range of cultural values that are present
- A summary of the pressures for change in the area/asset and the vulnerability of and issues that might affect the asset and its significance
- Definition of the management approach that it is proposed should be adopted towards the asset

Figure 5.8   An example of the wealth of decorative detail to housing within the Aldersbrook Estate Conservation Area (see Example 5.3).

- Identification of general and specific management policies to be set in place and implemented to care for the asset and the cultural values that are present
- General care, design or quality standards advice
- Specific care, design or quality standards advice, perhaps structured element by element, if dealing with buildings, or component by component for landscapes, and, then, for design advice additionally by alteration type
- Summary of the objectives of the guidance, the asset's value, the care, design and quality standards advice that has been given, and the intended impact of the advice
- Bibliography/further reading for those whose interest in the asset has been awakened
- Sources of further advice

It is worth noting and reflecting in passing on the marked similarities between this general framework and that set out for use in the production of local management agreements. As has been observed in a number of different ways throughout this book, this is typical of significance-based management tools and stems from the fundamental logic of the conservation planning approach.

One example of recently produced care and design guidance will suffice to demonstrate the use of the foregoing general framework in practice (Example 5.3 and Figure 5.8).

Example 5.3   Aldersbrook Estate (Figure 5.8)

In 2005, the London Borough of Redbridge published care and design guidance for the Aldersbrook Estate, which, roughly two years before, had been newly designated as a conservation area. The Aldersbrook Estate lies within a triangular-shaped block of land and was largely built between 1899 and 1910.

A small number of minor additions had occurred after that time, but since 1945 open land had been carefully protected and so new buildings in the second half of the twentieth century were limited to infill sites within the boundaries of the Estate. The essence of the character of the Aldersbrook Estate is its remarkable wealth and variation of external ornamentation to otherwise relatively similar dwellings which evolved within a short building period. It was this that the guidance sought to protect and enhance where it had become compromised or degraded. The guidance was structured in eight sections:

1 An introduction setting the scene for the guidance on the basis of the designation of the conservation area.

2 A chapter providing essential background, including the historic development of the estate, the legislative background and practical purpose behind designation of conservation areas, and the conceptual thinking that drove development of the guidance and its content.

3 An illustrated explanation of what makes the estate special, both in terms of character and significance. After a general discussion, this was set out on an external building element-by-element basis, pointing out both typical and special characteristics and aspects of cultural value.

4 A brief assessment of why the estate and its significance should be protected.

5 A more detailed illustrated analysis of the pressures for change facing the estate and the damage that these could cause.

6 The illustrated core of the care and design guidance: this commenced with general observations about the basics of successful care and then was expanded first elementally looking at:
   - chimneys and chimney pots
   - roofs
   - rainwater goods
   - fascias, eaves and bargeboarding
   - walls, gables, bays, rendering and pebbledashing
   - windows
   - porches
   - external doors
   - architectural ornamentation and decorative features
   - entrance lights, burglar alarms and other outside fittings
   - paintwork and colour
   - front boundaries and gardens
   - rear boundaries and gardens
   - signage
   - pavements
   - street lighting
   - interiors

and, thereafter, addressing design issues 'when making major changes', approaching these by alteration type, as relevant to the circumstances and issues facing the estate itself:

- sub-division of houses into multiple units
- conversions
- loft conversions, dormers and rooflights
- extensions and conservatories
- garages
- car parking within front gardens and the design and impact of 'crossovers' of public pavements
- aerials and satellite dishes
- re-instatement of lost features
- new build
- temporary buildings

7 Summary.
8 Further reading and sources of information.

Over and above the logical structure and development of the significance-based argument, experience shows that one of the most critical factors influencing the success, or otherwise, of guidance of this kind is being able to express significance and value in a way that appeals to the target audience and makes them want to take ownership of the principles espoused by the guidance.

Further reading

English Heritage (2003) *Managing Local Authority Heritage Assets*. London, English Heritage.
English Heritage (2006) *Guidance on Conservation Area Appraisals*. London, English Heritage.
English Heritage (2006) *Guidance on the Management of Conservation Areas*. London, English Heritage.

References

Audit Commission (2002) *Briefing: Learning from Inspections, Housing Repairs and Maintenance*. London, Audit Commission.
Australia ICOMOS (1999) *The Burra Charter – The Australia ICOMOS Charter for Places of Cultural Significance*. Australia ICOMOS Inc.
Brereton, C. (1991) *The Repair of Historic Buildings*. London, English Heritage.
British Standards Institute (1986) *BS 8210:1986, Guide to Building Maintenance Management*. London, BSI.
British Standards Institute (1998) *BS 7913:1998, Guide to the Principles of the Conservation of Historic Buildings*. London, BSI.
Clark, J., Darlington, J. and Fairclough, G. (2004) *Using Historic Landscape Characterisation*. London, English Heritage and Lancashire County Council.

Clark, K. (2001) *Informed Conservation*. London, English Heritage.

English Heritage (1995) *Developing Guidelines for the Management of Listed Buildings*. London, English Heritage.

English Heritage (2000) *Power of Place, the Future of the Historic Environment*. London, English Heritage.

English Heritage (2003) *Streamlining Listed Building Consent – Lessons from the Use of Management Agreements*. London, English Heritage.

English Heritage (2004) *Conservation Bulletin Issue 47 – Characterisation*. London, English Heritage.

English Heritage (2006a) *English Heritage Standard EHS 0004/2: Periodic Condition Surveys and Reports*. London, English Heritage. [Internal publication only.]

English Heritage (2006b) *Local Area Agreements and the Historic Environment*. London, English Heritage.

English Heritage (2007) *Conservation Principles, 2nd consultation document*. London, English Heritage.

English Heritage and Lancashire County Council (2004) http://www.english-heritage.org.uk/server/show/nav.1292

Feilden, B. (1982) *Conservation of Historic Buildings*. London, Architectural Press.

Feilden, B (1994) *Conservation of Historic Buildings*. London, Architectural Press.

Feilden, B. and Jokilehto, J. (1993) *Management Guidelines for World Cultural Heritage Sites*. Rome, International Centre for the Study of the Preservation and Restoration of Cultural Property (ICCROM).

Government Historic Buildings Advisory Unit (1998) *The Care of Historic Buildings and Ancient Monument: Guidelines for Government Departments and Agencies*. London, English Heritage and the Department of National Heritage.

HEFCE (1998) *Building Repairs and Maintenance Study in Higher Education Sector, National Report and Management Review Guide*. Bristol, Higher Education Funding Council for England (HEFCE).

Historic Scotland (1997) *Planning Advice Note 52: Planning in Small Towns*. Edinburgh, Historic Scotland.

Historic Scotland (2004) *Planning Advice Note 71: Conservation Area Management*. Edinburgh, Historic Scotland.

Holmes, R. (1994) Built asset management practice. In: *The CIOB Handbook of Facilities Management* (ed. A. Spedding). Ascot, Chartered Institute of Building (CIOB).

Kerr, J.S. (1996) *Conservation Plans for Places of European Significance*. National Trust of New South Wales.

MHLG (Ministry of Housing and Local Government) (1967) Civic Amenities Act 1967, Section 69 ff. London, HMSO.

Morris, W. (1877) *The Principles of the Society (for the Protection of Ancient Buildings) As Set Forth upon its Foundation*. Available on SPAB website http://www.spab.org.uk/html/what-is-spab/the-manifesto/

Pearson, M. and Marshall, D. (2005) *National Library of Australia, Conservation Management Plan*. Canberra, *National Library of Australia*. [Draft plan.]

Pearson, M. and Sullivan, S. (1995). *Looking After Heritage Places*. Melbourne, Melbourne University Publishing.

Pickard, R. and de Thyse, M. (2001) The management of historic centres: towards a common goal. In: *Management of Historic Centres* (ed. R. Pickard). London, Spon.

Ruskin, J. (1989) The lamp of memory. In: *The Seven Lamps of Architecture*. New York, Dover Publications, Chapter 6.

Sauer, C. (1925) Morphology of landscape. In: *University of California Publications in Geography*.

SPAB (Society for the Protection of Ancient Buildings) (undated) *SPAB's Purpose*. Available at: www.spab.org.uk

UNESCO (2003) *Mtskheta: A Heritage and Tourism Master Plan*. Paris, UNESCO.

Williams, B. (1994) *Facilities Economics*. Bromley, BEB Press.

Wood, B. (2003) *Building Care*. London, Blackwell Science.

Wordsworth, P. (2001) *Lee's Building Maintenance Management* (4th edn). London, Blackwell Science.

Chapter 6

Epilogue – Sustainability and the Built Cultural Heritage

In 1983, the United Nations established a World Commission on Environment and Development under the leadership of the former Norwegian Prime Minister Gro Harlem Brundtland to prepare strategies on sustainable development. In 1987, this Commission reported in a document called *Our Common Future* (more generally known as *The Brundtland Report*), which adopted the concept that sustainable development is '[development that] meets the needs of the present without compromising the ability of future generations to meet their own needs', and it is this phrase that has become the focal point of discussions on the concept (United Nations, 1987).

The idea of sustainable development is grounded in concerns about environmental sustainability, but it has developed to consider the interaction between environmental, economic and social values.

In the context of the conservation of the built cultural heritage, it is interesting to note that the basic 'sustainability' concept of the stewardship of valuable resources was espoused by both John Ruskin and William Morris. Writing in 1849 about buildings from the past, Ruskin suggested that 'They are not ours. They belong partly to those who built them and partly to all the generations of mankind who are to follow us' (Ruskin, 1989); and he emphasised that the intergenerational consideration referred to a responsibility to those from the past as well as the future when he observed, 'The dead still have their right in them'. William Morris, in stating the purpose of protecting buildings, wrote that it was to 'hand them down instructive and venerable to those that come after us' (Morris, 1877).

We could add to this, that the emphasis on understanding, valuing and honouring the work of past generations is also important – the sense that we might conceive of a responsibility to past generations, as well as future ones, is perhaps an aspect of 'sustainability' which is sometimes overlooked.

Charters such as Burra emphasise a sustainable approach to conservation:

> *the places that are likely to be of significance are those which help an understanding of the past or enrich the present, and which we believe will be of value to future generations* (Australia ICOMOS, 1999)

We can suggest that protecting the built cultural heritage does interact with all three aspects of the sustainability matrix, for example:

Social value – for instance, because of the sociological and psychological value to individuals, groups and nations of the physical connection to the past (and through this to notions of continuity, connectivity and identity). The educational potential of the built cultural heritage also has social value.

Environmental value – for instance, in respect of embodied energy in the use and reuse of these existing buildings, as the focus and driver for regeneration schemes, and for their aesthetic and amenity value.

Economic value – for instance, in tourist income, specifically and generally.

Setting this approach within the context of conservation management planning, we can say that:

> **Sustainable conservation** *is the proper management of use and change in and around historic places and spaces, so as to respect and enhance their value to society.*

Sustainability in this context is not just about how we sustain the protection of the built cultural heritage – there are still some interesting debates to be had about to what extent a fuller engagement with the ideas of sustainable development might drive a reassessment of the importance of, and the role of, the conservation of built cultural heritage, both in terms of what we protect and how we protect it. Such issues might include:

- How, and in what circumstances, we might trade off conservation values against others (socioeconomic benefits)
- The extent to which stakeholders are involved in deciding what is valuable and why
- Acknowledging, and incorporating in decision making, a range of values that are wider than are presently commonly used, and involving a wider constituency in the identification of those values
- Realising the possible benefits for the wider constituency. As Throsby observes, 'It may be suggested that equity of access to cultural capital should be regarded as just as important as equity in the intergenerational distribution of benefits from any other sort of capital.' (2002, p.10)

The 'conservation community' has engaged with some of these issues but is still perhaps too inward looking – for example, it is all very well talking about embodied energy but this does not address the question of the 'carbon footprint' of existing buildings. However, it can be seen that there has been an increasing move to a more holistic, integrative and inclusive view of how conservation ought to be conceived, and therefore how and what qualities ought to be protected and how they might be managed. To a large extent this thinking has been driven by the sustainability agenda and notions of integrated management. This has resulted in, for example, work derived from the notion of environmental capital and environmental capacity being recontextualised for the built environment, which has reinforced the importance of the notion of establishing cultural significance and vulnerability. Also the work on characterisation studies in the natural environment has been drawn on to inform approaches to the built environment.

The approach we have advocated and discussed in this book, for example in relation to the conservation plan, can be seen to address some of the concerns of sustainable development in that it emphasises the need to:

- Take a long-term view – including a consideration of threats in the future and encouraging plans and processes which mitigate against vulnerability.
- Be holistic in nature and content – in that it sets the historic place in its wider context and integrates issues and concerns.
- Understand a place and articulate and debate its values as a precursor to making decisions.
- Involve stakeholders not just in how the place is managed but also in deciding how important it is and why.
- Manage change whilst protecting that which is valued by society.
- Adopt a precautionary principle approach.
- Be rigorous and methodical in obtaining information and analysing it.
- Demonstrate transparency in decision making.
- Allow decision makers to be held accountable for decisions.

References

Australia ICOMOS (1999) *The Burra Charter – The Australia ICOMOS Charter for Places of Cultural Significance*. Australia ICOMOS Inc.

Morris, W. (1877) *The Principles of the Society (for the Protection of Ancient Buildings) As set Forth upon its Foundation*. Available on SPAB website at http://www.spab.org.uk/html/what-is-spab/the-manifesto/

Ruskin, J. (1989) The lamp of memory. In: *The Seven Lamps of Architecture*. New York, Dover Publications, Chapter 6.

Throsby, D. (2002) Cultural capital and sustainability concepts in the economics of cultural heritage. In: *Assessing the Values of Cultural Heritage, Research Report* (ed. Marta de la Torre). Los Angeles, The Getty Conservation Institute, pp. 101–117.

United Nations (1987) Report of the *World Commission on Environment and Development* New York. [Also published as *Our Common Future* by Oxford University Press, 1987.]

Index